FIFTH EDITION

2

W9-CIE-567

GRAMMAR *in* CONTEXT

Teacher's Edition

The cover photo shows the San Francisco–Oakland Bay Bridge over San Francisco Bay in California.

HEINLE
CENGAGE Learning

Australia • Brazil • Japan • Korea • Mexico • Singapore • Spain • United Kingdom • United States

HEINLE
CENGAGE Learning

Grammar in Context 2, Fifth Edition
Teacher's Edition

Publisher: Sherrise Roehr

Acquisitions Editor: Tom Jefferies

Development Editor: Sarah Sandoski

Associate Development Editor: Marissa
  Petrarca

Director of Global Marketing: Ian Martin

Director of U.S. Marketing: Jim McDonough

Product Marketing Manager: Katie Kelley

Marketing Manager: Caitlin Driscoll

Content Project Manager: Andrea Bobotas

Senior Print Buyer: Susan Spencer

Contributing Writers: Sarah J. Brown and
  Hilary Grant

Project Manager: Chrystie Hopkins

Production Services: Nesbitt Graphics, Inc.

Interior Design: Nesbitt Graphics, Inc.

Cover Design: Muse Group, Inc.

© 2010 Heinle, Cengage Learning

For permission to use material from this text or product, submit all requests online at **www.cengage.com/permissions**
Further permissions questions can be emailed to **permissionrequest@cengage.com**

Library of Congress Control Number: 2009936998
ISBN 13: 978-1-4240-7905-6
ISBN 10: 1-4240-7905-5

Heinle
20 Channel Center Street
Boston, Massachusetts 02210
USA

Cengage Learning is a leading provider of customized learning solutions with office locations around the globe, including Singapore, the United Kingdom, Australia, Mexico, Brazil, and Japan. Locate our local office at **international.cengage.com/region**

Cengage Learning products are represented in Canada by Nelson Education, Ltd.

Visit Heinle online at **elt.heinle.com**
Visit our corporate Web site at **www.cengage.com**

Printed in the United States of America.
1 2 3 4 5 6 7 8 9 10 — 13 12 11 10

Contents

Grammar in Context 2, Fifth Edition

Welcome to
Grammar in Context

TEACHER'S EDITION!

Grammar in Context, Fifth Edition, contains a rich variety of material, making it easy to customize to any program's needs. The new *Teacher's Edition* includes extra resources to make planning your syllabus and preparing lessons easier than ever before.

NEW! Pacing guides for every activity provide a timing framework useful for lesson planning.

NEW! Ten easy solutions for customizing *Grammar in Context, Fifth Edition,* to meet yours and your students' needs (see page v).

NEW! Presentation Ideas suggest alternative ways of presenting select grammar charts.

NEW! Practice Ideas include ways to adapt grammar exercises to target specific skills: reading, writing, listening, and speaking.

NEW! Online Lesson Planner saves you time by planning lessons online. This new tool provides instructors with complete, customizable lesson plans using the pacing guide from the *Teacher's Edition.* Go to elt.heinle.com/technology.

NEW! "Fast Track" option (highlighted by this icon:) identifies essential readings, charts, and exercises for courses that don't have the time to present and practice the full range of readings, grammar charts, and exercises available in *Grammar in Context, Fifth Edition.* Teaching these essential items gives students a basic understanding and practice of the most important grammar in each unit. Additional material can be used in the following ways:

- Struggling students can understand core grammar by doing extra practice exercises.

- Stronger students can be challenged by studying additional grammar charts and Expansion activities.

- Additional exercises may be used for students who have completed the in-class assignments ahead of other students.

Ten Tips for
Customizing *Grammar in Context,*
Fifth Edition, to fit your program:

1. Work within your curriculum.

Let your curriculum guide you on what to cover from this rich, comprehensive series. For example, if your program doesn't expect students to learn about *nonrestrictive clauses*, a teacher could skip the chart about *nonrestrictive clauses*. It may be enough to teach *contrary-of-fact clauses* in the present without getting into the past or mixed tenses. The Online Lesson Planner allows you to move, edit, and add to lessons to meet your program needs. These lesson plans can be done by individual teachers or shared across the program.

2. Do the Test/Review section at the start of each lesson.

One way to find out how much practice your students need is to give them the Test/Review section at the beginning of the lesson. If you find that most of your students can do this with relatively few errors, then you can skip the lesson altogether or focus only on the sticking points.

3. Assign the readings as homework.

All the readings are important in introducing the grammar in context and should not be skipped. To save class time, however, the readings can be done at home. The reading level is low enough that classroom instruction on how to read should not be necessary. The reading is not meant to challenge and improve one's reading skills; it is meant to illustrate the grammar in a stimulating context. In class, the teacher can ask questions about the reading or the vocabulary within to ensure that students read and understood the assignment. There can be a short discussion on the Before You Read questions, too, if time permits.

4. Set time limits for each fill-in-the blank exercise.

Set a maximum time limit for each exercise. Suggested times are given in the *Teacher's Edition.* Once the time limit has expired, ask students to put down their pens and move on to the next exercise. Students can complete the rest of the exercise at home.

5. Assign audio-based exercises for lab time.

Many exercises contain audio tracks (indicated with a listening icon ◀))). These exercises can take time to set up and run, so you may wish to assign these for lab credits or homework. You may also decide to do only one of these per class to add variety.

6. Use one of the "About You" exercises per class.

These exercises are fun to do; if you find your students' attention waning, you can insert one of these activities per lesson. If your students attend another class for speech and conversation, these exercises may be skipped.

7. Use Expansion Activities if there is time.

The Expansion Activities at the end are fun, but time is limited. If you do have extra time at the end of the lesson, choose the activity that seems the most enjoyable. Students are likely to remember the lesson better if there is a fun element.

8. Assign exercises for extra credit.

Students can go beyond the basic curriculum and do more of the exercises at home for extra credit.

9. Let students check answers at home.

Print the answer key for each unit from the Heinle Web site (elt.heinle.com/grammarincontext). Give the answer key at the start of each unit so that students can check their answers at home. Set aside ten minutes every week to do a quick troubleshooting of particular grammar points.

10. Use the *Teacher's Edition*.

Each level of the student book has an accompanying *Teacher's Edition*, which gives page-by-page teaching suggestions on how to present and teach each grammar point and corresponding exercises. The *Teacher's Edition* also identifies fast-track material to help you quickly identify essential material when you're pressed for time and have to prioritize what to cover.

Lesson 1

Lesson Overview

GRAMMAR

Ask: *What tense will we study in this lesson?* (the simple present tense) *What are some examples of the simple present tense?* Write the examples on the board. *What else will we study?* (frequency words) *Do you know any frequency words?* (*always, sometimes, often*, etc.) Have students give examples. Write the examples on the board.

CONTEXT

1. Ask: *What will we learn about in this lesson?* (pets, other animals, working dogs)

2. Activate students' prior knowledge. Ask: *Do any of you have pets?* Have students share information about their pets.

Presentation Ideas

The topic for this lesson can be enhanced with the following items:

1. Books on pets
2. Ads for pet supply stores
3. Pictures of your pet

Americans and Their Pets

READING

1. Have students look at the picture. Ask: *What is the dog doing?* (sleeping with its owner) *Do people from your culture treat their pets like this?*

2. Have students look at the title of the reading. Ask: *What is the reading about?* Have students use the title and picture to make predictions about the reading.

3. Preteach any vocabulary words your students may not know, such as *allow*, *cemetery*, and *attention*.

Reading Glossary

allow: to let; to permit
attention: work; care
cemetery: a burial place for the dead; graveyard

BEFORE YOU READ

 5-10 mins

1. Have students discuss the questions in pairs.
2. Ask for a few volunteers to share their answers with the class.

Practice Idea: Listening

To practice listening skills, have students first listen to the audio alone. Ask a few comprehension questions. Repeat the audio if necessary. Then have them open their books and read along as they listen to the audio.

Reading

CD 1 TR 01

 10-15 mins

1. Have students first read the text silently. Tell them to pay special attention to the verb *be* and other verbs in the simple present tense. Then play the audio and have students read along silently.

2. Check students' comprehension. Ask questions such as: *How do Americans feel about pets?* (They love them.) *Do more Americans own dogs or cats?* (dogs) *How do they treat their pets?* (like members of the family) *Do Americans spend a lot of money on their pets?* (yes) *Why are pets good for people?* (Pets are fun; contact with pets can be good for your health; pets keep lonely people company; etc.)

DID YOU KNOW?

Have students read the information, then ask: *What other dogs do you think are popular?* Then share the following information with them.

The Top Ten Dog Breeds in the United States

Labrador Retriever

Golden Retriever

German Shepherd

Beagle

Dachshund

Yorkshire Terrier

Boxer

Poodle

Chihuahua

Shih Tzu

1.1 *Be*—Forms and Uses

10-15 mins

1. Have students cover up grammar chart **1.1** on page 3. Activate students' prior knowledge. Write the uses of the verb *be* on the board. Ask volunteers to go up to the board and write examples. Or have students write examples in pairs and go over them as a class. For example, write:

    1. *description*
    2. *classification or definition*
    3. *location*

2. Have students look at grammar chart **1.1**. Ask students to compare their sentences with the example sentences. Confirm that students were able to provide an example for each use. Go over trouble spots with the whole class. Review the example sentences in the grammar chart.

3. Point out that to *be cold* and to *have a cold* have different meanings. *Be cold* means to feel a low temperature. *Have a cold* shows an illness.

Presentation Idea

Write example sentences for each use of *be* and have students decide what the use is. For example, write: *I am patient.* Students say: *description.* If students have difficulty, write the list of uses on the board.

EXERCISE 1

ANSWERS: **1.** are; **2.** is; **3.** is; **4.** are, are, are; **5.** is; **6.** are, are; **7.** is; **8.** are; **9.** are; **10.** are; **11.** is; **12.** is

5-10 mins

1. Have students read the direction line. Ask: *What words do we use here?* (is, are, am) Go over the example in the book. Then do #1 with the class. Ask: *What form of* be *goes here?* (are)

2. Have students complete Exercise 1 individually. Remind them to review grammar chart **1.1** on page 3 if necessary. Then have them check their answers in pairs. Monitor pair work. Check the answers as a class.

1.2 Contractions with *Be*

10-15 mins

1. Have students cover up grammar chart **1.2** on page 5. Write the list of pronouns and *be* verbs from the grammar chart on the board. Have volunteers make sentences. Say: *Make a sentence. Use contractions such as* I'm.

2. Then write: *My grandmother's lonely.* Ask: *Is this contraction correct?* (yes) Continue with: *A fox's a relative of a dog.* Ask: *Is this contraction correct?* (no) *Why can't we use a contraction here? Does anyone remember?* (We don't make contractions with *is* with nouns that end in *s, se, ce, ge, ze, sh, ch,* or *x.*)

    Now write: *Dogs're popular pets.* Ask: *Is this contraction correct?* (no) *Why can't we use a contraction here?* (In writing, we don't make a contraction with a plural noun and *are.*) Ask: *Is there a contraction for* am not? (no)

3. Have students look at grammar chart **1.2**. Say: *Compare our list with the list in the chart.*

4. Review the example sentences and explanations in the grammar chart.

EXERCISE 2

ANSWERS: 1, 2, 3, 4 (second and third blanks), **5, 7, 9, 11, 12**

5-10 mins

1. Have students read the direction line. Point out that students need to go back to Exercise 1 on page 4.

2. Have students complete Exercise 2 in pairs. Remind them to review grammar chart **1.2** on page 5 if necessary. Then check the answers as a class.

Practice Idea: Speaking

Go back to grammar chart **1.1** on page 3. Review the example sentences. Ask: *Which sentences can use a contraction?* Have students say the sentences using contractions.

EXERCISE 3

Answers: 1. are, aren't (OR 're not); **2.** 's, isn't (OR 's not); **3.** 'm, isn't (OR 's not); **4.** 's, isn't (OR 's not); **5.** 's, isn't (OR 's not); **6.** are, aren't; **7.** 's, isn't (OR 's not); **8.** 'm, 'm not; **9.** is, isn't (OR 's not)

10-15 mins

1. Have students read the direction line. Ask: *What goes in the second blank?* (the negative form) Go over the example in the book.

2. Have students complete the rest of Exercise 3 individually. Remind them to review grammar chart **1.2** on page 5 if necessary. Then have them compare their answers in pairs. Monitor pair work. Give help as needed. Then check the answers as a class.

EXERCISE 4

Answers: 1. 's; **2.** isn't (OR 's not), 's; **3.** are; **4.** are; **5.** 's; **6.** is, 's, old; **7.** It's; **8.** 's; **9.** is; **10.** This; **11.** 'm, 's; **12.** isn't (OR 's not), 's, old

5-10 mins

1. Have students read the direction line. Go over the example in the book. Then do #1 with the class.

2. Have students complete Exercise 4 individually. Remind them to review grammar chart **1.2** on page 5 if necessary. Have them compare their answers in pairs. Monitor pair work. Give help as needed. Then check the answers as a class.

Practice Idea: Writing

Have students work in pairs to write five to eight sentences about their own families and pets with the verb *be*. Ask students to use contractions.

Dog Walkers READING

1. Have students look at the picture. Ask: *What are the people doing?* (walking a dog) *Who are the people?* (dog walkers)

2. Have students look at the title of the reading. Ask: *What is the reading about?* Have students make predictions.

3. Preteach any vocabulary words your students may not know, such as *agency*, *customer*, and *Dalmatian*.

Reading Glossary

agency: a type of business that helps people do something

customer: a person or business that buys from another person or business; a client

Dalmatian: a white dog with black spots often kept as a pet by firefighters

BEFORE YOU READ

5-10 mins

1. Have students discuss the questions in pairs.

2. Ask for a few volunteers to share their answers with the class.

Reading

CD 1 TR 02

10-15 mins

1. Have students first read the text silently. Tell them to pay special attention to questions with *be*. Then play the audio and have students read along silently.

2. Check students' comprehension. Ask questions such as: *What's a dog walker?* (Someone who walks other people's dogs.) *Why does person B like her job?* (Her customers are always happy to see her, and she likes working outside.) *Who is person B talking about when she says* customers? (the dogs she walks) *Does person A want to become a dog walker?* (yes)

Presentation Idea

The topic for this reading can be enhanced with the following items:

1. Funny pictures of dog walkers with lots of dogs

2. Newspaper ads for dog walkers

1.3 Questions with *Be*

10-15 mins

1. Have students cover up grammar chart **1.3** on page 8. Activate prior knowledge. Write the statements from the grammar chart on the board. Have volunteers go to the board to write questions and short answers, or have students write questions and answers in pairs. Say: *Write* yes/no *questions and short answers for these statements.* Remind students to use contractions whenever possible.

2. Then write the statements from the second chart (page 9) on the board. Have students write *wh-* questions for each statement. Ask volunteers to write the questions on the board or have students work in pairs.

3. Have students look at grammar chart **1.3**. Say: *Now compare your work with the chart.* Go over any trouble spots with the class. Review the example sentences and explanations in the grammar chart.

4. Direct students to the Pronunciation Note on page 8. Model the rising intonation of the *yes/no* questions. Write a question on the board and show the rising intonation with an arrow.

5. Direct students to the Language Notes on page 9. Point out that most question words, except for *which* and *how much*, can contract with *is*. Review the list of common questions with *be*.

EXERCISE 5
Answers will vary.

10-15 mins

1. Tell students that this exercise is about them. Have students read the direction line. Ask: *What kind of questions are we going to ask?* (yes/no questions) *What kind of answers are we going to give?* (short answers) *Do we always make contractions in short answers?* (No. Not with affirmative short answers.) Go over the example in the book. Have students model the example.

2. Have students complete Exercise 5 individually. Remind them to review grammar chart **1.3** on pages 8–9 if necessary. Then have students take turns asking and answering the questions in pairs. Monitor pair work. Give help as needed.

EXERCISE 6
Answers will vary.

10-15 mins

1. Tell students that this exercise is about the class and them. Have students read the direction line. Ask: *What kind of questions are we going to ask?* (yes/no questions) *What kind of answers are we going to give?* (short answers) *Do we always make contractions in short answers?* (No. Not with affirmative short answers.) Go over the example in the book. Have students model the example.

2. Have students complete Exercise 6 individually. Remind them to review grammar chart **1.3** on pages 8–9 if necessary. Then have students take turns asking and answering the questions in pairs. Monitor pair work. Give help as needed.

(Practice Idea: Writing and Speaking)

Have students write three more *yes/no* questions about the class. Then have students ask and answer their questions in pairs.

EXERCISE 7

Answers will vary.

10-15 mins

1. Have students read the direction line. Say: *Answer the questions in complete sentences.* Model #1: *Gerbils are good pets for children.*

2. Have students complete Exercise 7 individually. Remind them to review grammar chart **1.3** on pages 8–9 if necessary. Then have students ask and answer the questions in pairs. Monitor pair work. Give help as needed.

(Practice Idea: Speaking)

Have students discuss the questions in groups and report their results to the class. Take a class survey about pets and animals.

 ### EXERCISE 8
CD 1
TR 03
ANSWERS: 1. is; **2.** 's; **3.** Is she; **4.** is; **5.** is she; **6.** 's; **7.** 's her name; **8.** How old is she; **9.** 's; **10.** Is it; **11.** 'm; **12.** 'm not; **13.** are; **14.** 'm not; **15.** aren't you home; **16.** she's; **17.** is she; **18.** 's; **19.** 're; **20.** 's

10-15 mins

1. Have students read the direction line. Go over the example.

2. Have students complete Exercise 8 individually. Remind them to review grammar charts **1.1** on page 3, **1.2** on page 5, and **1.3** on pages 8–9 if necessary. Play the audio and check answers as a class.

(Practice Idea: Listening)

To provide practice with listening skills, have students close their books and listen to the audio. Repeat the audio as needed. Ask comprehension questions, such as: *Is the dog male or female?* (female) *How old is the dog?* (three years old) *Why is the grandmother lonely?* (because nobody is home all day; everyone is at work) Then have students open their books and complete Exercise 8.

(Practice Idea: Speaking)

Have students practice the conversation in pairs. Have volunteers act out the conversation for the class.

 ### EXERCISE 9
CD 1
TR 04
ANSWERS: 1. are you; **2.** are you; **3.** 's; **4.** 'm not; **5.** 'm; **6.** What's; **7.** 's not; **8.** 's; **9.** It's; **10.** is; **11.** is; **12.** How old is he; **13.** 's; **14.** old; **15.** Are you; **16.** Who's; **17.** 's; **18.** 're; **19.** isn't she; **20.** 's; **21.** 's

10-15 mins

1. Have students read the direction line. Go over the example.

2. Have students complete Exercise 9 individually. Remind them to review grammar charts **1.1** on page 3, **1.2** on page 5, and **1.3** on pages 8–9 if necessary. Play the audio and check answers as a class.

(Practice Idea: Listening)

To provide practice with listening skills, have students close their books and listen to the audio. Repeat the audio as needed. Ask comprehension questions, such as: *Who made the call?* (Betty) *What's wrong with the cat?* (He's sick; he isn't hungry or thirsty; he's tired all the time.) Then have students open their books and complete Exercise 9.

Practice Idea: Speaking

Have students practice the conversation in pairs. Have volunteers act out the conversation for the class.

◄)) EXERCISE 10

CD 1 TR 05

ANSWERS: 1. 's; **2.** 's; **3.** 's; **4.** 's; **5.** are; **6.** isn't (OR 's not); **7.** are; **8.** 's; **9.** are they; **10.** are there; **11.** 's; **12.** 's; **13.** Is she; **14.** is; **15.** is she; **16.** 's; **17.** isn't (OR 's not); **18.** 'm; **19.** isn't he; **20.** 's; **21.** 'm; **22.** Are you; **23.** 'm not; **24.** 's; **25.** 's; **26.** Is it; **27.** is; **28.** it's

10-15 mins

1. Have students read the direction line. Go over the example. Remind students to use contractions whenever possible.

2. Have students complete Exercise 10 individually. Remind them to review grammar charts **1.1** on page 3, **1.2** on page 5, and **1.3** on pages 8–9 if necessary. Play the audio and check answers as a class.

Practice Idea: Listening

To provide practice with listening skills, have students close their books and listen to the audio. Repeat the audio as needed. Ask comprehension questions, such as: *What's a mutt?* (a mixed-breed dog) *Are mutts expensive?* (no) *Are the animals at shelters healthy?* (yes) *How do you know?* (The shelter's doctors check an animal's health before giving it to a family.) Then have students open their books and complete Exercise 10.

Practice Idea: Speaking

Have students practice the conversation in pairs. Have volunteers act out the conversation for the class.

Guide Dogs READING

1. Have students look at the photos. Ask: *What's happening in the photos?* (A visually impaired person is walking with a guide dog. A dog is running round obstacles/being trained.)

2. Have students look at the title of the reading. Ask: *What is the reading about?* Have students make predictions.

3. Preteach any vocabulary words your students may not know, such as *curb, intersection, distraction,* and *harness.* Point out the pictures of *harness* and *obstacle.*

Reading Glossary

curb: the edge and border area of a sidewalk; a curbstone
distraction: something that interrupts; a disturbance
harness: straps and a collar that horses and other animals wear to pull loads
intersection: a crossing of roads

BEFORE YOU READ

5-10 mins

1. Have students discuss the questions in pairs.

2. Ask for a few volunteers to share their answers with the class.

◄)) Reading

CD 1 TR 06

10-15 mins

1. Have students first read the text silently. Tell them to pay special attention to simple present tense verbs. Then play the audio and have students read along silently.

2. Check students' comprehension. Ask questions such as: *Do guide dogs work alone?* (No. They work as a team with their owner.) *What do guide dogs do at all intersections?* (stop and wait) *Should you pet guide dogs when you see them?* (No. They are working and need to concentrate.) *How do trainers reward their dogs?* (with physical and verbal affection) *When do guide dogs know they can play?* (when their harnesses are off)

Context Note

In addition to guide dogs, there are many other kinds of service dogs trained to assist people with various disabilities. There are hearing dogs that alert their owners to sounds. There are mobility dogs that may pull wheelchairs or physically support their owners. There are even seizure alert dogs that help their owners get to a safe place when they sense a seizure coming on.

1.4 The Simple Present Tense—Affirmative Statements

10-15 mins

1. Have students go back to the reading on page 14. Say: *Circle three examples of the base form and three examples of the* -s *form in the simple present tense. Look at the subject. When do you use the base form? When do you use the* -s *form?* Write students' examples on the board.

2. Review the examples and explanations of the simple present tense in the grammar chart on page 15. Go over when to use the base form (when the subject is *I, you, we, they,* or a plural noun). Go over when to use the *-s* form (when the subject is with *he, she, it,* or a singular noun). Point out that the *-s* form is used with *family, everyone, everybody, no one, nobody,* and *nothing.*

3. Point out the verbs that have irregular *-s* forms.

4. Review the uses of the simple present tense. Go over the examples and explanations in the chart. Then have students go back to the reading on page 14. Say: *Find an example of one or two of the uses.* Write students' examples on the board.

Presentation Idea

Have students go back to the reading on page 2 (*Americans and Their Pets*). Say: *Circle three verbs in the simple present tense base form and one verb in the* -s *form.* Then have students look at grammar chart **1.4**.

EXERCISE 11

ANSWERS: 1. have; **2.** sleeps; **3.** learn; **4.** makes; **5.** work; **6.** graduate; **7.** gives; **8.** get; **9.** needs; **10.** costs; **11.** talk; **12.** wants; **13.** barks; **14.** travel; **15.** have; **16.** has; **17.** protect; **18.** loves; **19.** knows; **20.** thinks

5-10 mins

1. Have students read the direction line. Go over the examples in the book.

2. Have students complete the exercise individually. Remind them to review grammar chart **1.4** on page 15 if necessary. Check the answers as a class.

1.5 Negative Statements with the Simple Present Tense =★

10-15 mins

1. Have students cover up grammar chart **1.5** on page 17. Write the following statements on the board:

   1. *The owner knows the destination.*
   2. *Some trainers use food to reward a dog.*
   3. *You have a cat.*
   4. *The dog stops at a curb.*
   5. *Guide dogs work when the harness is on.*

   Ask students to write a negative statement for each sentence.

2. Have students look at grammar chart **1.5**. Say: *Check your work.* Go over trouble spots with the whole class. Review the example sentences and explanations in the grammar chart.

Presentation Idea

Have students go back to the reading on page 14 (*Guide Dogs*). Ask students to find all the examples of negative statements from the reading. Write them on the board (*Guide dogs don't lead the owners; Their owners don't completely control the guide dogs;* etc.). Have volunteers explain the rules for forming negative statements in the simple present tense. Write the rules on the board.

EXERCISE 12

ANSWERS: **1.** don't play; **2.** don't use; **3.** doesn't work; **4.** don't see; **5.** doesn't go; **6.** don't eat; **7.** don't like; **8.** doesn't sleep; **9.** doesn't allow; **10.** don't need; **11.** don't have; **12.** doesn't like

⏱ 5–10 mins

1. Have students read the direction line. Ask: *What will we put in the blanks?* (the negative of the underlined verb) Remind students that they should use contractions whenever possible. Go over the example in the book.

2. Have students complete the exercise individually. Remind them to review grammar chart **1.5** on page 17 if necessary. Check the answers as a class.

Search and Rescue Dogs

READING

1. Have students look at the photo. Ask: *What's going on in the photo?* (A rescue dog is looking for something.)

2. Have students look at the title of the reading. Ask: *What is the reading about?* Have students make predictions.

3. Preteach any vocabulary words your students may not know, such as *disaster, earthquake,* and *flood.*

Reading Glossary

disaster: a sudden great act of destruction and loss
earthquake: sudden, violent movements of the earth's surface
flood: covering of dry land with water; an overflow

BEFORE YOU READ

⏱ 5–10 mins

1. Have students discuss the questions in pairs.

2. Ask for a few volunteers to share their answers with the class.

Reading

CD 1
TR 07

⏱ 10–15 mins

1. Have students first read the text silently. Tell them to pay special attention to questions with the simple present tense. Then play the audio and have students read along silently. Point out that *SAR* stands for *search and rescue*.

2. Check students' comprehension. Ask questions such as: *What do search and rescue dogs do?* (They help find missing people in disasters like earthquakes.) *How do they find people?* (by smelling them) *What kinds of dogs are usually search and rescue dogs?* (large dogs like Labrador Retrievers and Golden Retrievers)

Practice Idea: Listening

To practice listening skills, have students first listen to the audio alone. Ask a few comprehension questions. Repeat the audio if necessary. Then have them open their books and read along as they listen to the audio.

Context Note

Approximately 300 dogs and their handlers participated in search and rescue efforts after the World Trade Center disaster on September 11, 2001. Dogs representing 19 states, together with all the police canine units from New York, worked together to find victims in the debris and rubble. In addition, a number of canine search and rescue teams from all over the world also volunteered their services.

1.6 Questions with the Simple Present Tense

1. Have students cover up grammar chart **1.6** on page 19. Ask students to find examples of *yes/no* questions in the reading. Write them on the board. Make sure students find examples with both *do* and *does*.

2. Have students look at grammar chart **1.6**. Review the example sentences and explanations in the grammar chart.

3. Then have students go back to the reading on page 18. Say: *Find all the different kinds of wh- questions in the reading.* Write students' examples on the board (e.g., *What does* search *mean? What do these dogs do?*).

4. Have students look at grammar chart **1.6** on page 19. Review the example sentences and explanations in the grammar chart. Ask: *What* wh- *questions in the chart are not in the reading?* (*where* and *why*)

5. Review negative questions with *why*. Go over the examples in the chart and have students ask you questions about the class (e.g., *Why don't you stop class at 7:00? Why don't we have a break?*).

6. Direct students to the Language Note. Compare questions with *be* to questions with other verbs. Go over the examples in the chart. Then have students write *yes/no* and *wh-* questions about the class.

Practice Idea: Writing

Have students go back to the reading on page 14 (*Guide Dogs*). Ask students to work in pairs to write ten questions. Say: *Write yes/no, wh-, and negative questions.* Then have one pair exchange questions with another pair.

EXERCISE 13

CD 1
TR 08

ANSWERS: 1. do; **2.** Do; **3.** don't; **4.** don't you have; **5.** doesn't permit; **6.** Does; **7.** does; **8.** Do you have; **9.** need; **10.** Do; **11.** don't you want; **12.** doesn't want; **13.** doesn't she want; **14.** like; **15.** likes;

16. comes; **17.** sneezes; **18.** coughs; **19.** doesn't want

1. Have students read the direction line. Go over the example. Remind students to use contractions whenever possible.

2. Have students complete Exercise 13 individually. Remind them to review grammar chart **1.6** on page 19 if necessary. Play the audio and check answers as a class.

Practice Idea: Listening

To provide practice with listening skills, have students close their books and listen to the audio. Repeat the audio as needed. Ask comprehension questions, such as: *What kind of pet does the landlord permit?* (cats) *What is the cat owner doing in three months?* (getting married) *What does he have to do before then?* (find a new home for his cat) *Why?* (because his girlfriend is allergic to cats) Then have students open their books and complete Exercise 12.

Practice Idea: Speaking

Have students practice the conversation in pairs. Ask volunteers to act out the conversation for the class.

EXERCISE 14

ANSWERS: Part 1: 1. How old is your dog? **2.** What's your dog's name? **3.** Is it a male or a female? **4.** What does your dog eat? **5.** How often do you take your dog out? **6.** Does your dog do tricks?/ What kind of tricks does your dog do? **7.** Does your dog have toys?/What kind of toys does your dog have? **8.** Is your dog friendly? **9.** Does your dog bark a lot? **10.** Why do you like dogs?
Part 2: 1. How old is your cat? **2.** What's your cat's name? **3.** Is it a male or a female? **4.** Does your cat catch mice? **5.** Is your cat friendly? **6.** Does your cat sit on your lap a lot? **7.** Does your cat have toys?/What kind of toys does your cat have? **8.** Why do you like cats?

1. Tell students that in Part 1, they will have to interview a student who has a dog. Part 2 is for interviewing a student with a cat. Identify dog owners and cat owners in the classroom. Ask: *Who owns a dog? Who owns a cat?* Go over the examples. Have volunteers model the examples.

2. Have students complete the exercise in pairs. Remind them to review grammar chart **1.6** on page 19 if necessary. Monitor pair work. Give help as needed.

Practice Idea: Speaking

Do a class survey with the information from the interviews. Have students discuss their information in groups (people with dogs and people with cats) and then have them report their findings to the class.

1.7 *Wh-* Questions with a Preposition ✏️★

1. Have students cover up grammar chart **1.7** on page 21. Write the following on the board:

   1. *What does she talk _____?*
   2. *What does your cat sleep _____?*
   3. *Who does the dog sleep _____?*
   4. *Where do you come _____?*
   5. *Where are you _____?*

   Activate students' prior knowledge. Say: *Fill in the blanks with the missing words.* (**Answers: 1.** about; **2.** on; **3.** with; **4.** from; **5.** from)

2. Have students look at grammar chart **1.7**. Say: *Now compare your questions with the chart.* Review the example questions in the grammar chart.

3. Point out the formal *with whom.* Review questions and answers with time (e.g., *What time does the class begin? At 7:00.*).

EXERCISE 15 ✏️★

ANSWERS: **Answers may vary. 1.** Do you live alone?/With whom do you live? OR Who do you live with? **2.** Do you go to bed early?/What time do you go to bed? **3.** Does your teacher come

to class on time?/What time does your teacher (OR he/she) come to class? **4.** Does your teacher come from this city?/Where does your teacher (OR he/she) come from? **5.** Do you practice English outside of class?/With whom do you practice English? OR Who do you practice English with? **6.** Do you think about your future?/What else do you think about? **7.** Do you complain about English grammar?/What else do you complain about? **8.** Do you listen to the radio?/What station do you listen to? **9.** Does your teacher talk about spelling?/What else does your teacher (OR he/she) talk about? **10.** Are you interested in animals?/What animals are you interested in? **11.** Do you come from Mexico?/Where do you come from? **12.** Do you go to sleep before midnight?/What time do you go to sleep?

---

1. Tell students that they will be answering questions about themselves. Have students read the direction line. Ask: *What kind of question do we ask first?* (a *yes/no* question) Say: *Then ask a* wh- *question, if possible.* Go over the example in the book. Model the example with a volunteer. Answer "no" to the question.

2. Have students complete Exercise 15 in pairs. Remind them to review grammar chart **1.7** on page 21 if necessary. Monitor pair work. Go over any trouble spots with the class.

Practice Idea: Speaking

Do a class survey with the information from the interviews. Write the results on the board (e.g., Do you live alone? Yes: 5 No: 7).

🔊 **EXERCISE 16**

CD 1
TR 09

ANSWERS: **1.** Do; **2.** do they help; **3.** help; **4.** Do; **5.** do; **6.** do; **7.** are you; **8.** It's not; **9.** needs; **10.** do; **11.** play; **12.** takes; **13.** do

---

1. Have students read the direction line. Go over the example. Do #1 with the class.

2. Have students complete Exercise 16 individually. Remind students to review grammar charts **1.6** on page 19 and **1.7** on page 21 if necessary. Play the audio and check answers as a class.

Practice Idea: Listening

To provide practice with listening skills, have students close their books and listen to the audio. Repeat the audio as needed. Ask comprehension questions, such as: *What do guide dogs do?* (help people with disabilities; help blind people move from place to place, on foot and by public transportation) *What kind of people do guide dogs help?* (blind people, deaf people, people in wheelchairs) *When do guide dogs play?* (when the owner takes off the dog's harness) Then have students open their books and complete Exercise 16.

1.8 Questions About Meaning, Spelling, Cost, and Time

5-10 mins

1. Have students look at grammar chart **1.8** on page 23. Review the questions and explanations in the chart.

2. Then ask students to work in pairs to create sentences with *mean*, *spell*, *say*, and *take* to ask you, the teacher. Have volunteers ask you questions.

 EXERCISE 17

CD 1 TR 10

ANSWERS: 1. does it (OR kitten) mean; **2.** do you spell that (OR his name OR Romeo); **3.** does he sleep; **4.** Do you have; **5.** do you have; **6.** do you say; **7.** 's his name; **8.** is he; **9.** do they live; **10.** do they cost; **11.** Are; **12.** does he eat; **13.** Does he talk; **14.** does he say

10-15 mins

1. Tell students that they will be completing the questions in this exercise. Go over the example.

2. Have students complete Exercise 17 individually. Remind them to review grammar chart **1.8** on page 23 if necessary. Play the audio and check answers as a class.

Practice Idea: Listening

To provide practice with listening skills, have students close their books and listen to the audio. Repeat the audio as needed. Ask comprehension questions, such as: *What does* kitten *mean?* (baby cat) *How much do parrots usually cost?* (between $175 and $1,000) *What does Chico eat?* (fruit, rice, vegetables, nuts, and seeds) Then have students open their books and complete Exercise 17.

Practice Idea: Speaking

Have students practice the conversation in pairs. Ask volunteers to act out the conversation for the class.

 EXERCISE 18

CD 1 TR 11

ANSWERS: 1. don't; **2.** don't you have; **3.** aren't you at home; **4.** don't; **5.** Don't they; **6.** Do you have; **7.** Are they; **8.** do they cost; **9.** aren't; **10.** 's; **11.** don't; **12.** aren't; **13.** don't; **14.** do you have; **15.** do you spell

10-15 mins

1. Have students read the directions. Go over the example. Remind students to use contractions whenever possible.

2. Have students complete Exercise 18 individually. Remind them to review grammar charts **1.6** on page 19, **1.7** on page 21, and **1.8** on page 23 if necessary. Play audio and check answers as a class.

Practice Idea: Listening

To provide practice with listening skills, have students close their books and listen to the audio. Repeat the audio as needed. Ask comprehension questions, such as: *Do you need a lot of time to own a dog?* (Yes, dogs need a lot of attention.) *How much do some tropical fish cost?* (over $100) *What kind of fish is an Oranda?* (a kind of goldfish) Then have students open their books and complete Exercise 18.

Marianne and Sparky READING

1. Have students look at the photo. Ask: *What is the dog doing?* (riding in a bag) *What is the dog wearing?* (a hat and sunglasses)

2. Have students look at the title of the reading. Ask: *What is the reading about?* Have students make predictions.

3. Preteach any vocabulary words your students may not know, such as *dog groomer* and *kennel*.

Reading Glossary

dog groomer: a person who makes dogs look neat and clean

kennel: a place where dogs are kept, usually while their owners are away

BEFORE YOU READ

5-10 mins

1. Have students discuss the questions in pairs.

2. Ask for a few volunteers to share their answers with the class.

CD 1
TR 12

10-15 mins

Reading ═★

1. Have students first read the text silently. Tell them to pay special attention to frequency words. Then play the audio and have students read along silently.

2. Check students' comprehension. Ask questions such as: *Who is Marianne?* (a friend of Elena's) *Who is Sparky?* (Marianne's dog) *Does Marianne call her dog on the telephone?* (Yes. She talks to him through the answering machine.) *Who takes care of her dog when she's at work?* (a dog walker) *Where does Marianne like to go with Sparky when the weather is nice?* (to a beach for dogs and their owners) *Does Elena think Marianne and other Americans should treat their pets the way they do?* (probably not)

1.9 Simple Present Tense with Frequency Words ═★

5-10 mins

1. Have students cover up grammar chart **1.9** on page 27. Write the following frequency words on the board in random order:

> *rarely/seldom/hardly ever*
> *usually/generally*
> *always*
> *never/not ever*
> *often/frequently*
> *sometimes/occasionally*

Draw a 0%–100% scale on the board. Ask volunteers to place the frequency words on the scale.

2. Have students look at grammar chart **1.9**. Say: *Check our scale on the board with the scale in the book.* Review the example sentences in the grammar chart.

3. Explain to students that frequency words are used with the simple present tense to show regular activity.

4. Review frequency expressions such as *every day*, *once a week*, *from time to time*, etc.

EXERCISE 19

ANSWERS: Answers may vary. 1. writes; **2.** is; **3.** is; **4.** buys; **5.** is; **6.** sleeps; **7.** travels

5-10 mins

1. Tell students that this exercise is based on the reading. Have students read the direction line. Go over the example.

2. Have students complete the rest of the exercise individually. Remind them to review grammar chart **1.9** on page 27 if necessary. Go over the answers as a class.

EXERCISE 20

Answers will vary.

5-10 mins

1. Say: *Complete the sentences based on what's true for you.* Have students read the direction line. Go over the example in the book.

2. Have students complete the exercise individually. Remind them to review grammar chart **1.9** on page 27 if necessary. Then have students compare answers with a partner.

Practice Idea: Writing

Say: *What do you do in the United States that you don't do in your native country? Write comparisons. Use frequency words (e.g., Here I eat in fast-food restaurants once a week. In Colombia, I never eat in fast-food restaurants.).*

EXERCISE 21

Answers will vary.

5-10 mins

1. Tell students that this exercise is about customs and habits in their native culture. Have students read the direction line. Go over the example in the book.

2. Have students complete the exercise individually. Remind them to review grammar chart **1.9** on page 27 if necessary. Then have students compare answers in pairs or groups.

Practice Idea: Speaking

On the board, make a grid of the nationalities represented in the class and the item numbers (1–5) from Exercise 21. Write the frequency word under each nationality for each item of the exercise.

	El Salvador	Morocco	Saudi Arabia
1.	rarely	never	never
2.			
3.			
4.			
5.			

EXERCISE 22

ANSWERS: 1. B; **2.** A; **3.** A; **4.** B; **5.** B

5-10 mins

1. Have students read the direction line. Go over the example in the book.

2. Have students complete the exercise individually. Then go over answers with the class. Make two lists on the board: frequency words that go before the verb and frequency words that go after the verb.

1.10 Position of Frequency Words and Expressions

5-10 mins

1. Have students look at grammar chart **1.10** on page 29. Have students compare the lists the class made on the board with the examples in the grammar chart.

2. Review the example sentences in the grammar chart. Point out that *sometimes, usually,* and *often* can come at the beginning of sentences. Tell students not to put *always, never, rarely,* or *seldom* at the beginning of the sentence.

3. Explain to students that frequency expressions can come at the beginning or at the end of a sentence. If a frequency expression comes at the beginning, you can use a comma to separate it from the rest of the sentence.

EXERCISE 23

ANSWERS: 1. Often she talks to Sparky on the telephone./She often talks to Sparky on the telephone. **2.** Sometimes she puts Sparky in a pet hotel./She sometimes puts Sparky in a pet hotel. **3.** Usually she takes her dog on vacation./She usually takes her dog on vacation. **4.** She's always with her dog. **5.** Sparky never goes out in the rain without a coat.

10-15 mins

1. Have students read the direction line. Ask: *What kind of word are we going to add to make the sentence true?* (a frequency word) Go over the example in the book.

2. Have students complete the exercise individually. Remind them to review grammar chart **1.10** on page 29 if necessary. Then have students compare answers in pairs. Monitor pair work.

EXERCISE 24

Answers will vary.

5-10
mins

1. Have students read the direction line. Model
   the example for the students and have a
   volunteer also model the example.

2. Have students complete the exercise
   individually. Remind them to review grammar
   chart **1.10** on page 29 if necessary. Then have
   students compare answers with a partner.
   Monitor pair work. Give help as needed.

EXERCISE 25

Answers will vary.

10-15
mins

1. Have students read the direction line. Model
   the example for the students and have
   a volunteer also model the example. Tell
   students they are going to write sentences
   about themselves.

2. Have students complete the exercise
   individually. Remind them to review grammar
   chart **1.10** on page 29 if necessary. Then have
   students compare answers with a partner.
   Monitor pair work. Give help as needed.

1.11 Questions with *Ever*

10-15
mins

1. Have students look at grammar chart **1.11** on
   page 31. Say: *When we want an answer that
   has a frequency word, use* ever *in the question.*

Go over the examples for *do/does.* Go around
the room and ask students questions with *ever*
(e.g., *Do you ever walk to school? Do you ever
bring your lunch? Do they ever talk in class?*).

2. Say: *You can use* ever *in sentences with* be, *too.*
   Go over the examples. Go around the class
   asking questions with *be* and *ever* (e.g., *Are you
   ever sad? Are they ever quiet? Is he ever late?*).

3. Point out that in short answers the frequency
   word comes between the subject and the verb.
   Tell students that the verb after *never* is always
   affirmative. Go over the example in the chart.

EXERCISE 26

ANSWERS: Answers may vary. Possible answers:
1. Yes, she <u>always</u> does. **2.** Yes, she <u>often</u> does.
3. No, they <u>never</u> do. **4.** Yes, they <u>always</u> do. **5.** Yes,
they <u>usually</u> do. **6.** No, they <u>rarely</u> do. **7.** Yes, they
<u>sometimes</u> are. **8.** Yes, they <u>usually</u> are.

10-15
mins

1. Have students read the direction line. Say:
   *Answer the questions with short answers and
   the frequency words in parentheses.* Go over the
   example in the book.

2. Have students complete the statements
   individually. Remind them to review grammar
   chart **1.11** on page 31 if necessary. Then have
   students take turns asking and answering
   the questions. Monitor pair work. Give help as
   needed. Briefly check answers as a class.

EXERCISE 27

Answers will vary.

10-15
mins

1. Tell students that this exercise is about their
   customs and habits. Have students read the
   direction line. Say: *Complete the statements
   for yourself. Then ask a partner.* Go over the
   example in the book. Model the example
   with a volunteer. Then have two volunteers
   model #1.

2. Have students complete the statements
   individually. Remind them to review grammar
   chart **1.11** on page 31 if necessary. Then have
   students take turns asking and answering
   questions. Monitor pair work. Give help as
   needed.

1.12 Questions with *How Often* and Answers with Frequency Expressions

 5-10 mins

1. Have students cover up grammar chart **1.12** on page 32. Write some frequency expressions on the board (e.g., *once a week, every day, every week,* and *twice a month*). Go around the room and ask questions with *How often?* (e.g., *How often do we come to class? How often do you visit your parents? How often do you call your grandmother? How often do you watch TV?*)

2. Now have students look at grammar chart **1.12**. Go over the examples and explanations.

EXERCISE 28

ANSWERS: Student responses will vary. Correct question constructions: 1. How often do you check your e-mail? **2.** How often do you shop for groceries? **3.** How often do you exercise? **4.** How often do you get a haircut? **5.** How often do you use your dictionary? **6.** How often do you use public transportation? **7.** How often do you use the Internet? **8.** How often do you go to the dentist? **9.** How often do you watch the news on TV? **10.** How often do you go to the teacher's office?

 10-15 mins

1. Tell students that they're going to ask their partners about their customs and habits. Go over the example. Have two volunteers model the example.

2. Have students complete the exercise in pairs. Remind them to review grammar chart **1.12** on page 32 if necessary. Monitor pair work. Give help as needed.

Practice Idea: Speaking

Create two rings of students. Have half of the students stand in an outer ring around the classroom. Have the other half stand in an inner ring, facing the outer ring. Instruct students to ask and answer the questions from Exercise 28. Call out *turn* every minute or so. Students in the inner ring should move one space clockwise. Students now ask and answer with their new partners. Say: *Ask questions in random order.* Make sure students look at each other when they're speaking.

Summary of Lesson 1

 20-30 mins

1. **Observe the simple present tense with the verb *be*.** Review the examples. Then have students write their own sentences. Say: *Write the following with* is *and* are:

   1. *affirmative statement*
   2. *negative statement*
   3. yes/no *question*
   4. *short answer*
   5. wh- *question*
   6. *negative question*

   If necessary, have students review Lesson 1.

2. **Observe the simple present tense with other verbs.** Review the examples. Then have students write their own sentences. Say: *Write the following with the base form and with the* -s *form*:

   1. *affirmative statement*
   2. *negative statement*
   3. yes/no *question*
   4. *short answer*
   5. wh- *question*
   6. *negative question*

   If necessary, have students review: **Lesson 1**.

3. **Frequency Words** On the board, write a scale with the frequency words in scrambled order. Have the students unscramble the scale. If necessary, have students review:

   1.9 Simple Present Tense with Frequency Words (p. 27)
   1.10 Position of Frequency Words and Expressions (p. 29)

4. **Questions with Frequency Words** Have students write five questions with *ever* and *how often* to ask their classmates. Let students mingle in the room as they ask their questions. Have volunteers share the information. If necessary, have students review:

   1.11 Questions with *Ever* (p. 31)
   1.12 Questions with *How Often* and Answers with Frequency Expressions (p. 32)

Editing Advice

10–15 mins

Have students close their books. Write the first few sentences without editing marks or corrections on the board. For example:

1. *My daughter has 10 years.*
2. *Please open the window. I have hot.*

Ask students to correct each sentence and provide a rule or explanation for each correction. This activity can be done individually, in pairs, or as a class. After students have corrected each sentence, tell them to turn to pages 34–35. Say: *Now compare your work with the Editing Advice in the book.*

Editing Quiz

ANSWERS: 1. does a therapy dog do; **2.** makes; **3.** We often go; **4.** sits; **5.** C; **6.** does that make; **7.** C; **8.** loves; **9.** usually smile; **10.** does a dog become; **11.** have; **12.** C; **13.** C; **14.** have; **15.** doesn't bark; **16.** is six OR is six years old; **17.** C; **18.** has; **19.** C; **20.** does the training cost; **21.** C; **22.** C; **23.** does it take; **24.** depends; **25.** Do; **26.** C; **27.** C; **28.** We go once a week (OR Once a week we go); **29.** is located; **30.** I always bathe; **31.** does TDI mean; **32.** C; **33.** C; **34.** is thirsty; **35.** do you know; **36.** I'm thirsty.

10–15 mins

1. Tell students they are going to put the Editing Advice into practice. Have students read the direction line. Ask: *Do all the shaded words and phrases have mistakes?* (no) Go over the examples with the class. Then do #1 together.

2. Have students complete the quiz individually. Then have them compare answers with a partner before checking answers as a class.

3. For the items students had difficulties with, have them go back and find the relevant grammar chart and review it. Monitor and give help as necessary.

Lesson 1 Test/Review

50–60 mins

Use the Assessment CD-ROM with Exam*View*®, Online Workbook, and the Web site for additional practice, review, and assessment materials.

PART 1

ANSWERS: 1. knows, doesn't know; **2.** has, doesn't have; **3.** lives, doesn't live; **4.** is, isn't; **5.** understand, don't understand; **6.** are, aren't; **7.** like, don't like; **8.** need, don't need; **9.** loves, don't like (OR love)

1. Part 1 may be used as an in-class test to assess student performance, in addition to the Assessment CD-ROM with Exam*View*®. Have students read the direction line. Go over the examples. Say: *Remember to use contractions.*

2. Have students complete the exercise individually. Collect for assessment.

3. If necessary, have students review:

    1.2 Contractions with *Be* (p. 5)
    1.4 The Simple Present Tense— Affirmative Statements (p. 15)
    1.5 Negative Statements with the Simple Present Tense (p. 17)

PART 2

ANSWERS: 1. Does Elena have a dog? No, she doesn't. **2.** Does Sofia live in the U.S.? No, she doesn't. **3.** Does Sofia have an American friend? No, she doesn't. **4.** Do you ever write letters? **5.** Do you ever go to the zoo? **6.** Are American customs strange for Marianne? No, they aren't.

1. Part 2 may also be used as an in-class test to assess student performance, in addition to the Assessment CD-ROM with Exam*View*®. Tell students that they will be writing *yes/no* questions and short answers. Have students read the direction line. Go over the example.

2. Have students complete individually. Collect for assessment.

3. If necessary, have students review:

    1.3 Questions with *Be* (pp. 8–9)
    1.6 Questions with the Simple Present Tense (p. 19)
    1.11 Questions with *Ever* (p. 31)

PART 3

ANSWERS: 1. often does Marianne (OR she) travel; **2.** doesn't she understand; **3.** does Sofia write; **4.** does it cost; **5.** doesn't she have; **6.** does she carry a picture of Sparky; **7.** does she walk her dog;

8. does she take her dog; **9.** do they need; **10.** do they save; **11.** does a purebred dog cost

1. Part 3 may also be used as an in-class test to assess student performance, in addition to the Assessment CD-ROM with Exam*View*®. Have students read the direction line. Go over the example.

2. Have students complete the exercise individually. Collect for assessment.

3. If necessary, have students review:

   1.6 Questions with the Simple Present Tense (p. 19)

   1.8 Questions about Meaning, Spelling, Cost, and Time (p. 23)

   1.11 Questions with *Ever* (p. 31)

   1.12 Questions with *How Often* and Answers with Frequency Expressions (p. 32)

PART 4

ANSWERS: 1. How do you spell "kitten"? **2.** What does "puppy" mean? **3.** How do you say "cat" in Spanish? **4.** How much does a parrot cost? **5.** How long does it take to train a dog?

1. Part 4 may also be used as an in-class test to assess student performance, in addition to the Assessment CD-ROM with Exam*View*®. Have students read the directions. Review the example.

2. Have students complete the questions individually. Collect for assessment.

3. If necessary, have students review:

   1.6 Questions with the Simple Present Tense (p. 19)

   1.8 Questions About Meaning, Spelling, Cost, and Time (p. 23)

Expansion

These expansion activities provide opportunities for students to interact with one another and further develop their speaking and writing skills. Encourage students to use grammar from this lesson whenever possible.

CLASSROOM ACTIVITIES

10-15 mins per activity

1. Say: *This chart lists different customs. Which customs are practiced here in the U.S. and which are practiced in your native cultures?* Have students complete the charts individually. Then put students in groups to compare.

2. Have students discuss each animal in pairs or groups and decide which ones are good pets. Have pairs/groups share their decisions with the class.

TALK ABOUT IT

15-20 mins

Write on the board: *dogs/cats* Ask: *Why do dogs and cats make good pets? What are dogs/cats like?* Elicit adjectives to describe them (e.g., friendly, intelligent). Write the students' ideas on the board. Then have students discuss each question about pets and animals in pairs or groups. Then have them report back to the class.

WRITE ABOUT IT

30-40 mins

1. Brainstorm with the class a list of ways that Americans treat pets. Write them on the board. Then have students choose another country and brainstorm ideas about how people in that country treat animals. Write the ideas on the board. Then have students help you begin writing a paragraph on the board describing the differences between how Americans treat pets and how people in the other country treat pets. Have students write their own paragraphs individually or in pairs.

2. Have students read the direction line and the model paragraph. Tell students they can use the list of customs on page 40 or use any of their own thoughts and ideas. With the class, choose one or two of the customs from the list and have students choose a different country and say how those customs are different there. Write their ideas on the board. Then begin a paragraph on the board following the model in the book. Have students help you develop the paragraph comparing customs between the U.S. and the other country. Then have students write their own comparisons individually. Encourage them to write more than one paragraph. Collect compositions for assessment and/or have students present their paragraphs to a group.

Practice Idea: Writing

Have students exchange first drafts with a partner. Ask students to help their partners edit their drafts. Refer students to the Editing Advice on pages 34–35.

OUTSIDE ACTIVITIES

1. Tell students to take a notebook and a pen/pencil and go to a park and observe people with dogs. Tell them to write their observations. Then have them bring their notebooks to class and discuss their observations with their classmates in groups.

2. Have students interview an English-speaking friend or neighbor who has a pet and find out five interesting things about this pet. Have students write their interview questions in class before the interview if necessary. Have them bring the results of their interview to the class to share in pairs or groups.

3. Tell students to rent a movie about a dog and write a summary of the movie. Have students share their summaries with the class by posting them around the class for everyone to read.

INTERNET ACTIVITIES

1. Tell students to use a search engine and type in *pet supplies*. Have them find a Web site that advertises pet supplies and find out what people buy for their pets. Tell them to make a list of all the unusual things people buy for their pets. Ask volunteers to share their findings with the rest of the class. Then vote on the strangest pet product.

2. Tell students to find information about a breed of dog or cat that they like. (Tell them to try the Web site of the American Kennel Club, or AKC, for example.) Have students create a poster of their favorite breed of dog or cat. Ask them to include a picture if possible. Display the posters around the classroom.

3. Tell students to use a search engine and type in *animal shelter* and the name of the city where they live (or the nearest big city). Have them find information about what this shelter does. In class, have them discuss the animal shelters in the area and the information they found.

Lesson 2

Lesson Overview

GRAMMAR

Ask: *What tense did we study in Lesson 1?* (the simple present tense) *What tenses will we study in this lesson?* (the present continuous and the future tense) Ask volunteers to give examples of the present continuous and the future tenses. Write them on the board. Then ask: *Can anyone give examples of action and nonaction verbs?*

CONTEXT

1. Ask: *What will we learn about in this lesson?* (getting older) Activate students' prior knowledge. *What's life like for senior citizens in the U.S.? Is it different from life in your native countries?*

2. Have students share their knowledge and personal experiences.

Presentation Ideas

The topic for this lesson can be enhanced with the following items:

1. Brochures from retirement communities
2. Copies of *AARP* (American Association of Retired Persons) magazine

Retirement Living READING

1. Have students look at the photo. Ask: *Can you do what this woman is doing? How old do you think she is?*

2. Have students look at the title of the reading. Ask: *What is the reading about?* Have students use the title and photo to make predictions about the reading.

3. Preteach any vocabulary words your students may not know, such as *village* and *widower*.

Reading Glossary

village: a group of houses forming a settlement smaller than a town or city

widower: a husband whose wife has died

BEFORE YOU READ

1. Have students discuss the questions in pairs.

5-10 mins

2. Ask for a few volunteers to share their answers with the class.

Reading ≡★

CD 1 TR 13

10-15 mins

1. Have students first read the text silently. Explain that this is a conversation between Jack (a 62-year-old man who is taking a tour of a retirement village) and the manager of the retirement village. Tell students to pay special attention to present continuous tense verbs. Then play the audio and have students read along silently.

2. Check students' comprehension. Ask questions such as: *What kinds of houses do they have at the retirement village?* (single-family homes, townhouses, and apartments) *Are there many activities at the village?* (yes) *What are people learning in the computer class?* (how to design Web pages) *Are there more men or more women at the retirement village?* (more women) *How often does the singles group meet?* (once a week)

Practice Idea: Listening

To practice listening skills, have students first listen to the audio alone. Ask a few comprehension questions. Repeat the audio if necessary. Then have students open their books and read along as they listen to the audio.

2.1 Present Continuous Tense ≡★

10-15 mins

1. Have students go back to the reading on pages 44–45. Say: *Find examples of the present continuous tense with am, is, and are.* Write students' sentences on the board.

2. Ask: *How do we form the present continuous?* (*be* + verb *-ing*) Write it on the board.

3. Ask: *When do we use the present continuous?* (to describe an action in progress at this moment; to describe a state or condition using *sit, stand, wear,* and *sleep*) Write students' responses on the board. Ask students to find an example of each use from the reading.

4. Ask students to explain how to form contractions. Have them find examples from the reading and write them on the board. Then write the following on the board:

   They are playing cards.
   Jack is taking a tour.
   He is asking questions.
   The manager is asking questions.

   Ask students to make contractions using the subject and verb.

5. Review how to form the negative. Have them find examples from the reading and write them on the board. Then write the following on the board:

   Jack is doing yoga.
   Most people are watching TV.
   I'm playing tennis.

   Have students make the sentences into negative statements.

6. Have students look at grammar chart **2.1** on page 46. Say: *Compare your work with the grammar chart.* Review the examples and explanations.

7. Point out that they shouldn't repeat the verb *be* after the connectors *or* and *and*.

EXERCISE **1** =★

ANSWERS: **1.** 's taking; **2.** 's looking; **3.** is giving; **4.** are dancing; **5.** are using; **6.** 's lifting; **7.** are playing; **8.** are swimming; **9.** isn't (OR 's not) reading, 's putting; **10.** 's reading, watching, isn't (OR 's not) taking; **11.** aren't doing

 5-10 mins

1. Have students read the direction line. Go over the example in the book. Remind students to use contractions whenever possible.

2. Have students complete Exercise 1 individually. Remind them to review grammar chart **2.1** on page 46 if necessary. Check the answers as a class.

Practice Idea: Writing

Have students rewrite the sentences in Exercise 1 using the negative form of the verb

EXERCISE

ANSWERS: **Answers may vary. Possible answers:**
1. 's shining/isn't shining; **2.** 's raining/isn't raining; **3.** 'm (not) writing; **4.** 'm (not) using; **5.** 're doing/ aren't doing; **6.** 's helping/isn't helping; **7.** 's wearing/isn't wearing; **8.** 'm (not) using; **9.** 're practicing/aren't practicing; **10.** 'm (not) wearing; **11.** 's standing/(isn't standing); **12.** 'm (not) sitting

5-10 mins

1. Have students read the direction line. Say: *You're going to make true statements for what's happening now in the class and outside.* Go over the examples in the book. Model the exercise with your own information.

2. Have students complete Exercise 2 individually. Remind them to review grammar chart **2.1** on page 46 if necessary. Then have students compare answers with a partner. Monitor pair work. Give help as needed.

Practice Idea: Writing

Have students work in pairs to write five more true statements about what's happening in the class right now.

Life After Retirement READING

1. Have students look at the photo. Ask: *What is this woman doing?* (She is working on a computer.)

2. Have students look at the title of the reading. Ask: *What is the reading about?* Have students use the title and photo to make predictions about the reading.

3. Preteach any vocabulary words your students may not know, such as *avenue, pension, volunteer, pantry,* and *hobby.*

Reading Glossary

avenue: a path or road

hobby: an activity done for pleasure or relaxation

pantry: a small room next to the kitchen used to store food, dishes, and cooking equipment

pension: a regular payment made by a business or government to a person who has retired from a job

volunteer: to agree to do something of one's own free will rather than by necessity

BEFORE YOU READ

5–10 mins

1. Have students discuss the questions in pairs.
2. Ask for a few volunteers to share their answers with the class.

Reading

CD 1
TR 14

10–15 mins

1. Have students first read the text silently. Tell them to pay special attention to present continuous tense verbs. Then play the audio and have students read along silently.
2. Check students' comprehension. Ask questions such as: *What are more and more Americans doing after retirement?* (Many are starting new careers.) *What is Judy Pearlman doing now?* (making dolls) *What kind of classes is Charles Haskell taking?* (art classes) *What else are retirees doing in their free time?* (volunteering)

> **Practice Idea: Listening**
>
> To practice listening skills, have students first listen to the audio alone. Ask a few comprehension questions. Repeat the audio if necessary. Then have students open their books and read along as they listen to the audio.

2.2 Using the Present Continuous for Longer Actions

5–10 mins

1. Have students look at grammar chart **2.2** on page 49. Say: *We use the present continuous tense to describe actions that are happening now, but we also use it to describe long-term actions and trends.* Go over the examples and explanations in the chart.

2. Ask volunteers to make sentences that describe trends in the world now (e.g., *Women are having fewer babies. Children are watching more TV.*).

EXERCISE 3

ANSWERS: Answers may vary. Possible answers:
1. are retiring; **2.** 're not spending; **3.** 're starting;
4. are living; **5.** are discovering; **6.** are returning

5–10 mins

1. Tell students that this exercise is based on the reading on pages 48–49. Have students read the direction line. Ask: *What do we write in the blanks?* (the present continuous tense) Go over the example in the book.

2. Have students complete Exercise 3 individually. Remind them to review grammar chart **2.2** on page 49 if necessary. Have students compare answers in pairs. Monitor pair work. Check answers as a class.

EXERCISE 4

Answers will vary.

10–15 mins

1. Tell students that they will be making three long-term statements about themselves. Say: *The statements have to be about your life as a student.* Have students read the direction line. Point out the list of verbs provided. Go over the examples in the book. Model three statements about your own life. Write them on the board.

2. Have students complete Exercise 4 individually. Remind them to review grammar chart **2.2** on page 49 if necessary. Then have students compare sentences in groups. Monitor group work. Have volunteers share some of their sentences with the class.

EXERCISE 5

Answers will vary.

10–15 mins

1. Tell students that they will be making three long-term statements about things that are changing in their lives. Have students read the direction line. Go over the examples in the book. Model three statements about your own life. Write them on the board.

2. Have students write sentences individually. Remind them to review grammar chart **2.2** on page 49 if necessary. Then have students compare their statements in pairs. Monitor pair work. Have volunteers share some of their sentences with the class.

> ### Practice Idea: Writing
>
> Have students write a letter or an e-mail to a friend in a different city about their lives now. Say: *Use some of the statements from Exercises 4 and 5 and add new ones.*

EXERCISE 6

Answers will vary.

10-15 mins

1. Have students read the direction line. Say: *Complete the activity for your native country or another country. You can use affirmative or negative sentences.* Model item 1 (e.g., *Older people are getting more respect than before.*).

2. Have students complete Exercise 6 in groups. Remind them to review grammar chart **2.2** on page 49 if necessary. If possible, have students from different countries work together. Monitor group work. Give help as needed. Have volunteers share their answers with the class.

> ### Practice Idea: Speaking
>
> Have a class debate about one of the statements from the exercise. Divide the class into two groups. Assign one side of the argument to each group. Have groups prepare their arguments and present them to the opposing group.

2.3 Questions with the Present Continuous Tense =★

10-15 mins

1. Have students cover up grammar chart **2.3** on page 52. Write the following two sentences on the board:

> *Jerry is designing something.*
> *They are taking courses at college.*

Say: *For each sentence, write a yes/no question, a short answer, and a wh- question.*

2. Have students look at grammar chart **2.3**. Say: *Compare your sentences to the ones in the book.* Review the statements and questions. Go over any trouble spots.

3. Direct students to the Language Notes. Point out that a preposition can come at the end of a question (e.g., *What is he thinking about?*). Explain that we usually answer the question *What . . . doing?* with another verb (e.g., *What's she doing? She's watching TV.*).

4. Review the negative statements and questions in the chart. Have students go around the room making negative statements and questions. Say: *I'm going to make a negative statement. I want you to make a negative question.* Model the exercise with a volunteer (e.g., Teacher: *Sam isn't studying.*
Student: *Why isn't Sam studying?*).
Then instruct the volunteer to make a negative statement, and have another student ask a negative question. Continue the statement-question chain.

EXERCISE 7 =★

ANSWERS: 1. Are you considering; **2.** Is Marge designing; **3.** Is she taking; **4.** Is everyone doing; **5.** Are Judy and Charles taking; **6.** Am I asking

10-15 mins

1. Have students read the direction line. Go over the example in the book.

2. Have students complete Exercise 7 individually. Remind them to review grammar chart **2.3** on page 52 if necessary. Check the answers as a class.

EXERCISE 8 =★

ANSWERS: 1. Why is Judy (OR she) having more fun now? **2.** Where is she (OR Judy) traveling? **3.** What kind of career are you starting? **4.** What new things are seniors (OR they) studying? **5.** Why is your father (OR he) thinking about retirement? **6.** What kind of career is your mother (OR she) looking for? **7.** Why aren't you planning to retire? **8.** Why are people living longer nowadays? **9.** What kinds of things are you doing (that interest you)?

1. Have students read the direction line. Ask: *What kind of questions are we going to write here?* (wh- questions) Go over the example in the book. Remind students that they don't have to write an answer.

2. Have students complete Exercise 8 individually. Remind them to review grammar chart **2.3** on page 52 if necessary. Have students compare answers in pairs. Monitor pair work.

Practice Idea: Speaking

To provide speaking practice, have students use each item to create a short dialogue. Instruct students to make a *yes/no* question from the statement and ask a partner. The partner answers with a *yes* short answer. Then students ask the information question for the item, and the partner answers the question.

For example:
A: *Is Judy having more fun now?*
B: *Yes, she is.*
A: *Why is Judy having more fun now?*
B: *Because she loves her new hobbies.*
Then have students complete the written exercise.

Practice Idea: Writing and Speaking

Have students write five statements about themselves in the present continuous tense. Say: *Write about long-term actions.* Then have students exchange papers. Say: *Take turns asking and answering questions.*

For example:
A: *I'm watching a lot of TV in the evening.*
B: *Why are you watching a lot of TV?*
A: *I'm bored.*

EXERCISE **9**

CD 1
TR 15   **ANSWERS: 1.** 'm looking; **2.** are you looking at; **3.** are you thinking; **4.** 're working; **5.** Are they working; **6.** 're traveling; **7.** 're taking; **8.** 'm watering; **9.** 's talking; **10.** aren't (OR 're not) complaining;

11. 're just looking; **12.** 's watching; **13.** are they watching; **14.** are you planning; **15.** 's planning

1. Say: *A man (Jack) is talking to his neighbor (Alan) about moving to a retirement village.* Have students read the direction line. Go over the example in the book.

2. Have students complete Exercise 9 individually. Remind them to review grammar charts **2.1** on page 46, **2.2** on page 49, and **2.3** on page 52 if necessary. Then have students compare answers in pairs. Play the audio and check answers as a class.

Practice Idea: Listening

To provide practice with listening skills, have students close their books and listen to the audio. Repeat the audio as needed. Ask comprehension questions, such as: *What is Jack doing?* (looking at some brochures) *Where are the brochures from?* (a retirement village) *What is Jack thinking about doing?* (moving into a retirement village) Then have students open their books and complete Exercise 9.

Practice Idea: Speaking

Have students practice the conversation in pairs. Then ask volunteers to act out the conversation for the class.

 EXERCISE 10

CD 1
TR 16   **ANSWERS: Answers may vary. Possible answers: 1.** are you reading (OR are you doing), Are you enjoying; **2.** 's Grandma going, Isn't it raining; **3.** 's she talking to, 's she talking, isn't she using (OR isn't she talking on); **4.** Is my accent improving, am I doing better; **5.** are you cooking, Is, burning; **6.** are they watching, aren't they doing; **7.** are you going (OR are you going to Grandma's house); **8.** are you retiring, Are you planning to travel, 'm going, working

1. Have students read the direction line. Go over the example in the book. Do item 1 with the class.

2. Have students complete the rest of Exercise 10 individually. Remind them to review grammar charts **2.1** on page 46 and **2.3** on page 52 if necessary. Then have students compare answers in pairs. Play the audio and check answers as a class. Then have partners practice the mini-dialogues.

Practice Idea: Speaking

Have students write additional lines to extend the mini-conversations. Then have volunteers role-play the mini-conversations in front of the class.

Technology and the Generation Gap READING

1. Have students look at the photo. Ask: *What is this woman doing?* (She is using a cell phone/sending a text message.)

2. Have students look at the title of the reading. Ask: *What is the reading about?* Have students use the title and photo to make predictions about the reading.

3. Preteach any vocabulary words your students may not know, such as *remind*, *old-fashioned*, and *driver's license*.

Reading Glossary

driver's license: an official document that you need to be able to drive a car

old-fashioned: not up-to-date or modern, an old style or way of doing things

remind: to tell someone about something they planned to do so that they don't forget to do it

BEFORE YOU READ

5-10 mins

1. Have students discuss the questions in pairs.

2. Ask for a few volunteers to share their answers with the class.

CD 1
TR 17

Reading

1. Have students first read the text silently. Tell them to pay special attention to the present continuous tense and the present simple tense. Then play the audio and have students read along silently.

10-15 mins

2. Check students' comprehension. Ask questions such as: *Why does Marco need to go home early?* (for a driving lesson with his dad) *Why does Marco send so many text messages?* (because it saves time) *Why doesn't Marco's grandma like writing without punctuation?* (because she's an English teacher) *What is Marco's grandma studying?* (photo editing)

Practice Idea: Listening

To practice listening skills, have students first listen to the audio alone. Ask a few comprehension questions. Repeat the audio if necessary. Then have students open their books and read along as they listen to the audio.

DID YOU KNOW?

Have students read the information. Then ask them how many text messages they send. Discuss why 13- to 17-year-olds prefer texting over e-mailing.

2.4 Contrasting the Simple Present and the Present Continuous ≡★

10-15 mins

1. Have students cover up grammar chart **2.4** on page 58. Make a matching activity. Write the following sentences on the board:

Simple Present Tense

1. *Grandma often e-mails her friends.*
2. *Many people text without punctuation.*
3. *Most people have a computer.*

a. *a general truth*
b. *a habitual activity*
c. *a custom*

Present Continuous Tense

1. *I'm making a family album.*
2. *You're writing so slowly.*
3. *People are retiring earlier these days.*

a. *an action that is in progress now*
b. *a longer action in progress at this general time*
c. *recent trends in society*

Say: *Match the examples to the explanations.*
(**Matching Answers:** Simple Present: **1.** b; **2.** c;
3. a; Present Continuous: **1.** b; **2.** a; **3.** c)

2. Have students look at grammar chart **2.4**.
Say: *Check your work.* Go over the rest of the
example sentences.

3. Compare the two tenses. Review the verb
live in the two tenses. Have volunteers make
similar sentences with *live*. Repeat steps
with the questions. Ask volunteers to create
questions with the simple present and present
continuous.

EXERCISE **11**

ANSWERS: 1. eat; **2.** 'm gaining; **3.** 'm trying; **4.** eat;
5. 're drinking; **6.** are you doing; **7.** 'm filling; **8.** are
you using; **9.** make; **10.** make; **11.** make; **12.** does
your father do; **13.** works; **14.** 's he doing;
15. 's playing; **16.** takes; **17.** 's the teacher going;
18. 's going; **19.** 's carrying; **20.** starts; **21.** gets;
22. 're sleeping; **23.** get; **24.** do you sleep; **25.** fall;
26. 'm taking; **27.** take

1. Have students read the direction line. Say: *You
have to decide between the simple present and
present continuous.* Go over the example in the
book. Do the next item with the class.

2. Have students complete the rest of Exercise 11
individually. Remind them to review grammar
chart **2.4** on page 58 if necessary. Go over
answers as a class.

Practice Idea: Speaking

Have students practice the mini-conversations
(or create similar conversations) in pairs. Ask
volunteers to role-play the mini-conversations in
front of the class.

2.5 Action and Nonaction Verbs

1. Have students cover up grammar chart **2.5**
on page 61. Write the following verbs on the
board: *run, like, hate, need, play, drive, know,
eat, understand, smell, walk, talk, feel,* and *cost.*

2. Say: *Some verbs are action verbs. They show
mental or physical activity. Some verbs are
nonaction verbs. They describe a state, condition,
or a feeling. Look at the verbs on the board.
Which ones are action verbs and which ones
are nonaction verbs?* Ask students to create
two lists in their notebooks. Give them a few
minutes to sort through the verbs. Then go
over the verbs with the class. (Action verbs:
run, play, drive, eat, walk, talk; Nonaction verbs:
like, hate, need, know, understand, smell, feel)

3. Review the pairs *look/see, listen/hear,* and
meet/know. Write the sentences from the chart
on the board. Ask students to say whether the
verbs are action or nonaction. Then review
think about and *think that.* Write the sentences
from the book on the board, and ask students
to say in which instance *think* is an action or
nonaction verb. Do the same with the rest of
the verbs in the chart.

4. Have students look at grammar chart **2.5**. Say:
*We usually use the simple present tense with
nonaction verbs.*

 ## EXERCISE **12**

CD 1
TR 18

ANSWERS: 1. works OR is working; **2.** loves; **3.** rides;
4. likes; **5.** Is she working; **6.** 's sailing; **7.** 'm using;
8. bring; **9.** Do you expect; **10.** need; **11.** 's the
teacher saying; **12.** 's talking; **13.** don't understand;
14. 'm not listening; **15.** 'm thinking; **16.** think;
17. 'm thinking; **18.** are you writing; **19.** 'm writing;
20. love; **21.** Do they live; **22.** visit; **23.** Do you ever
send; **24.** isn't working OR doesn't work;
25. prefer; **26.** know; **27.** 's she wearing;
28. 's wearing; **29.** looks; **30.** Does she always
wear; **31.** wears; **32.** doesn't wear; **33.** Do you see;
34. 's wearing; **35.** has; **36.** looks; **37.** know;
38. thinks; **39.** does he teach; **40.** 's looking;
41. doesn't have; **42.** wants; **43.** are you studying;
44. Are you doing; **45.** 'm doing; **46.** need;
47. don't understand; **48.** talks; **49.** does your
mother do; **50.** Is she; **51.** does she do; **52.** doesn't
have; **53.** 's taking; **54.** 's painting; **55.** volunteers
OR is volunteering; **56.** volunteer OR are
volunteering

1. Have students read the direction line. Say: *You
have to decide between the simple present and
present continuous.* Go over the example in the
book.

2. Have students complete Exercise 12 individually. Remind them to review grammar chart **2.5** on page 61 if necessary. Play the audio and check the answers as a class.

Practice Idea: Listening

To provide practice with listening skills, have students close their books and listen to the audio. Say: *In this selection, you'll hear eight short conversations.* Repeat the audio as needed. Ask comprehension questions, such as: *In conversation 1, what does person A's grandfather do with his time?* (he volunteers) *How often?* (twice a week) *Who does he help?* (blind people) Then have students open their books and complete Exercise 12.

Practice Idea: Speaking

Have students practice the mini-conversations (or create similar conversations) in pairs. Have volunteers role-play the conversations in front of the class.

 EXERCISE 13

CD 1
TR 19

ANSWERS: 1. Do you want; **2.** 'm cooking; **3.** have; **4.** 'm waiting; **5.** are you doing; **6.** 'm studying; **7.** want; **8.** need; **9.** talk; **10.** have; **11.** 's visiting; **12.** 'm preparing; **13.** sounds; **14.** are planning; **15.** thinks; **16.** don't think; **17.** never put; **18.** always take care; **19.** doesn't know; **20.** falls; **21.** needs; **22.** never remembers; **23.** hear

10-15 mins

1. Have students read the direction line. Say: *You have to decide between the simple present and present continuous.* Point out that this conversation is between two friends, Patty and Linda. Go over the example in the book. Point out the drawing of a woman using a walker on page 65.

2. Have students complete Exercise 13 individually. Remind them to review grammar chart **2.5** on page 61 if necessary. Play the audio and check the answers as a class.

Practice Idea: Listening

To provide practice with listening skills, have students close their books and listen to the audio. Repeat the audio as needed. Ask comprehension questions, such as: *Can Patty meet Linda for coffee?* (no) *Why not?* (She's cooking dinner.) *What's Linda doing?* (studying for a test) Then have students open their books and complete Exercise 13.

Practice Idea: Speaking

Have students practice the conversation in pairs. Then ask volunteers to act out the conversation for the class.

The Graying of America

READING

1. Have students look at the title of the reading and the photos. Ask: *What is the reading about?* Have students use the title and the photos to make predictions about the reading.

2. Preteach any vocabulary words your students may not know, such as *shortage* and *influence.*

Reading Glossary

influence: the power to change or persuade others
shortage: a state of not having enough, a lack of something

BEFORE YOU READ

5-10 mins

1. Have students discuss the questions in pairs.

2. Ask for a few volunteers to share their answers with the class.

 Reading ═★

CD 1
TR 20

10-15 mins

1. Have students first read the text silently. Tell them to pay special attention to future tense verbs. Then play the audio and have students read along silently.

2. Check students' comprehension. Ask questions such as: *What part or segment of the population is growing fastest?* (the elderly) *What are the two reasons this is happening?* (Life expectancy is rising, and the baby boomers are getting older.) *Why are younger people going to pay more taxes?* (Fewer people will be working.) *Why will some people move from the suburbs to the city?* (Their children will be out of school, and there are more activities for older people in the cities.)

> ## Practice Idea: Listening
>
> To practice listening skills, have students first listen to the audio alone. Ask a few comprehension questions. Repeat the audio if necessary. Then have students open their books and read along as they listen to the audio.

Context Note

When workers retire, they receive payments from Social Security based on the length of time they or their spouses worked. Social Security is funded through a tax on earnings. This payment is presently keeping 48 percent of retirees out of poverty. But in about 40 years, experts say that the funds in Social Security will not be able to cover the number of benefits needed. There are currently 35 million retired people. In 2050 there will be more than 85 million. The problem is that there aren't enough workers to pay into Social Security.

2.6 The Future Tense with *Will*

10-15 mins

1. Have students look at grammar chart **2.6** on page 67. Go over the examples and the explanations in the grammar chart. Review how to form the future with *will* (*will* + base form), how to make contractions with the subject (subject pronoun + *'ll*), and how to form the negative (*will* + *not* + verb). Explain that *will not* contracts to *won't*.

2. Review how to form questions (*will* + subject + verb OR *wh-* word + *will* + subject + verb).

Review how to form negative questions beginning with *why* (*why* + *won't* + subject + verb).

3. Have students write between three and five sentences in the future tense on any topic. Ask volunteers to share them with the class. Go over any trouble spots.

EXERCISE 14

ANSWERS: Answers may vary. Possible answers:
1. will grow OR will increase, **2.** will be; **3.** will, go OR live OR be; **4.** Will, take; **5.** will, be; **6.** will, be

---

5-10 mins

1. Tell students that the information in the exercise is based on the reading on pages 66–67. Have students read the direction line. Go over the example in the book.

2. Have students complete Exercise 14 individually. Remind them to review grammar chart **2.6** on pages 67–68 if necessary. Check the answers as a class.

EXERCISE 15

CD 1 TR 21

ANSWERS: Answers may vary. Possible answers:
1. 'll; **2.** be; **3.** 'll be; **4.** won't be; **5.** 'll stop OR be; **6.** will you wash; **7.** will you buy (OR get); **8.** 'll make OR 'll start; **9.** 'll eat; **10.** will you go; **11.** Will you send/Will you mail; **12.** will; **13.** 'll; **14.** will you send; **15.** 'll take OR 'll bring OR 'll have; **16.** will you get OR will you find; **17.** 'll have; **18.** Will you take; **19.** will be; **20.** 'll send; **21.** 'll miss

---

10-15 mins

1. Say: *In this exercise, a daughter is saying goodbye to her 60-year-old parents, who are taking a trip in their recreational vehicle.* Point out the photo on page 69 of an RV. Have students read the direction line. Go over the example in the book. Remind students that several answers may be correct.

2. Have students complete Exercise 15 individually. Remind them to review grammar chart **2.6** on pages 67–68 if necessary. Then have students compare answers in pairs. Monitor pair work. Give help as needed. Play the audio and have students compare their answers.

Practice Idea: Listening

To provide practice with listening skills, have students close their books and listen to the audio. Say: *In this exercise, a daughter is saying goodbye to her 60-year-old parents, who are taking a trip in their recreational vehicle.* Repeat the audio as needed. Ask comprehension questions, such as: *How long will the woman's parents be gone?* (for the summer months) *How will the parents wash their clothes?* (with a washing machine in the RV) *Does the RV have a microwave?* (yes) Then have students open their books and complete Exercise 15.

Practice Idea: Speaking

Have students practice the dialogue in pairs. Then have students create a skit or role-play the dialogue. Ask volunteers to perform in front of the class.

2.7 The Future Tense with *Be Going To*

🕐 10-15 mins

1. Have students go back to the reading on pages 66–67. Say: *There's another way to express the future. Can you give me some examples from this reading?* Write the students' examples on the board. Ask: *How do we form the future with* be going to? (*be* + *going to* + verb) How do we form the negative? (*be* + *not* + *going to* + verb)

2. Have students look at grammar chart **2.7**. Go over the examples and explanations. Point out that *going to go* is usually shortened to *going*. Give examples (e.g., *We're going to go to New York tomorrow. We're going to New York tomorrow.*).

3. Explain that when *in* is used with the future, it means *after* (a period of time). Give examples (e.g., *We're going to take a break in 10 minutes.*).

4. Go over the Pronunciation Notes. Explain that *going to* is often pronounced by native speakers as *gonna*. Point out that although we say *gonna*, we don't use it in formal written English.

EXERCISE 16

ANSWERS: Answers may vary. Possible answers:
1. is going to rise OR is going to increase OR is going to grow; **2.** are going to pay OR are going to have; **3.** is, going to be; **4.** Are, going to take; **5.** are going to be

🕐 5-10 mins

1. Have students read the direction line. Ask: *What do we write on the blanks?* (the future with *be going to*) Go over the example in the book.

2. Have students complete Exercise 16 individually. Remind them to review grammar chart **2.7** on page 70 if necessary. Check the answers as a class.

🔊 EXERCISE 17

CD 1
TR 22

ANSWERS: 1. are you going to do; **2.** 'm going to explore; **3.** are you going to explore; **4.** 'm going to take; **5.** Are you going to work; **6.** 'm going to do; **7.** 's going to retire; **8.** aren't they going to need; **9.** 's going to graduate; **10.** 's going to get; **11.** 'm going to miss; **12.** 'm going to miss; **13.** 'm not going to miss

🕐 10-15 mins

1. Say: *A woman is talking to her coworker about retiring.* Have students read the direction line. Go over the example in the book.

2. Have students complete Exercise 17 individually. Remind them to review grammar chart **2.7** on page 70 if necessary. Then have students compare answers in pairs. Play the audio and check answers as a class.

Practice Idea: Listening

To provide practice with listening skills, have students close their books and listen to the audio. Say: *A woman is talking to her coworker about retiring early.* Repeat the audio as needed. Ask comprehension questions, such as: *Why is person A excited?* (Person A is going to retire at the end of this year.) *What kind of classes is person A going to take?* (art classes) *Is person A going to work?* (no) Then have students open their books and complete Exercise 17.

Practice Idea: Speaking

Have students practice the conversation in pairs. Then have students create a new conversation in pairs. Ask volunteers to role-play their conversations in front of the class.

EXERCISE 18
Answers will vary.

 10-15 mins

1. Say: *Now you get to ask me anything you want!* Have students read the direction line. Say: *What tense will your questions be in?* (the future with *be going to*) Go over the examples in the book.

2. Have students complete Exercise 18 individually. Remind them to review grammar chart **2.7** on page 70 if necessary. Then answer questions from each of the students.

Practice Idea: Writing and Speaking

Have students write three questions for three other people in the class. Have students take turns asking and answering questions. Ask volunteers to report anything interesting they learned about their classmates.

Context Note

Some types of questions are considered too personal and therefore impolite in American culture. Tell students they shouldn't ask questions about age, salary, the cost of clothing or other items, love relationships, or religion.

2.8 Choosing *Will* or *Be Going To* ≡★

10-15 mins

1. Have students cover up grammar chart **2.8** on page 72. Copy the chart below onto the board.

Uses	*Will*	*Be Going To*
Prediction		
Facts about the Future		
Scheduled event		

Ask students to work in pairs to fill in the chart with example sentences using *will* and *be going to.* Remind students that sometimes you can use both *will* and *be going to.*

2. Have students look at grammar chart **2.8**. Say: *Compare your sentences with the sentences from the chart in the book.* Review the chart.

3. Direct students to the Language Notes. Point out that we can also use the present continuous to express the future. Review the examples sentences in the chart.

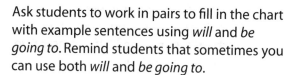

Presentation Idea

Have students cover up grammar chart **2.8**. Write the example sentences on the board for both *will* and *be going to.* On another part of the board, write a list of the uses of the future in scrambled order. Ask students to read the sentences and match them with the appropriate uses.

EXERCISE 19 ≡★

ANSWERS: 1. 'm going to pass; **2.** 'll return; **3.** will arrive OR 's going to arrive; **4.** 'll go; **5.** 'll stay; **6.** won't have to OR aren't going to have to; **7.** Are you going to give; **8.** 'm going to/will; **9.** are you going to give OR will you give; **10.** 'm going to buy OR 'll buy; **11.** will she be OR is she going to be; **12.** 'll be OR 's going to be; **13.** 're going to have OR 'll have; **14.** Will it be OR Is it going to be; **15.** 'll help OR 'm going to help; **16.** 'll pick; **17.** 'll prepare; **18.** 'll be OR 'm going to be; **19.** 'll find OR 'm going to find; **20.** 'll wait; **21.** 'll always love OR 'm always going to love; **22.** is going to move; **23.** 'm going to help; **24.** 'll look; **25.** 'm going (to go); **26.** 'll get; **27.** 'll bring; **28.** 'm going to get; **29.** will you take OR are you going to take; **30.** 's going to help OR 'll help; **31.** 'm not going to tell OR won't tell; **32.** 'll know OR 's going to know; **33.** 'll have to OR 're going to have to; **34.** will bark OR 's going to bark

 10-15 mins

1. Say: *In this exercise, you'll choose to use* will *or* be going to. Have students read the direction line. Go over the example with the class. Have volunteers complete #1.

2. Have students complete Exercise 19 individually. Remind them to review grammar chart **2.8** on page 72 if necessary. Go over the answers as a class.

> ### Practice Idea: Speaking
>
> Have students practice the mini-conversations in pairs. Ask volunteers to role-play the conversations in front of the class.

2.9 Future Tense + Time/ *If* Clause

5-10 mins

1. Have students cover up grammar chart **2.9** on page 75. Write several sentences from the grammar chart on the board. Point out that these sentences are made up of two clauses, the time clause and the main clause. Underline the time clause and double underline the main clause. Ask: *What tense is used in the time clause?* (simple present) *What tense is used in the main clause?* (future)

2. Have students look at grammar chart **2.9**. Review all of the examples and explanations.

3. Direct students to the Punctuation Note. Point out that the main clause can come before or after the time/*if* clause. Explain that when the time/*if* clause goes first they must use a comma. Go over the examples.

EXERCISE 20

ANSWERS: 1. When I retire, I'm not going to live with my children. OR I'm not going to live with my children when I retire. **2.** When I'm old, I'll take care of myself. OR I'll take care of myself when I'm old. **3.** If I'm not healthy, I'll live with my children. OR I'll live with my children if I'm not healthy. **4.** If I don't have money, I'll get help from the government. OR I'll get help from the government if I don't have money. **5.** After my parents die, I'll move to another city. OR I'll move to another city after my parents die. **6.** If I get a pension, I won't need to depend on my children. OR I won't need to depend on my children if I get a pension. **7.** Before I retire, I'm going to save my money. OR I'm going to save my money before I retire.

5-10 mins

1. Say: *In this exercise, we will connect two sentences using the word in parentheses.* Have students read the direction line. Go over the example in the book. Point out that they will need to change the tense of the verb in the time clause. Remind students that if they write the time clause or *if* clause first, they must use a comma.

2. Have students complete the exercise individually. Remind them to review grammar chart **2.9** on page 75 if necessary. Check the answers as a class.

EXERCISE 21

Answers will vary.

10-15 mins

1. Say: *In this exercise, you're going to write about your future.* Have students read the direction line. Go over the examples in the book. Model the exercise with your own examples. Write some of the board.

2. Have students complete the exercise individually. Remind them to review grammar chart **2.9** on page 75 if necessary. Then have students compare answers in pairs. Monitor pair work. Give help as needed.

> ### Practice Idea: Writing
>
> Have students write a letter or an e-mail to a friend in another city or country. Say: *Talk about your future plans. Use* will *and* be going to *and time/*if *clauses.*

EXERCISE 22

CD 1
TR 23

ANSWERS: 1. 's going to go; **2.** 'll be OR 's going to be; **3.** 's going to get; **4.** is he going to do; **5.** will you do OR are you going to do; **6.** 's going to be OR 'll be; **7.** 'll outlive OR 's going to outlive; **8.** 'll probably need OR 's probably going to need; **9.** 'll cross; **10.** 're; **11.** 're going to live OR 'll live; **12.** 'm; **13.** 'll take OR 'm going to take; **14.** 'll change; **15.** 're; **16.** 'll see; **17.** 'll drive

10-15 mins

1. Say: *In this exercise, you'll choose to use* will *or* be going to. *Remember that in many cases, you can use both.* Have students read the direction line. Go over the example with the class.

---

2. Have students complete Exercise 22 individually. Remind them to review grammar charts **2.7** on page 70, **2.8** on page 72, and **2.9** on page 75 if necessary. Then have students compare answers in pairs. Play the audio and have students compare their answers.

Practice Idea: Listening

To provide practice with listening skills, have students close their books and listen to the audio. Say: *A Korean student is talking to an American about getting old.* Repeat the audio as needed. Ask comprehension questions, such as: *Who is the American going to visit this afternoon?* (the American's grandfather) *What is the grandfather going to do next week?* (go to Hawaii to play golf) *What is the grandfather going to do in June?* (get married) Then have students open their books and complete Exercise 22.

Practice Idea: Speaking

Have students practice the conversation in pairs. Then ask volunteers to act out the conversation for the class.

EXERCISE 23

CD 1
TR 24

ANSWERS: 1. are you going to do OR will you; **2.** retire; **3.** sell; **4.** 'm going to move OR 'm moving; **5.** are you going to do OR will you do; **6.** 'm going to buy; **7.** 'm; **8.** 'm going to start; **9.** 'm going to get OR 'll get; **10.** sell; **11.** are you going to do OR will you; **12.** retire; **13.** retire; **14.** save; **15.** 'll have OR 're going to have; **16.** don't think; **17.** comes; **18.** 're not going to have OR won't have; **19.** 'll worry; **20.** comes; **21.** wait; **22.** 're; **23.** 'll be OR 're going to be; **24.** 're; **25.** 'll introduce; **26.** talk; **27.** 'll change OR 're going to change

1. Have students read the direction line. Explain that this is a conversation between two coworkers. Go over the example with the class.

2. Have students complete Exercise 23 individually. Remind them to review grammar

charts **2.7** on page 70, **2.8** on page 72, and **2.9** on page 75 if necessary. Then have students compare answers in pairs. Play the audio and check the answers as a class.

Practice Idea: Listening

To provide practice with listening skills, have students close their books and listen to the audio. Explain that this is a conversation between two coworkers. Repeat the audio as needed. Ask comprehension questions, such as: *What's person B going to do this year?* (retire) *When will person B turn 65 years old?* (in September) *Where does person B want to live?* (in Florida; in a condo) Then have students open their books and complete Exercise 23.

Practice Idea: Speaking

Have students practice the conversation in pairs. Then ask volunteers to act out the conversation for the class.

Practice Idea: Speaking

Have students create a conversation about retirement between two people they know, such as their parents.

Summary of Lesson 2

USE OF TENSE

1. Have students cover up the first chart in the summary. Ask: *When do we use the simple present tense?* Write the students' answers on the board. Ask students to give example sentences.

   If necessary, have students review:

   2.4 Contrasting the Simple Present and the Present Continuous (p. 58)

2. Have students cover up the second chart in the summary. Ask: *When do we use the present continuous?* Write the students' answers on the board. Ask students to give example sentences. If necessary, have students review:

   2.1 Present Continuous Tense (p. 46)
   2.2 Using the Present Continuous for Longer Actions (p. 49)
   2.3 Questions with the Present Continuous Tense (p. 52)
   2.4 Contrasting the Simple Present and the Present Continuous (p. 58)
   2.5 Action and Nonaction Verbs (p. 61)

3. Have students cover up the third chart in the summary. Ask: *When do we use* will *and* be going to? Write the students' answers on the board. Ask students to give example sentences. If necessary, have students review:

   2.6 The Future Tense with *Will* (pp. 67–68)
   2.7 The Future Tense with *Be Going To* (p. 70)
   2.8 Choosing *Will* or *Be Going To* (p. 72)
   2.9 Future Tense + Time/*If* Clause (p. 75)

Editing Advice

10-15 mins

Have students close their books. Write the first few sentences without editing marks or corrections on the board. For example:

1. *She working now.*
2. *I am liking your new car.*

Ask students to correct each sentence and provide a rule or explanation for each correction. This activity can be done individually, in pairs, or as a class. After students have corrected each sentence, tell them to turn to pages 80–81. Say: *Now compare your work with the Editing Advice in the book.*

Editing Quiz

ANSWERS: 1. C; **2.** C; **3.** taking; **4.** is studying; **5.** is going to; **6.** gets; **7.** C; **8.** am I going to; **9.** I think; **10.** needs; **11.** will be happy; **12.** Am I going to have OR Will I have; **13.** retire; **14.** I'll cross; **15.** C

10-15 mins

1. Tell students they are going to put the Editing Advice into practice. Have students read the direction line.

Ask: *Do all the shaded words and phrases have mistakes?* (no) Go over the examples with the class. Then do #1 together.

2. Have students complete the quiz individually. Then have them compare answers with a partner before checking answers as a class.

3. For the items students had difficulties with, have them go back and find the relevant grammar chart and review it. Monitor and give help as necessary.

Lesson 2 Test/Review

50-60 mins

Use the Assessment CD-ROM with Exam*View*®, Online Workbook, and the Web site for additional practice, review, and assessment materials.

PART 1

ANSWERS: 1. 're moving OR 're going to move; **2.** have; **3.** 's coming OR 's going to come; **4.** need OR 're going to need; **5.** is he coming OR is he going to come; **6.** 's going to come OR 'll come OR 's coming; **7.** gets; **8.** has; **9.** always likes; **10.** brings; **11.** needs; **12.** Will your father get OR Is your father going to get; **13.** finds; **14.** 's going to live; **15.** doesn't like; **16.** are going to stay OR are going to stay; **17.** is helping OR is going to help; **18.** 'll come; **19.** 're going to use OR 're using; **20.** want; **21.** will be; **22.** hear; **23.** 's calling; **24.** wants; **25.** 'll call; **26.** 'll see

1. Part 1 may be used as an in-class test to assess student performance, in addition to the Assessment CD-ROM with Exam*View*®. Have students read the direction line. Point out that this exercise is a phone conversation between Mary and Sue. Go over the example with the class.

2. Have students complete the exercise individually. Collect for assessment.

3. If necessary, have students review Lesson 2.

PART 2

ANSWERS: 1. isn't (OR 's not) talking; **2.** isn't (OR 's not) going to move; **3.** doesn't need; **4.** won't go; **5.** won't move; **6.** doesn't have; **7.** doesn't like

1. Part 2 may also be used as an in-class test to assess student performance, in addition to the Assessment CD-ROM with Exam*View*®. Have students read the direction line. Ask: *What do we write in the blanks?* (the negative form of the underlined verb) Go over the example with the class.

2. Have students complete the exercise individually. Collect for assessment.

3. If necessary, have students review:
   - **2.1** Present Continuous Tense (p. 46)
   - **2.6** The Future Tense with *Will* (pp. 67–68)
   - **2.7** The Future Tense with *Be Going To* (p. 70)

PART 3

ANSWERS: 1. Is her sister helping her pack? Yes, she is. **2.** Does he work at home? Yes, he does. **3.** Does her present apartment have an extra room for her father? No, it doesn't. **4.** Will her friends move the furniture? No, they won't. **5.** Is her husband staying home this week? Yes, he is. **6.** Is Sue going to move? No, she isn't.

1. Part 3 may also be used as an in-class test to assess student performance, in addition to the Assessment CD-ROM with Exam*View*®. Have students read the direction line. Ask: *What kind of questions do we write?* (*yes/no* questions) Point out that the answers should be based on the conversation in Part 1. Go over the example with the class.

2. Have students complete the exercise individually. Collect for assessment.

3. If necessary, have students review:
   - **2.3** Questions with the Present Continuous Tense (p. 52)
   - **2.6** The Future Tense with *Will* (pp. 67–68)
   - **2.7** The Future Tense with *Be Going To* (p. 70)

PART 4

ANSWERS: 1. Why are they going to move to a bigger apartment? **2.** Why does her husband need an extra room? **3.** Why doesn't she need her friend to help her move? **4.** When is her father going to come? **5.** Why is Bill (OR he) calling Mary? **6.** When will they use professional movers?

1. Part 4 may also be used as an in-class test to assess student performance, in addition to the Assessment CD-ROM with Exam*View*®. Have students read the direction line. Ask: *What kind of questions are you going to write?* (*wh-* questions) Go over the examples with the class. Remind students that an answer isn't necessary.

2. Have students complete the exercise individually. Collect for assessment.

3. If necessary, have students review:
   - **2.3** Questions with the Present Continuous Tense (p. 52)
   - **2.6** The Future Tense with *Will* (pp. 67–68)
   - **2.7** The Future Tense with *Be Going To* (p. 70)

Expansion

These expansion activities provide opportunities for students to interact with one another and further develop their speaking and writing skills. Encourage students to use grammar from this lesson whenever possible.

CLASSROOM ACTIVITIES

10-15 mins per activity

1. Have students complete the checklist on their own. Then have students get into groups to discuss their predictions (e.g., *I think people are going to have fewer children than they do today. These days, both men and women work. They don't have time or money for big families. I agree/disagree.*). Monitor group work. Give help as needed.

2. Have students complete the checklist on their own. Then have students get into groups to ask and answer questions about their plans. Instruct students to ask *wh-* questions and *yes/no* questions. Encourage them to use the future tense. Monitor work. Give help as needed.

TALK ABOUT IT

15-20 mins

Write on the board: *Getting older* Ask: *What are some of the difficulties older people face? What are some of the positive aspects of being older?* Write the students' ideas on the board. Then have students discuss each question in pairs or groups. Then have them report back to the class.

WRITE ABOUT IT

20-30
mins

1. Have students read the direction line and the sample beginning. Briefly model the activity with the class. Write a little about what your life will be like in 10 years on the board (e.g., *In 10 years, I will only work part-time. I will buy a house in Puerto Rico and live there during the winter.*). Then have students write their own paragraph. Collect for assessment and/or have students present their paragraphs to a group.

2. Have students read the direction line and the sample paragraph. Have students write down who they are going to write about. Then have them tell a partner about that person's life. Have them write their paragraphs individually. Encourage them to write as much as they can. Collect for assessment and/or have students present their paragraphs to a group.

Practice Idea: Writing

Have students exchange first drafts with a partner. Ask students to help their partners edit their drafts. Refer students to the Editing Advice on pages 80–81.

OUTSIDE ACTIVITIES

1. Tell students to give the list from Classroom Activity 1 to an American and find out his or her predictions. Have them report to the class something interesting that the American told them.

2. Tell students to keep a small notebook and a pen with them at all times for a week and write down all the behaviors of older people that seem strange to them. Tell students to observe food, clothes, shopping, recreation, relationships between parents and children, behaviors on public transportation, etc. Have them write what people are doing as they are observing. For example:

   An old woman is standing on the bus. No one is giving her a seat.

   An old man is jogging in the park.

Have students discuss their observations in a group. Say: *Discuss behaviors you observed that are different from behaviors in your native country or culture.*

INTERNET ACTIVITIES

1. Tell students to find a Web site for the elderly and find out what kinds of products and services are available for senior citizens. Tell them they can search under *senior citizens* or try the *National Council of Senior Citizens* (NCSC) or *American Association of Retired Persons* (AARP). Say: *Find at least five products or services that you think would be very helpful for an elderly person.* Have volunteers talk about their findings. Vote on the most useful product or service.

2. Tell students to look for a life expectancy calculator on the Internet and calculate how long they will probably live. Do a class survey to find out who's going to live the longest.

3. Tell students to use a search engine and type in *baby boomers*. Tell them to find an article about the baby boomers and bring it to class. Have students give a short oral summary of the articles they found.

4. Tell students to use the Internet to find information about a retirement community in the area where they live. Tell them to get information about the cost, types of activities, and types of housing. Have students create a presentation of the retirement community they researched. Ask them to include information on cost, types of activities, and types of housing. Vote on the best place to live.

Lesson 3

Lesson Overview

GRAMMAR

1. Briefly review other tenses students have learned. Ask: *What tense did we study in Lesson 1?* (simple present tense) *What tenses did we study in Lesson 2?* (present continuous and future)

2. Ask: *What will we study in this lesson?* (the habitual past with *used to* and the simple past tense) *Can anyone make a sentence with* used to? (e.g., *I used to go to the gym every day*.) Have students give examples. Write the examples on the board. Then ask volunteers for sentences in the simple past.

CONTEXT

1. Ask: *What will we learn about in this lesson?* (equality) Activate students' prior knowledge. Ask: *What is equality?*

2. Have students share their knowledge and personal experiences.

Presentation Ideas

The topic for this lesson can be enhanced with the following items:

1. A recording of the "I Have a Dream" speech by Martin Luther King, Jr.
2. Pictures of Dr. King and Rosa Parks
3. Pictures of Civil Rights marches, riots, and other related events

Equal Rights for All   READING

1. Have students look at the photo of Rosa Parks. Ask: *Does anyone know who Rosa Parks was?* Have students make predictions about who she was/what she did if they don't know. Direct students' attention to the photos on page 89. Ask: *Does anyone know who these people are?*

2. Have students look at the title of the reading. Ask: *What is the reading about?* Have students use the title and photos to make predictions.

3. Preteach any vocabulary words your students may not know, such as *rights, inferior, reserve, arrest*, and *boycott*.

Reading Glossary

arrest: to seize or hold something by legal authority

boycott: a refusal for political reasons to buy certain products or do business with a certain store or company

inferior: lower in quality

reserve: to hold or keep for oneself or for somebody specific

rights: permission to do something guaranteed by law

BEFORE YOU READ

5-10 mins

1. Have students discuss the questions in pairs. Try to pair students of different cultures together.

2. Ask a few volunteers to share their answers with the class.

Reading ─★

CD 1 TR 25

10-15 mins

1. Have students read the text silently. Tell them to pay special attention to simple past tense verbs and *used to* + base form. Then play the audio and have students read along silently.

2. Check students' comprehension. Ask questions such as: *When did slavery end in the U.S.?* (in 1865) *In what ways did blacks continue to suffer discrimination even after slavery ended?* (Businesses and schools were segregated.) *Who refused to give her bus seat to white people?* (Rosa Parks)

DID YOU KNOW?

Have students read the information. Then ask them what they know about Mahatma Gandhi.

Share the following information with them:

Mahatma Gandhi was born and raised in India and then later studied law in England. After his studies, he worked in South Africa, where he witnessed firsthand the terrible prejudices that people of color faced. He worked to end the injustices immigrant Indian workers endured there and was often sent to jail. It was in South Africa that he began to develop his philosophy of passive resistance. Back in India, he took the lead in the struggle for independence from Britain. He often fasted to end the violence between the British, Hindu, and Muslims. He was assassinated in 1948.

Practice Idea: Listening

To practice listening skills, have students first listen to the audio alone. Ask a few comprehension questions. Repeat the audio if necessary. Then have them open their books and read along as they listen to the audio.

Practice Idea: Speaking

Have students talk in pairs or groups about champions of civil rights from their native countries (e.g., Mahatma Gandhi, the students of Tiananmen Square) or of their own countries' "firsts."

3.1 Habitual Past with Used To

🕐
5-10 mins
1. Have students go through the reading on pages 88–89 and find examples of *used to*. Write students' examples on the board (e.g., *Many businesses there used to have signs in their windows that said: "Blacks Not Allowed."*). Ask: *How do you form the habitual past with used to?* (*used to* + base form) Ask students questions about the sentences, such as: *Do these businesses still have the signs? Are there still separate sports teams for blacks? Do buses still reserve front seats for whites?*

2. Have students look at grammar chart **3.1**. Say: Used to *shows a habit or custom from the past.*

The custom is no longer practiced. Go through the examples. Point out that the negative is *didn't use to.*

3. Compare the use of the simple past (an event that happened once in the past) and *used to* (a custom that was followed over time in the past). Go over the examples in the Language Note.

EXERCISE 1
Answers will vary.

🕐
10-15 mins
1. Tell students that this exercise is about the things they used to do as a child. Have students read the direction line. Go over the example in the book. Have a volunteer complete #1 for the class.

2. Have students complete Exercise 1 individually. Remind them to review grammar chart **3.1** on page 90 if necessary. Then have them compare their answers in pairs. Monitor pair work. If necessary, check the answers as a class.

Practice Idea: Speaking

Review how to make a question with *used to*. Write on the board: *Did you use to cry a lot when you were a child?* Remind students that in questions, as in negatives, *use to* is written without the *d*. In pairs, have students ask each other questions from Exercise 1 and answer them (e.g., *Did you use to enjoy school when you were a child? Yes, I did.*).

EXERCISE 2
Answers will vary.

🕐
10-15 mins
1. Have students read the direction line. Go over the example in the book. Say: *You will name something you used to do or know, etc., in the past but that you don't do or know now.* Model the example for the class. Have a volunteer model the example as well.

2. Have students complete Exercise 2 individually. Remind them to review grammar chart **3.1** on page 90 if necessary. Then have them compare their answers in pairs. Monitor pair work.

Practice Idea: Speaking

Have students create a question for each item in Exercise 2 (e.g., *What did you use to do when you were a child? What kind of stories did you use to enjoy when you were a child?*). Then have students ask a new partner the questions.

EXERCISE 3

Answers will vary.

10-15 mins

1. Have students read the direction line. Say: *What did you use to do, and what do you do now? Use your own ideas or the ideas listed here.* Go over the examples in the book. Model the exercise for the class. Write a few sentences about yourself on the board.

2. Have students complete Exercise 3 individually. Remind them to review grammar chart **3.1** on page 90 if necessary. Then have them compare their answers in pairs. Monitor pair work.

Practice Idea: Speaking

Say: *Find out something new from three of your classmates.* Have students mingle around the room asking and answering questions about the past (e.g., *Do you live in a house? I used to live in an apartment, but now I live in a house.*). Then have students report to the class the information they learned about the three classmates.

EXERCISE 4

ANSWERS: Answers may vary. Possible answers:
1. spend my money; **2.** be a lazy student;
3. live with my family OR live with friends OR live with people; **4.** watch TV all the time; **5.** go out (after work); **6.** have long hair; **7.** walk everywhere OR bike everywhere OR take a bus everywhere; **8.** weigh a lot OR be fat OR be overweight; **9.** do what my parents told me OR take orders OR have people tell me what to do; **10.** use cash to buy things

10-15 mins

1. Ask: *Do you think you're a different person now than you were in the past?* Tell them they are going to make sentences about a man whose life has changed. Have students read the direction line. Go over the example.

2. Have students complete Exercise 4 individually. Remind them to review grammar chart **3.1** on page 90 if necessary. Then have them compare their answers in pairs. Monitor pair work.

Practice Idea: Speaking

Have students discuss how their lives are different now from five years ago in groups. Ask: *Who has changed a lot? Who is still the same?*

George Dawson— Life Is So Good READING

1. Have students look at the photo. Ask: *Who was George Dawson?* Have students make predictions.

2. Preteach any vocabulary words your students may not know, such as *witness*, *wonder*, and *trouble*.

Reading Glossary

trouble: difficulty, distress, especially by accident
witness: to see, to observe an incident
wonder: to express an interest in knowing

BEFORE YOU READ

5-10 mins

1. Have students discuss the questions in pairs. Try to pair students of different cultures together.

2. Ask for a few volunteers to share their answers with the class.

 Reading ─★
CD 1
TR 26

10-15 mins

1. Have students first read the text silently. Tell them to pay special attention to the simple past tense. Then play the audio and have students read along silently.

2. Check students' comprehension. Ask questions such as: *How many centuries did Mr. Dawson live in?* (three) *Why did he have to go to work*

when he was four years old? (His family was very poor.) *Where did he work most of the time when he was an adult?* (on a dairy farm) *When did he learn to write?* (when he was 98 years old) *Who helped him write his biography?* (an elementary school teacher) *What was the main message in his book?* (Life is good.)

Practice Idea: Listening

To practice listening skills, have students first listen to the audio alone. Ask a few comprehension questions. Repeat the audio if necessary. Then have them open their books and read along as they listen to the audio.

3.2 Past Tense of *Be*

10-15 mins

1. Have students cover up grammar chart **3.2** on pages 93–94. Activate prior knowledge. Ask: *What are the two forms of the past tense of* be? (*was, were*)

2. Write the following on the board:

   Life _____ hard for George Dawson.
   He _____ poor.
   His grandparents _____ slaves.
   There _____ discrimination in the South.
   There _____ many changes in the twentieth century.
   Dawson's life _____ (not) easy.
   Education and books _____ (not) available to Dawson as a child.
   Dawson _____ born in 1898.
   Dawson _____ married four times.

   Say: *Fill in the blanks with the correct verb.*

3. Have students look at grammar chart **3.2**. Say: *Check your work with the chart.* Review the examples and explanations in the grammar chart. Review the contractions for *was not* (*wasn't*) and *were not* (*weren't*). Have students work in pairs to write sentences for the adjectives in the chart that end in *-ed*.

4. Compare the affirmative and negative statements and questions.

EXERCISE 5

ANSWERS: 1. born; **2.** was; **3.** were; **4.** hard; **5.** were; **6.** 98; **7.** were; **8.** unhappy

5-10 mins

1. Tell students that this exercise is based on the reading on pages 92–93. Have students read the direction line. Go over the example in the book.

2. Have students complete the rest of Exercise 5 individually. Remind them to review grammar chart **3.2** on pages 93–94 if necessary. Then have them compare their answers in pairs. Finally, check the answers as a class.

EXERCISE 6

ANSWERS: 1. was; **2.** wasn't; **3.** were; **4.** was; **5.** Was there, was; **6.** Was she; **7.** was she; **8.** weren't they; **9.** wasn't he; **10.** wasn't; **11.** was George Dawson/(OR he); **12.** Was there

5-10 mins

1. Have students read the direction line. Go over the example in the book.

2. Have students complete the exercise individually. Remind them to review grammar chart **3.2** on pages 93–94 if necessary. Go over the answers as a class.

3.3 The Simple Past Tense of Regular Verbs

5-10 mins

1. Have students go back to the reading on pages 92–93. Say: *Find verbs in the past that end in -ed* (*lived, started, worked, chopped*, etc.). Write the verbs on the board. Then ask students to tell you the base form of the verbs. Write them next to the past tense (*live, start, work, chop*).

2. Have students look at grammar chart **3.3** on page 95. Explain that to form the simple past of regular verbs, we add *-ed*. If the verb ends in *-e*, add only *-d*. Review the examples in the chart. Remind students that the past forms are the same for all persons. If necessary, review the spelling and pronunciation rules for the past tense form in Appendix A.

3. Explain that verbs that come after *to* are in the infinitive form, not the past, so their endings do not change.

EXERCISE 7

5-10 mins

1. Have students read the direction line. Ask: *What do we write in the blanks?* (the past tense of the verb) Go over the example.

2. Have students complete Exercise 7 individually. Remind them to review grammar chart **3.3** on page 95 if necessary. Then check the answers as a class.

EXERCISE 8

5-10 mins

1. Have students read the direction line. Go over the example.

2. Have students complete the exercise individually. Remind them to review grammar chart **3.3** on page 95 if necessary. Check the answers as a class.

Context Note

Direct students to the photo on page 96. In 1954, the Supreme Court declared separate but equal education unconstitutional. After this decision, blacks and whites began attending the same schools.

Practice Idea: Speaking

Have students prepare a short presentation about an event in U.S. history or in the history of their native countries. Have students create a timeline of the events. Brainstorm ideas with the class. Ask volunteers to talk about their events in front of the class.

3.4 The Simple Past of Irregular Verbs

10-15 mins

1. Have students cover up grammar chart **3.4** on page 97. Write the following sentences on the board:

Dawson _____ (have) a close family.
He _____ (go) to classes when he was 98.
Carl Henry _____ (teach) him to read.

Say: *Fill in the blanks with the past tense of the verb in the parentheses.*

2. Then have students look at grammar chart **3.4**. Say: *Check the verb forms in the grammar chart.* Explain that many past tense verbs are irregular and that their forms must be memorized.

3. To help students memorize the simple past tense of irregular verbs, give students quizzes on the irregular forms. Group the verbs by spelling patterns, and space the quizzes as appropriate. Tell students that there is an alphabetical list of irregular verbs in Appendix M.

EXERCISE 9

5-10 mins

1. Tell students that this exercise is about George Dawson. Have students read the direction line. Say: *If you don't know the past tense of these irregular verbs, find them on the chart on page 97.* Go over the example in the book.

2. Have students complete the exercise individually. Remind them to review grammar chart **3.4** on page 97 if necessary. Check the answers as a class.

EXERCISE 10

5-10 mins

1. Tell students that this exercise is about Martin Luther King, Jr. Have students read the direction line. Say: *If you don't know the past tense of these irregular verbs, find them on the chart on page 97.* Go over the example in the book.

2. Have students complete the exercise individually. Remind them to review grammar chart **3.4** on page 97 if necessary. Check the answers as a class.

Barack Obama and *Dreams from My Father* READING

1. Have students look at the photo. Ask: *What do you know about Barack Obama?*

2. Preteach any vocabulary words your students may not know, such as *belong* and *adore*.

Reading Glossary

adore: to love and admire
belong to: to feel part of a group of people, to identify with a certain group of people

BEFORE YOU READ

5-10 mins

1. Have students discuss the questions in pairs. Try to pair students of different cultures together.

2. Ask for a few volunteers to share their answers with the class.

Reading

CD 1 TR 27

10-15 mins

1. Have students first read the text silently. Tell them to pay special attention to the negative form of past tense verbs. Then play the audio and have students read along silently.

2. Check students' comprehension. Ask questions such as: *Did Barack Obama grow up with his father?* (No, he didn't.) *How old was he when he returned to Hawaii?* (10) *Whom did he live with when he returned to Hawaii?* (his grandparents) *When did his grandmother die?* (one day before the election)

Practice Idea: Listening

To practice listening skills, have students first listen to the audio alone. Ask a few comprehension questions. Repeat the audio if necessary. Then have them open their books and read along as they listen to the audio.

3.5 Negative Statements

5-10 mins

1. Have students cover up grammar chart **3.5** on page 100. Ask students to go back to the reading on page 99. Say: *Circle the negative verbs in the past tense.* Write students' examples on the board.

2. Tell students to look at grammar chart **3.5**. Write on the board: *didn't* + base form. Explain that this is how the negative is formed for all verbs, regular and irregular.

3. Review all of the example sentences in the chart.

EXERCISE 11

ANSWERS: 1. didn't write; **2.** wasn't born; **3.** didn't live; **4.** didn't know; **5.** didn't go; **6.** didn't see; **7.** didn't grow up; **8.** didn't study; **9.** didn't become; **10.** didn't die

---

5-10 mins

1. Tell students that this exercise is about Barack Obama. Have students read the direction line. Go over the example in the book.

2. Have students complete Exercise 11 individually. Remind them to review grammar chart **3.5** on page 100 if necessary. Check answers as a class.

Questions and Answers about Barack Obama READING

1. Have students look at the photo. Ask: *When did Barack Obama become president?*

2. Preteach any vocabulary words your students may not know, such as *law office* and *law*.

Reading Glossary

law: the rules and regulations in a community
law office: a firm where attorneys work

BEFORE YOU READ

5-10 mins

1. Have students discuss the questions in pairs. Try to pair students of different cultures together.

2. Ask for a few volunteers to share their answers with the class.

Reading

**CD 1
TR 28**

10-15
mins

1. Have students first read the text silently. Tell them to pay special attention to past tense questions and answers. Then play the audio and have students read along silently.

2. Check students' comprehension. Ask questions such as: *When did Barack Obama get married?* (in 1989) *What did he teach?* (law) *When did he live in Springfield?* (when he was a senator from Illinois)

Practice Idea: Listening

To practice listening skills, have students first listen to the audio alone. Ask a few comprehension questions. Repeat the audio if necessary. Then have them open their books and read along as they listen to the audio.

3.6 Questions with the Simple Past Tense

10-15
mins

1. Have students cover up grammar chart **3.6** on page 102. Write the following affirmative sentences on the board:

    Obama lived with his grandparents.
    Obama went to Africa.

    Say: *Write yes/no questions, short answers, and wh- questions for these two sentences.*

2. Then write the following negative sentences on the board:

    Obama didn't live with his father.
    His father didn't stay in the U.S.

    Say: *Write negative questions with* why *for these two negative statements.*

3. Have students look at grammar chart **3.6**. Say: *Now compare your questions with the questions in the grammar chart.* Write on the board: Did + *subject* + *base form* ... ?

Explain that this is how *yes/no* questions are formed in the simple past for all verbs—regular and irregular. Review negative and affirmative short answers.

4. Write on the board: Wh- *word* + did + *subject* + *base form* ... ? Explain that this is how *wh-* questions are formed in the simple past for all verbs—regular and irregular.

5. Write: Why + didn't + *subject* + *base form* ... ? Explain that this is how negative questions are formed in the simple past for all verbs—regular and irregular.

EXERCISE 12

ANSWERS: 1. Did his mother die before he became president? Yes, she did. **2.** Did his mother go to Kenya? No, she didn't. **3.** Did Michelle Robinson (OR she) become his law partner? No, she didn't. **4.** Did he meet his wife in Hawaii? No, he didn't. **5.** Did he live in Indonesia? Yes, he did. **6.** Did he lose the election for representative of Illinois? Yes, he did. **7.** Did he teach law (at the University of Chicago)? Yes, he did.

10-15
mins

1. Tell students that this exercise is about Barack Obama. Have students read the direction line. Tell them they are going to write a question and an answer. Go over the example.

2. Have students complete the exercise individually. Remind them to review grammar chart **3.6** on page 102 if necessary. Then have them compare answers in pairs. Check answers as a class.

EXERCISE 13

ANSWERS: 1. Where did his mother meet his father? They met in college. **2.** Why did his mother (OR she) go to Indonesia? She went to be with her husband. **3.** When did Obama (OR he) return to Hawaii? He returned in 1971. **4.** Where did he study law? He studied law at Harvard University. **5.** What kind of book did he write? He wrote a book about his life. **6.** When did Obama (OR he) become president? He became president in 2009. **7.** When did Obama's grandmother (OR she) die? She died in November 2008. **8.** Why didn't Obama (OR he) work in Hawaii? He didn't work there because he lived in Illinois.

10-15
mins

1. Tell students that this exercise is about Barack Obama. Have students read the direction line. Tell them they are going to write a question and an answer. Go over the example in the book.

2. Have students complete the exercise individually. Remind them to review grammar chart **3.6** on page 102 if necessary. Then have students check answers in pairs. Check answers as a class.

Practice Idea: Speaking

Have students ask and answer the questions from Exercises 11 and 12 in pairs. Have them ask the questions in random order.

EXERCISE 14

CD 1
TR 29

ANSWERS: 1. was; **2.** Did you see; **3.** did; **4.** did he speak; **5.** spoke; **6.** Did a lot of people go; **7.** went; **8.** died; **9.** came; **10.** told; **11.** did you do; **12.** didn't believe; **13.** cry; **14.** went; **15.** watched; **16.** was; **17.** was; **18.** came; **19.** shot; **20.** didn't know; **21.** was; **22.** became; **23.** Did this date become; **24.** became; **25.** wrote

10-15 mins

1. Tell students that this exercise is a conversation between a student and her teacher. Have students read the direction line. Go over the example in the book.

2. Have students complete Exercise 14 individually. Remind them to review grammar chart **3.6** on page 102 if necessary. Play the audio and then check the answers as a class.

Practice Idea: Listening

To provide practice with listening skills, have students close their books and listen to the audio. Say: *In this conversation, a student is interviewing her teacher about Martin Luther King Jr.* Repeat the audio as needed. Ask comprehension questions, such as: *Where was Martin Luther King Jr., when he made his famous speech in 1963?* (Washington, D.C.) *How many people were in Washington to hear his speech?* (250,000) *Who told the teacher's class about King's death?* (the high school principal) Then have students open their books and complete Exercise 14.

Practice Idea: Speaking

Have students practice the conversation in pairs. Then ask volunteers to act out the conversation for the class, or have students ask you questions about an important historical event during your lifetime.

EXERCISE 15
Answers will vary.

10-15 mins

1. Have students read the direction line. Say: *Your partner will ask you questions about things you have done this past week.* Go over the example. Model #2 with another student.

2. Have students complete the checklist individually. Remind them to review grammar chart **3.6** on page 102 if necessary. Then have students exchange lists and ask and answer questions in pairs.

Practice Idea: Speaking

Create two rings of students. Have half of the students stand in an outer ring around the classroom. Have the other half stand in an inner ring, facing the outer ring. Instruct students to ask each other *yes/no* questions in random order from Exercise 15 (e.g., *Did you make a long-distance phone call this week? Did you go to the post office this week?*). Call out *turn* every minute or so. Students in the inner ring should move one space clockwise. Students now interview their new partners. Make sure students look at each other when they're asking and answering questions.

Summary of Lesson 3

20-30 mins

1. **Simple Past Tense** Have students cover up the summary. Write the following on the board:

(be)
1. *Dawson* _____ *happy.*
2. *He* _____ *rich.*
3. _____ *he from a large family?*

4. *Yes, he _____.*
5. *Where_____he born?*
6. *Why_____he in school?*

(live)
1. *Dawson_____for 103 years.*
2. *He_____in the time of slavery.*
3. *_____ he _____ in the North?*
4. *No, he _____.*
5. *Where _____ he _____?*
6. *Why _____ he _____ in the North?*

(feel)
1. *Dawson _____ happy.*
2. *He _____ lonely.*
3. *_____ he _____ good when he learned to read?*
4. *Yes, he _____.*
5. *How _____ he _____ about his life?*
6. *Why _____ he _____ lonely?*

Have students come up to the board and complete each sentence with the correct form of the simple past tense. [**Answers:** (be) **1.** was; **2.** wasn't; **3.** was; **4.** was; **5.** was; **6.** wasn't; (live) **1.** lived; **2.** didn't live; **3.** Did, live; **4.** didn't; **5.** did, live; **6.** didn't, live; (feel) **1.** felt; **2.** didn't feel; **3.** Did, feel; **4.** did; **5.** did, feel; **6.** didn't, feel]

If necessary, have students review:
3.2 Past Tense of *Be* (pp. 93–94)
3.3 The Simple Past Tense of Regular Verbs (p. 95)
3.4 The Simple Past Tense of Irregular Verbs (p. 97)
3.5 Negative Statements (p. 100)
3.6 Questions with the Simple Past Tense (p. 102)

2. **Habitual Past with *Used To*** Have students cover up the summary. Write the following on the board:

   1. *Obama _____ in Hawaii.*
   2. *Black children and white children _____ to separate schools. Now schools are for all children.*

Have students complete each sentence with the correct form of the habitual past with *used to*. If necessary, have students review:
3.1 Habitual Past with *Used To* (p. 90)

Editing Advice

 10-15 mins

1. Have students close their books. Write the first few sentences without editing marks or corrections on the board. For example:

   He born in Germany.
   He was died two years ago.

2. Ask students to correct each sentence and provide a rule or explanation for each correction. This activity can be done individually, in pairs, or as a class. After students have corrected each sentence, tell them to turn to pages 106–107. Say: *Now compare your work with the Editing Advice in the book.*

Editing Quiz

ANSWERS: 1. did we study; **2.** didn't you come; **3.** work; **4.** was tired; **5.** C; **6.** learned; **7.** C; **8.** C; **9.** C; **10.** was born; **11.** didn't learn; **12.** C; **13.** died; **14.** C; **15.** used; **16.** studied; **17.** I used to study; **18.** there was; **19.** C; **20.** did it make OR were; **21.** didn't live; **22.** Was there; **23.** C; **24.** write

 10-15 mins

1. Tell students they are going to put the Editing Advice into practice. Have students read the direction line. Ask: *Do all the shaded words and phrases have mistakes?* (No) Go over the examples with the class. Then do #1 together.

2. Have students complete the quiz individually. Then have them compare answers with a partner before checking answers as a class.

3. For the items students had difficulties with, have them go back and find the relevant grammar chart and review it. Monitor and give help as necessary.

50-60 mins Use the Assessment CD-ROM with Exam*View*®, Online Workbook, and the Web site for additional practice, review, and assessment materials.

PART 1

ANSWERS: 1. ate; **2.** put; **3.** gave; **4.** wrote; **5.** sent; **6.** listened; **7.** read; **8.** took; **9.** brought; **10.** talked; **11.** knew; **12.** found; **13.** stood; **14.** left; **15.** sat; **16.** went; **17.** made; **18.** heard; **19.** felt; **20.** fell; **21.** got

1. Part 1 may be used as an in-class test to assess student performance, in addition to the Assessment CD-ROM with Exam*View*®. Have students read the direction line. Say: *Some verbs may be regular and some may be irregular.* Collect for assessment.

2. If necessary, have students review:
   3.3 The Simple Past Tense of Regular Verbs (p. 95)
   3.4 The Simple Past Tense of Irregular Verbs (p. 97)

PART 2

ANSWERS: 1. wasn't; **2.** didn't go; **3.** didn't tell; **4.** didn't stand; **5.** didn't come; **6.** didn't take; **7.** didn't have; **8.** didn't write; **9.** didn't spend

1. Part 2 may also be used as an in-class test to assess student performance, in addition to the Assessment CD-ROM with Exam*View*®. Have students read the direction line. Review the example. Ask: *What do we write in the blank?* (the negative of the underlined word) Collect for assessment.

2. If necessary, have students review:
   3.1 Habitual Past with *Used To* (p. 90)
   3.2 Past Tense of *Be* (pp. 93–94)
   3.5 Negative Statements (p. 100)

PART 3

ANSWERS: 1. did he become a minister? **2.** was he born? **3.** did they go to separate schools? **4.** didn't some restaurants (OR they) permit black people to eat there? **5.** was he in jail because of his protests? **6.** did he win the Nobel Peace Prize? **7.** did she work?

8. was she tired? **9.** did she go home by bus? **10.** didn't she want to obey the law? **11.** did the police take her to jail? **12.** did he learn to read? **13.** didn't he feel lonely? **14.** didn't he know his father very well? **15.** did he win the election? **16.** was Obama's (OR his) father born? **17.** did he write

1. Part 3 may also be used as an in-class test to assess student performance, in addition to the Assessment CD-ROM with Exam*View*®. Have students read the direction line. Go over the example. Remind students that they do not have to write an answer. Collect for assessment.

2. If necessary, have students review:
   3.6 Questions with the Simple Past (p. 102)

PART 4

Answers will vary.

1. Part 4 may also be used as an in-class test to assess student performance, in addition to the Assessment CD-ROM with Exam*View*®. Have students read the direction line. Say: *How is your life different? Write about two things that you used to do in the past that are different from what you do today.* Collect for assessment.

2. If necessary, have students review:
   3.1 Habitual Past with *Used To* (p. 90)

Expansion

These expansion activities provide opportunities for students to interact with one another and further develop their speaking and writing skills. Encourage students to use grammar from this lesson whenever possible.

CLASSROOM ACTIVITIES

10-15 mins per activity

1. Have students complete the checklist on their own. Then have students get into pairs to discuss their activities (e.g., *What kind of CD did you buy? I bought a jazz CD.*). Monitor pair work. Give help as needed.

Practice Idea: Speaking

Don't have students exchange books to read the checklists. Have students tell each other what they did and didn't do. Then have students discuss their activities (e.g., *What kind of CD did you buy? I bought a jazz CD.*). Monitor pair work. Give help as needed.

2. Say: *Let's find out how well you know each other.* Tell students to write two or three things they did in the past week on the index card. Then have students guess who wrote each one.

Practice Idea: Speaking

On an index card, have students write a false statement about something they did in the past and two true statements about something they did (e.g., *I went to France five times. I met the president of my country. I lived in the Amazon.*). Students should write their names on the card. Then read the statements, and have students guess which statement is false.

3. Ask: *What do you know about your classmates' past?* Tell students to write two or three things they used to do on the index card. Then have students guess who wrote each one.

4. This activity can be done with the whole class or in groups. Model the activity for the students. Bring in a picture of yourself when you were younger and tell students how you have changed. Then have students do the same in pairs or groups.

Practice Idea: Speaking

Have students make a poster of themselves when they were younger. Tell students to include pictures. Ask students not to include their names. Put the posters up around the class. Have students walk around to view the posters. Ask students to guess who is who and to make comparisons (e.g., *José used to wear glasses. Now he wears contacts.*).

5. Have students complete the sentence individually and then discuss their answers in pairs or groups. If possible, try to put students together in groups from different cultures or countries. Then have volunteers share what they wrote with the class.

6. Have students write questions in pairs. Then have them the class what they would ask George Dawson.

TALK ABOUT IT

15-20 mins

Write two columns on the board: *Now—20 years ago* Ask: *What has changed in our lives? What did you used to do 20 years ago that you don't do now?* Write the students ideas on the board. Then have students discuss each question in pairs or groups. Have them report back to the class. If possible, try to put students together in groups or pairs from different cultures or countries.

WRITE ABOUT IT

20-30 mins

Have students read the direction line and the sample paragraph about childhood. Have students choose one of the topics and brainstorm a list of ideas for their composition. Then have them find a partner who has chosen the same topic and share the ideas on their list. Then have students write their own composition. Collect for assessment and/or have students present their paragraphs to a group.

Practice Idea: Writing

Have students exchange first drafts with a partner. Ask students to help their partners edit their drafts. Refer students to the Editing Advice on pages 106–107.

OUTSIDE ACTIVITY

Tell students to interview an American-born person. Tell them they should ask this person to tell them about changes he or she sees in American society and to compare how he or she used to live with how he or she lives now. With the class, brainstorm questions for the interview. (e.g., *How did you use to call people? How did you use to get your information? How did you use to see movies?*). Have students report interesting information to the class.

INTERNET ACTIVITIES

1. Tell students to use the Internet to find information about one of the people below. Then have them tell the class why this person was (or is) famous.

   Jesse Jackson   Frederick Douglass
   Malcolm X   Jesse Owens
   Jackie Robinson   Nat Turner
   Mahatma Gandhi

2. Tell students to use a search engine and type in *I Have a Dream* to find Martin Luther King Jr.'s most famous speech. Have them summarize his dream and share their summaries with the class, orally or in writing.

3. Tell students to find a description of George Dawson's book *Life Is So Good*. (Suggest they try using Web sites such as amazon.com or barnesandnoble.com.) Have students print it and bring it to class. Then have them discuss the book in groups.

4. Have students find a description of Barack Obama's book *Dreams from My Father*. Have students print it and bring it to class. Then have them discuss the book in groups.

Lesson 4

Lesson Overview

GRAMMAR

1. Briefly review what students learned in Lesson 3. Ask: *What did we study in Lesson 3?* (the habitual past with *used to* and the simple past tense)

2. Ask: *What are we going to study in this lesson?* (possessive forms, object pronouns, reflexive pronouns, and questions) *What are possessive forms?* (e.g., **Mary's** coat. **My** hat. It's **mine**.) Have students give examples. Write the examples on the board. Ask: *What are object pronouns?* (pronouns that are the object in a sentence, such as *He loves me.*) *Give me some examples of reflexive pronouns.* (*myself, herself*)

CONTEXT

1. Ask: *What are we going to learn about in this lesson?* (weddings) Activate students' prior knowledge. Ask: *What do you know about American weddings?*

2. Have students share their knowledge and personal experiences.

Presentation Ideas

The topic for this lesson can be enhanced with the following items:

1. A wedding album (yours or someone else's)
2. Bridal and wedding magazines
3. A wedding planner book

A Traditional American Wedding READING

1. Have students look at the illustration. Say: *This is a traditional bridal party. Who are these people? What's happening?*

2. Have students look at the title of the reading. Ask: *What is the reading about?* Have students use the title and picture to make predictions about the reading.

3. Preteach any vocabulary words your students may not know such as: *maid of honor, bridesmaid, groomsman, ceremony,* and *bouquet.* Point out the illustrations of the bride and groom and the wedding party on page 116.

Reading Glossary

bouquet: a bunch of flowers
bridesmaid: a bride's attendant
ceremony: a formal event usually with rituals
groomsman: a man who is an attendant to the groom
maid of honor: a bride's main attendant at her wedding

BEFORE YOU READ

5-10 mins

1. Have students discuss the questions in pairs. Try to pair students of different cultures together.

2. Ask for a few volunteers to share their answers with the class.

Reading

CD 2
TR 01

10-15 mins

1. Have students first read the text silently. Tell them to pay special attention to object pronouns and possessive forms. Then play the audio and have students read along silently.

2. Check students' comprehension. Ask questions such as: *How long do couples spend planning for their weddings?* (one year) *Who chooses the maid of honor?* (the bride) *Why can't the groom see the bride before the wedding?* (It's bad luck.) *What happens when the bride enters?* (Everyone turns to look. Sometimes people stand.)

DID YOU KNOW?

Have students read the information. Ask them what they think the most popular month for weddings is in their country. Tell them that the least popular months for weddings in the U.S. are March, February, and January. Only 5.13 percent of weddings take place in January.

Practice Idea: Listening

To practice listening skills, have students first listen to the audio alone. Ask a few comprehension questions. Repeat the audio if necessary. Then have them open their books and read along as they listen to the audio.

Context Note

It's a custom in American weddings for the bride to have "something old, something new, something borrowed, and something blue." Each item is a good-luck token. The old symbolizes a connection with the past (the bride's family), the new with the future (her life with her husband). The borrowed item from a happily married couple will bring the bride good luck, and the color blue in the past symbolized virtue and fidelity.

4.1 Possessive Forms of Nouns ≡★

5-10 mins

1. Have students close their books. Say: *We use possessive forms to show ownership or relationship.* Give an example, such as *The teacher's desk is big.* Put students into pairs. Write grammar chart **4.1** on the board. Keep the middle column (*Ending*) empty. Say: *Study the nouns and the examples of possessives. Try to guess the rule for the ending.* Have volunteers write the rules on the board.

2. Then ask students to look at grammar chart **4.1** on page 117 to compare their chart with the chart in the book.

3. Make sure to point out that possession by inanimate objects is expressed in the following way: "the _____ of _____ ."

EXERCISE 1 ≡★

ANSWERS: 1. 's; **2.** 's; **3.** '; **4.** '; **5.** 's; **6.** 's; **7.** '; **8.** 's

5-10 mins

1. Have students read the direction line. Go over the example in the book. Have a volunteer do #1 for the class.

2. Have students complete Exercise 1 individually. Remind them to review grammar

chart **4.1** on page 117 if necessary. Go over the answers as a class.

Practice Idea: Writing

Have students work in pairs to make ten sentences about the class and the classroom (e.g., *The door of the class is brown. Serena's jacket is pretty.*). Monitor pair work.

EXERCISE 2 ≡★

ANSWERS: 1. bride's grandmother; **2.** floor of the church; **3.** windows of the church; **4.** bride's mother; **5.** name of the church; **6.** men's tuxedos; **7.** color of the limousine; **8.** girls' dresses; **9.** color of the flowers; **10.** parents' house

5-10 mins

1. Have students read the direction line. Go over the examples in the book. Ask: *When do you use the possessive form with apostrophe + s?* (with people or animals)

2. Have students complete Exercise 2 individually. Remind them to review grammar chart **4.1** on page 117 if necessary. Then have them compare their answers in pairs. Go over the answers as a class.

Practice Idea: Speaking

Divide students into small groups. Give each group a picture of a wedding party, a bride and groom, etc. Have groups make sentences about the pictures using the possessive form of nouns (e.g., *The color of the cake is white.*).

4.2 Possessive Adjectives ≡★

5-10 mins

1. Have students cover up grammar chart **4.2** on page 119. Activate prior knowledge. Ask: *What are the subject pronouns?* (*I, you, he,* etc.) Write them on the board. Then ask: *Do you know what the possessive adjectives are for these pronouns?* (*my, your, his,* etc.) Write them on the board next to the subject pronouns.

2. Have students look at grammar chart **4.2**. Say: *Compare our lists with the grammar chart.* Go over any errors.

3. Review the examples in the chart. Point out that possessive adjectives must be followed by a noun (e.g., *Your gift is wonderful,* NOT *Your is wonderful.*).

4. Point out that English learners sometimes confuse *his* and *her*. Instruct students not to confuse *its* and *it's*, and *their* and *they're*. Explain that although these words are pronounced the same, their spellings and meanings are different.

EXERCISE 3

ANSWERS: 1. My; **2.** her; **3.** his; **4.** Their; **5.** Their; **6.** our; **7.** your

5-10 mins

1. Have students read the direction line. Go over the example in the book.

2. Have students complete Exercise 3 individually. Remind them to review grammar chart **4.2** on page 119 if necessary. Then have them compare their answers in pairs. Go over the answers as a class.

Practice Idea: Writing

Say: *Write about your family and friends. Use Exercise 3 as a model.* Have students write five to seven sentences about their families using possessive adjectives. Then have students compare sentences in pairs.

EXERCISE 4

CD 2
TR 02
ANSWERS: 1. my; **2.** her; **3.** Our; **4.** its; **5.** their; **6.** his

10-15 mins

1. Tell students that this exercise is a conversation about a wedding. Have students read the direction line. Go over the example in the book.

2. Have students complete Exercise 4 individually. Remind them to review grammar chart **4.2** on page 119 if necessary. Play the audio and check answers as a class.

Practice Idea: Listening

To provide practice with listening skills, have students close their books and listen to the audio. Repeat the audio as needed. Ask comprehension questions, such as: *What is she going to wear to her sister's wedding?* (her new blue dress) *Where is the wedding going to be?* (at a church) *Where are the newlyweds going for their honeymoon?* (They're going to stay at a friend's cottage.) Then have students open their books and complete Exercise 4.

Practice Idea: Speaking

Have students practice the conversation in pairs. Ask volunteers to role-play all or some of the conversation in front of the class.

4.3 Possessive Pronouns

⏱
5-10 mins

1. Have students cover up grammar chart **4.3** on pages 120–121. Activate prior knowledge. Say: *OK. Let's review. What are the subject pronouns?* Write them on the board. *What are the possessive adjectives?* (my, your, his, etc.) Write them on the board. Then ask: *Do you know what the possessive pronouns are?* (mine, yours, his, hers, etc.) Write them on the board next to the possessive adjectives.

2. Have students look at grammar chart **4.3**. Say: *Compare our lists with the grammar chart.* Go over any errors.

3. Review the examples in the chart. Ask: *What does a pronoun take the place of ?* (a noun) *What does a possessive pronoun take the place of ?* (a possessive adjective + noun) Say: *We use possessive pronouns to avoid repetition of a noun.* Go over the examples in the chart. For example, say: *Her dress is white. Mine is blue. What does* mine *mean?* (my dress)

4. Explain that after a possessive noun, the noun can be omitted. Go over the example in the book.

5. Point out that there is no corresponding possessive pronoun for *it/its*.

EXERCISE 5

ANSWERS: 1. mine; **2.** Mine; **3.** yours; **4.** My; **5.** his; **6.** Theirs; **7.** Ours; **8.** her; **9.** Hers; **10.** His

10-15 mins

1. Tell students that this exercise is a conversation about a wedding. Have students read the direction line. Go over the example in the book.

2. Have students complete Exercise 5 individually. Remind them to review grammar chart **4.3** on pages 120–121 if necessary. Play the audio and check answers as a class.

Practice Idea: Listening

To provide practice with listening skills, have students close their books and listen to the audio. Repeat the audio as needed. Ask comprehension questions, such as *Who got married last month?* (person B's brother) *Where was person B's wedding?* (in a garden) *Does person A like formal or informal weddings?* (informal weddings) Then have students open their books and complete Exercise 5.

Practice Idea: Speaking

Have students practice the conversation in pairs. Ask volunteers to role-play all or some of the conversation in front of the class.

EXERCISE 6

ANSWERS: 1. I'm; **2.** I; **3.** My; **4.** My, me; **5.** mine

 5-10 mins

1. Have students read the direction line. Ask: *What do we write in the blanks?* (*I, I'm, me, my,* or *mine*)

2. Have students complete Exercise 6 individually. Remind them to review grammar charts **4.2** on page 119 and **4.3** on pages 120–121 if necessary. Check the answers as a class.

EXERCISE 7

ANSWERS: 1. Our; **2.** We; **3.** We're; **4.** us; **5.** ours

 5-10 mins

1. Have students read the direction line. Ask: *What do we write in the blanks?* (*we, we're, us, our,* or *ours*)

2. Have students complete Exercise 7 in pairs. Remind them to review grammar charts **4.2** on page 119 and **4.3** on pages 120–121 if necessary. Monitor pair work. Give help as needed. Check the answers as a class.

EXERCISE 8

ANSWERS: 1. You're; **2.** You; **3.** Yours; **4.** Your; **5.** you

 5-10 mins

1. Have students read the direction line. Ask: *What do we write in the blanks?* (*you, you're, your,* or *yours*)

2. Have students complete Exercise 8 in pairs. Remind them to review grammar charts **4.2** on page 119 and **4.3** on pages 120–121 if necessary. Monitor pair work. Give help as needed. Check the answers as a class.

EXERCISE 9

ANSWERS: 1. His; **2.** He's; **3.** He; **4.** His; **5.** him

 5-10 mins

1. Have students read the direction line. Ask: *What do we write in the blanks?* (*he, he's, his,* or *him*)

2. Have students complete Exercise 9 in small groups. Remind them to review grammar charts **4.2** on page 119 and **4.3** on pages 120–121 if necessary. Monitor pair work. Give help as needed. Check the answers as a class.

EXERCISE 10

ANSWERS: 1. Her; **2.** her; **3.** She; **4.** She's, Her; **5.** Hers

 5-10 mins

1. Have students read the direction line. Ask: *What do we write in the blanks?* (*she, she's, her,* or *hers*)

2. Have students complete Exercise 10 in small groups. Remind them to review grammar charts **4.2** on page 119 and **4.3** on

pages 120–121 if necessary. Monitor pair work. Give help as needed. Check the answers as a class.

EXERCISE 11

ANSWERS: 1. It's; **2.** It; **3.** Its; **4.** it; **5.** It's

1. Have students read the direction line. Ask: *What do we write in the blanks?* (*it, it's,* or *its*)

2. Have students complete Exercise 11 individually. Remind them to review grammar charts **4.2** on page 119 and **4.3** on pages 120–121 if necessary. Check the answers as a class.

EXERCISE 12

ANSWERS: 1. their; **2.** theirs; **3.** They're; **4.** They; **5.** them

1. Have students read the direction line. Ask: *What do we write in the blanks?* (*they, they're, their, theirs,* or *them*)

2. Have students complete Exercise 12 individually. Remind them to review grammar charts **4.2** on page 119 and **4.3** on pages 120–121 if necessary. Check the answers as a class.

4.4 Questions with *Whose*

1. Have students cover up grammar chart **4.4** on page 123. Pick up a student's book from his/her desk. Ask: *Whose book is this?* (e.g., Tina's book) Write it on the board. Then ask: *What was the question I asked?* Have a volunteer write it on the board.

2. Have students look at grammar chart **4.4**. Say: Whose + *noun asks about ownership (possession).*

EXERCISE 13

ANSWERS: 1. Whose car is that? **2.** Whose gifts are those? **3.** Whose necklace is she wearing? **4.** Whose suit are you wearing? **5.** Whose advice do you follow? **6.** Whose dress did the bride borrow?

1. Have students read the direction line. Go over the example in the book.

---

2. Have students complete the exercise individually. Remind them to review grammar chart **4.4** on page 123 if necessary. Go over the answers with the class.

> **Practice Idea: Writing**
>
> Have students write five statements similar to the statements from Exercise 13 (e.g., *They're my keys. That's my friend's car. Those are my teacher's gifts.*). Then have students exchange papers with a partner to make questions for the statements (*Whose keys are these? Whose car is that? Whose gifts are those?*). Monitor pair work. Give help as needed.

4.5 Object Pronouns

1. Have students cover up grammar chart **4.5** on pages 125–126. Write the subject pronouns on the board. Activate prior knowledge. Say: *OK. Here are the subject pronouns. Can you write the object pronouns?* Have a volunteer write them on the board.

2. Have students look at grammar chart **4.5**. Say: *Compare our list with the grammar chart.* Go over any errors.

3. Review the examples in the chart. Ask: *What do subject pronouns take the place of?* (the subject of a sentence) *What do object pronouns take the place of?* (the object of a sentence) Say: *We can use an object pronoun to take the place of an object after the verb of a sentence.*

4. Explain that object pronouns can also take the place of an object after a preposition. Ask: *What prepositions do you know?* (*of, about, to, from, in,* etc.) Go over the examples in the book. Point out that we use *them* for plural people and plural things.

5. Then go back to the reading on pages 116–117. Ask students to circle the examples of verb + object pronoun and preposition + object pronoun.

EXERCISE 14

ANSWERS: 1. her, him; **2.** it; **3.** it, her; **4.** it; **5.** them;
6. him

5-10 mins

1. Have students read the direction line. Ask: *What do we write in the blanks?* (an object pronoun) Go over the example in the book.

2. Have students complete the exercise individually. Remind them to review grammar chart **4.5** on pages 124–125 if necessary. Go over the answers with the class.

EXERCISE 15

CD 2
TR 04

ANSWERS: 1. them; **2.** it; **3.** they; **4.** their; **5.** Their;
6. them; **7.** them; **8.** Their; **9.** she; **10.** her; **11.** it;
12. they; **13.** me; **14.** they; **15.** you; **16.** him;
17. he; **18.** her; **19.** them; **20.** them; **21.** me;
22. them; **23.** you

10-15 mins

1. Tell students that this exercise is a conversation about a wedding. Have students read the direction line. Do a brief review of subject pronouns, object pronouns, and possessive adjectives. Ask volunteers to write them on the board. Go over the example in the book.

2. Have students complete Exercise 15 in pairs. Remind them to review grammar charts **4.2** on page 119 and **4.5** on pages 124–125 if necessary. Play the audio and check the answers.

Practice Idea: Listening

To provide practice with listening skills, have students close their books and listen to the audio. Repeat the audio as needed. Ask comprehension questions, such as: *When was Lisa's wedding?* (last Saturday) *Was her wedding big?* (yes) *Did her parents pay for the wedding?* (No. They helped a little.) *Whose dress did Lisa wear?* (her mother's) *Where did they go on their honeymoon?* (Hawaii) Then have students open their books and complete Exercise 15.

Practice Idea: Speaking

Have students work in pairs to practice the conversation or to create their own conversations about weddings they have attended in their own lives. Ask volunteers to role-play the conversations in front of the class.

New Wedding Trends   READING

1. Have students look at the photo. Ask: *Do you know of anyone who has gotten married on the beach or in any other interesting place? What are these people doing in this photo? Do you know of any unusual wedding customs from other cultures?*

2. Have students look at the title of the reading. Ask: *What is the reading about?* Have students use the title and photos to make predictions about the reading.

3. Preteach any vocabulary words your students may not know such as *unique, vow,* and *cherish.*

Reading Glossary

cherish: to love most dearly

unique: singular, one of a kind

vow: a solemn promise

BEFORE YOU READ

5-10 mins

1. Have students discuss the questions in pairs. Try to pair students of different cultures together.

2. Ask for a few volunteers to share their answers with the class.

Reading

CD 2
TR 05

10-15 mins

1. Have students first read the text silently. Tell them to pay special attention to direct and indirect objects after verbs. Then play the audio and have students read along silently.

2. Check students' comprehension. Ask questions such as: *Where are some places couples are having their weddings?* (beaches and mountain tops) *Why do couples send their guests "save-the-date" cards?* (so they can make plans to attend the wedding)

What are some traditions in African-American weddings? (jumping over a broom; wearing traditional African clothing) *What do couples always do after a wedding?* (send thank-you cards to their guests)

4.6 Direct and Indirect Objects

10-15 mins

1. Have students cover up grammar chart **4.6** on page 129. To present Pattern A, write the following sentence on the board: *We gave the couple a wedding gift.*

   Say: *Some verbs are followed by both direct and indirect objects. What are the direct and indirect objects in this sentence?* (d.o.—a wedding gift; i.o.—the couple) *Which comes first—the direct object or the indirect object?* (the indirect object)

   Then present Pattern B. Say: *We can also write the sentence like this:*

   We gave a wedding gift to the couple.

   Ask: *How is this sentence pattern different from the first one?* (the direct object comes <u>before</u> the indirect object; the indirect object has a *to* in front of it)

2. Then ask students to look at grammar chart **4.6**. Review the patterns and explanations for direct and indirect objects.

3. Explain that some verbs (*bring, give, offer,* etc.) can use either Pattern A or Pattern B. Direct students to the list of verbs in the grammar chart. Point out that when the direct object is a pronoun, Pattern B must be used (e.g., *He gave it to her.* NOT *He gave her it.*).

4. Then direct students to the second list of verbs. Say: *Put the direct object before the indirect object after these verbs* (announce, describe, explain, etc.). Point out that we can't use Pattern A with these verbs. For example, it's incorrect to say, *Please explain me wedding customs.*

5. Now ask students to go back to the reading on pages 127–128 to find verbs with direct and indirect objects. Have students say if the order of the verb and objects are Pattern A or Pattern B (e.g., *A clergyperson reads the bride and groom their vows.—Pattern A*).

CD 2
TR 06

EXERCISE 16

ANSWERS: 1. the groom a lovely poem OR a lovely poem to the groom; **2.** her a poem OR a poem to her; **3.** you an invitation; **4.** them a letter OR a letter to them; **5.** my problem to them; **6.** them a lovely present OR a lovely present to them; **7.** it to you; **8.** them to you

---

10-15 mins

1. Tell students that this exercise is a conversation about a wedding. Have students read the direction line. Go over the example in the book. Ask: *Can we write: Give me it?* (No. If the direct object is a pronoun, it always goes before the indirect object.)

2. Have students complete Exercise 16 individually. Remind them to review grammar chart **4.6** on page 129 if necessary. Play the audio and check the answers as a class.

4.7 *Say* and *Tell*

1. Have students cover up grammar chart **4.6** on page 130. Activate prior knowledge. Ask: *Does anyone know the difference between the two verbs* say *and* tell? Write the two verbs on the board. Say: *They mean the same thing, but we use them differently.*

2. Create a matching exercise. Write the examples from the grammar chart on the board. On the other side of the board, write the explanations in a mixed-up order:

   1. *She said her name.*
   2. *She told me her name.*
   3. *She said her name to me.*
   4. *They told the musicians to start the music.*

   a. *We say something to someone.*
   b. *We tell someone something.*
   c. *We tell someone to do something.*
   d. *We say something.*

   Have students match the examples with the explanations. (Matching Answers: **1.** d; **2.** b; **3.** a; **4.** c)

3. Then ask students to look at grammar chart **4.7**. Say: *Now check your work.* Review the examples and explanations for *say* and *tell*.

4. Have students find an example of *say* and an example of *tell* in the reading on pages 127–128. Have students describe which pattern the sentences follow—*a, b, c,* or *d*.

EXERCISE 17 =★

ANSWERS: 1. told; **2.** tell; **3.** Tell; **4.** say; **5.** say; **6.** told; **7.** say; **8.** told, said

1. Have students read the direction line. Go over the examples in the book.

2. Have students complete the exercise individually. Remind them to review grammar chart **4.7** on page 130 if necessary. Go over the answers with the class.

Economizing on a Wedding (READING)

1. Have students look at the photo. Ask: *Who is this woman? What is she doing?* (making a dress)

2. Have students look at the title of the reading. Ask: *What is the reading about?* Have students use the title and photo to make predictions about the reading.

3. Preteach any vocabulary words your students may not know, such as *economize* and *secondhand*.

Reading Glossary

economize: to spend less than before
secondhand: owned or used by someone in the past

BEFORE YOU READ

1. Have students discuss the questions in pairs. Try to pair students of different cultures together.

2. Ask for a few volunteers to share their answers with the class.

Reading =★

CD 2
TR 07

1. Have students first read the text silently. Tell them to pay special attention to the reflexive pronouns. Then play the audio and have students read along silently.

2. Check students' comprehension. Ask questions such as: *Why do couples often pay for their own weddings?* (They're older.) *Instead of spending $1,000 on a dress, what does the author suggest brides do?* (Buy a secondhand dress or make it themselves.) *What does one couple suggest for music?* (Hire a DJ for dancing instead of a live band.) *Is January a popular time to get married?* (no) *What's the best way to save money on a wedding?* (Don't invite a lot of people.)

DID YOU KNOW?

Have students read the information and ask: *What's the average age of marriage for men and women in your countries?* Then tell the following information:

Although American women and men are marrying at a later age now than they did during the 1950s, Americans historically have always married at relatively later ages. From the 1890s to 1940, the average ages of marriage for American men and women were about the same as they are today.

Context Note

About 43 percent of couples spend more on their wedding than they had planned on spending. Many wedding debts now last longer than the actual marriages.

Context Note

The United States has the highest marriage rates—and the highest divorce rates—of any other industrialized nation. Americans marry at a rate that is twice that of most Western European countries.

4.8 Reflexive Pronouns =★

10-15
mins

1. Have students cover up grammar chart **4.8** on pages 132–133. Then have students go back to the reading on pages 131–132. Say: *Find the reflexive pronouns in the reading. Circle them. Then find the subject of the sentence or phrase that contains the reflexive pronoun and underline it* (e.g., *They often pay for things themselves.*). Write students' examples on the board. Say: *When the object and the subject of the sentence are the same, we use a reflexive pronoun for the object.*

2. Write the following two sentences on the board:

   The groom loves her.

   The bride loves herself.

   Say: *Look at these two sentences. What is the difference between the two?* (In the first example, the object (*her*) is not the same person as the subject (*the groom*). In the second, the object (*the bride*) and the subject (*herself*) are the same.)

3. Review the forms of the reflexive pronouns. Write a list of the subject pronouns on the board. Ask volunteers to write the reflexive pronouns.

Point out that *you* has both a singular reflexive pronoun (*yourself*) and a plural reflexive pronoun (*yourselves*).

4. Have students look at grammar chart **4.8**. Review the examples and explanations in the chart. Go over the reflexive pronoun as a direct object, as an indirect object, and as the object of a preposition.

5. Point out that the reflexive pronoun is often used to mean "alone" (without help). Often "(all) by" is added for emphasis. Direct students to the idiomatic expressions. Give students more examples. Have students make their own sentences using idiomatic expressions.

CD 2
TR 08

EXERCISE 18 =★

ANSWERS: 1. ourselves; **2.** myself; **3.** himself; **4.** myself; **5.** myself; **6.** myself; **7.** myself; **8.** themselves; **9.** herself; **10.** myself

10-15
mins

1. Tell students that this exercise is about a husband and wife, Frank and Sylvia. Ask students what some of the difficulties are for married couples. Have students read the direction line. Go over the example in the book.

2. Have students complete Exercise 18 individually. Remind them to review grammar chart **4.8** on pages 132–133 if necessary. Play the audio and check the answers as a class.

Practice Idea: Listening

To provide practice with listening skills, have students close their books and listen to the audio. Repeat the audio as needed. Ask comprehension questions, such as: *Does Frank help Sylvia with the housework?* (no) *Does Frank buy Sylvia lots of presents?* (no) *Does Frank like to go to the movies by himself?* (no) *Why doesn't Frank want to go to a counselor?* (because he doesn't like to tell people about his problems) Then have students open their books and complete Exercise 18.

EXERCISE 19

Answers will vary.

10-15 mins

1. Have students read the direction line. Ask: *What do you like to do by yourself?* Go over the examples. Model the exercise for the class (e.g., *I like to go to the movies by myself.*). Write your sentences on the board.

2. Have students complete the exercise individually. Remind them to review grammar chart **4.8** on pages 132–133 if necessary. Then have students compare sentences in pairs. Monitor pair work.

EXERCISE 20

ANSWERS: 1. they; 2. They; 3. their; 4. them; 5. their; 6. it; 7. they; 8. them; 9. themselves; 10. her; 11. his; 12. her; 13. his; 14. him; 15. her; 16. our; 17. ourselves; 18. me; 19. yourself; 20. itself

10-15 mins

1. Tell students that this exercise is about the married couple, Frank and Sylvia. Have students read the direction line. Go over the example. Model the exercise for the class.

2. Have students complete the exercise individually. Remind them to review grammar

charts **4.2** on page 119, **4.5** on pages 124–125, **4.6** on page 129, and **4.8** on pages 132–133 if necessary. Then have students compare their answers with a partner. Monitor pair work.

Questions and Answers about an American Wedding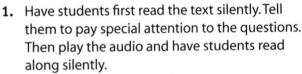

1. Have students look at the photo. Ask: *What do you think the woman is doing?* (opening gifts)

2. Have students look at the title of the reading. Ask: *What kind of questions do you have about American weddings?* Write students' questions on the board.

3. Preteach any vocabulary words your students may not know, such as *cookware* and *appliances*.

Reading Glossary

appliance: a device used for a specific function, usually electrical and used in the home

cookware: utensils that are used for cooking, such as pots and pans

BEFORE YOU READ

5-10 mins

1. Have students discuss the questions in pairs. Try to pair students of different cultures together.

2. Ask for a few volunteers to share their answers with the class.

Reading
CD 2
TR 09

10-15 mins

1. Have students first read the text silently. Tell them to pay special attention to the questions. Then play the audio and have students read along silently.

2. Check students' comprehension. Ask questions such as: *What kinds of gifts do brides get at a shower?* (towels, cookware, linens, and small appliances) *Who pays for the hotel for the bridesmaids?* (the bride) *Is the groom's brother always the best man?* (No, it can be a friend or another relative.) *How much do friends usually spend on a wedding gift?* (about $100)

Context Note

Many couples hire a wedding consultant or wedding planner to help with planning and organizing their big event. Wedding planners typically charge anywhere from 10 percent to 15 percent of the total wedding budget for their services.

4.9 Questions about the Subject or Complement =★

1. Have students go to the reading on pages 135–136. Ask them to look at the questions in the reading. Say: *Underline the questions with* do *or* does *(e.g.,* When do they have the shower?*). Are these questions about the subject or the complement?* (the complement—*two to four weeks before the wedding*) *Circle the questions with a verb in the -s form (e.g.,* Who pays for the wedding?*). Are these questions asking about the subject or the complement?* (the subject—*the bride's parents/the bride and groom*)

2. Have students look at grammar chart **4.9** on pages 136–137. Explain that when we use *do* or *does* in a question, we are asking about the complement of the sentence, not the subject. Say: *When we use the -s form in a question (without* do, does, *or* did*) we are asking a question about the subject.* Read the examples and the explanation.

3. Have students look back at the reading on pages 135–136 to compare questions about the subject with questions about the complement.

4. Point out that although *What happened?* is a subject question, the answer usually has another verb (not *happen* or an auxiliary verb).

5. Review the forms to use after *who, which* + noun, and *how many*.

6. Have students label the questions in the comparison chart on page 137. Ask: *Which questions are about the complement and which questions are about the subject?*

7. Direct students to the Language Note. Explain that *whom* is very formal. Native speakers typically use *who*.

EXERCISE 21

ANSWERS: 1. Who holds the rings? **2.** Whose car has a "just married" sign? **3.** How many people say, "Congratulations?" **4.** Which woman wore a black dress? **5.** Who pays for the bridesmaids' dresses?

1. Have students read the direction line. Go over the example in the book. Say: *These questions are all questions about the subject.*

2. Have students complete Exercise 21 individually. Remind them to review grammar chart **4.9** on pages 136–137 if necessary. Go over the answers as a class.

EXERCISE 22

ANSWERS: Student responses will vary. Correct question constructions: 1. Who explains the grammar? **2.** How many students speak Spanish? **3.** What usually happens after class? **4.** Who needs help with this lesson? **5.** Which students walk to school? **6.** Who has a digital camera? **7.** Who lives alone? **8.** Whose last name has more than ten letters?

1. Have students read the direction line. Say: *First you'll write the questions. Then we'll answer the questions as a class.* Go over the examples in the book.

2. Have students write the questions individually. Remind them to review grammar chart **4.9** on

pages 136–137 if necessary. Then answer the questions as a class.

EXERCISE 23

ANSWERS: **Student responses will vary. Correct question constructions: 1.** Who moved last year? **2.** Who understood the explanation? **3.** Whose family took a trip recently? **4.** Who brought a dictionary to class today? **5.** Who passed the last test? **6.** Which students came late today? **7.** Which student arrived first today? **8.** How many students did today's homework? **9.** How many students studied English in elementary school? **10.** How many students brought a cell phone to class?

1. Have students read the direction line. Say: *You're going to write questions about the subject. Will your questions include* do, does, *or* did? (no) Go over the example in the book. Say: *After you write the questions, we'll answer them as a class.*

2. Have students write the questions individually. Remind them to review grammar chart **4.9** on pages 136–137 if necessary. Answer the questions as a class.

EXERCISE 24

ANSWERS: **1.** When does she throw it? **2.** Which women try to catch it? **3.** On which hand does he put the ring?/Which hand does he put the ring on? **4.** What kind of music does the band (OR it) play? **5.** Who dances with the bride? **6.** What kind of presents do they give? **7.** Who cries at the wedding? **8.** What happens after the dinner?

1. Have students read the direction line. Ask: *Are the questions about the subject?* (No. Some are about the complement.) Go over the examples in the book.

2. Have students write the questions individually. Remind them to review grammar chart **4.9** on pages 136–137 if necessary. Then have students compare answers in pairs. Check the answers as a class.

CD 2
TR 10

EXERCISE 25

ANSWERS: **Answers may vary. Possible answers: 1.** cooks in your house; **2.** cleans your house; **3.** children do you have; **4.** children go to school; **5.** one goes to private school; **6.** do you recommend; **7.** does she work for

1. Tell students that the conversation in this exercise is between two women talking about their families. Direct students' attention to the photo. Then have students read the direction line. Go over the example in the book.

2. Have students complete Exercise 25 individually. Remind them to review grammar chart **4.9** on pages 136–137 if necessary. Then have students compare answers in pairs. Play the audio and check the answers as a class.

Practice Idea: Listening

To provide practice with listening skills, have students close their books and listen to the audio. Repeat the audio as needed. Ask comprehension questions such as: *Who helps at home while person B is at work or at school?* (her husband) *How many children does person B have?* (five) *Who is her babysitter?* (the neighbor) Then have students open their books and complete Exercise 25.

Practice Idea: Speaking

Have students work in pairs to practice the conversation or write a conversation about their own family lives. Ask volunteers to role-play the conversation in front of the class.

EXERCISE 26

ANSWERS: **1.** Who(m); **2.** Who; **3.** Whose; **4.** Who's

1. Have students read the direction line. Say: *More than one answer may be right. You may use the question words more than once.*

2. Have students complete the exercise individually. Remind them to review grammar charts **4.4** on page 123 and **4.9** on pages 136–137 if necessary. Go over the answers as a class.

20-30 mins

1. **Pronouns and Possessive Forms** Have students cover up the summary. Write the list of subject pronouns on the board. Write the headings of the other lists (*Object Pronoun, Possessive Adjective,* etc.). Ask students to fill in the rest of the chart. On the board, write the example sentences below the chart in the book without the pronouns:

   > *Robert and Lisa are my friends.*
   > *_____ come from Canada.*
   > *I like _____.*

   Have students fill in the blanks. Do the same with the *wh-* question words. If necessary, have students review:

   4.2 Possessive Adjectives (p. 119)
   4.3 Possessive Pronouns (pp. 120–121)
   4.5 Object Pronouns (pp. 124–125)
   4.8 Reflexive Pronouns (pp. 132–133)
   4.9 Questions about the Subject and Complement (pp. 136–137)

2. **Possessive Form of Nouns** Rewrite the examples from the summary without the possessive form:

   > *the dress of the bride*
   > *the house of the father*

   Ask students to make the examples into possessive nouns. If necessary, have students review:

   4.1 Possessive Forms of Nouns (p. 117)

3. *Say* **and** *Tell* Rewrite the examples from the summary without *say* and *tell*. For example:

   > *He _____ his name.*
   > *He _____ me his name.*

   Ask students to fill in the blanks with *said* or *told.* If necessary, have students review:

   4.7 *Say* and *Tell* (p. 130)

4. **Questions About the Subject** Write the following statements on the board:

   > *Jamie has the rings. (who)*
   > *Three bridesmaids have pink dresses.*
   >   *(how many)*
   > *That bridesmaid has a red dress. (which)*
   > *Those bridesmaids have pink flowers. (which)*
   > *A man kissed the bride. (who)*
   > *That man kissed the bride. (which)*

Ask students to make questions about the subject for each statement.

If necessary, have students review:

4.9 Questions about the Subject and the Complement (pp. 136–137)

Editing Advice

15-20 mins

Have students close their books. Write the first few sentences without editing marks or corrections on the board. For example:

1. *Your late. You're class started ten minutes ago.*
2. *His married. He's wife is a friend of mine.*

Ask students to correct each sentence and provide a rule or explanation for each correction. This activity can be done individually, in pairs, or as a class. After students have corrected each sentence, tell them to turn to pages 142–143. Say: *Now compare your work with the Editing Advice in the book.* Have students read through all the advice.

Editing Quiz

ANSWERS: 1. C; **2.** her; **3.** C; **4.** ourselves; **5.** the situation to them; **6.** C; **7.** Sara's grandfather; **8.** happened; **9.** him; **10.** Her; **11.** He's; **12.** C; **13.** C; **14.** C; **15.** C; **16.** they're; **17.** C; **18.** C; **19.** Sara's aunts; **20.** Whose; **21.** C; **22.** mother's; **23.** C; **24.** C; **25.** C; **26.** My; **27.** C; **28.** pictures; **29.** them to us; **30.** them; **31.** Sarah and I; **32.** Her; **33.** It's; **34.** C; **35.** C; **36.** them OR it; **37.** C; **38.** C; **39.** Who knows

15-20 mins

1. Tell students they are going to put the Editing Advice into practice. Have students read the direction line. Ask: *Do all the shaded words and phrases have mistakes?* (No) Go over the examples with the class. Then do #1 together.

2. Have students complete the quiz individually. Then have them compare answers with a partner before checking answers as a class.

3. For the items students had difficulties with, have them go back and find the relevant grammar chart and review it. Monitor and give help as necessary.

Lesson 4 Test/Review

 Use the Assessment CD-ROM with Exam*View*®, Online Workbook, and the Web site for additional practice, review, and assessment materials.

50-60 mins

PART 1

ANSWERS: 1. b; **2.** a; **3.** a; **4.** b; **5.** b; **6.** c; **7.** c; **8.** b; **9.** c; **10.** d; **11.** d; **12.** d; **13.** d; **14.** a; **15.** c

1. Part 1 may be used as an in-class test to assess student performance, in addition to the Assessment CD-ROM with Exam*View*®. Have students read the direction line. Instruct them to write the letter for the correct answer in the blank. Collect for assessment.

2. If necessary, have students review Lesson 4.

PART 2

ANSWERS: 1. said; **2.** told; **3.** told; **4.** said; **5.** told; **6.** told; **7.** said; **8.** said

1. Part 2 may also be used as an in-class test to assess student performance, in addition to the Assessment CD-ROM with Exam*View*®. Have students read the direction line. Collect for assessment.

2. If necessary, have students review:

   4.7 *Say* and *Tell* (p. 130)

PART 3

ANSWERS: 1. does the bride throw the bouquet; **2.** try to catch the bouquet; **3.** does the groom put the ring; **4.** does the groom kiss; **5.** ring has a diamond; **6.** (last) name does the bride use; **7.** took pictures at your wedding; **8.** dress did you borrow; **9.** wedding was bigger; **10.** came to the wedding; **11.** cut the cake

1. Part 3 may also be used as an in-class test to assess student performance, in addition to the Assessment CD-ROM with Exam*View*®. Have students read the direction line. Go over the examples. Remind students that some of the questions are about the complement and some are about the subject. Ask: *Which example has a question about the subject?* (the 2nd example) *How do you know?* (It doesn't contain *do, does*, or *did*.) Collect for assessment.

2. If necessary, have students review:

   4.9 Questions about the Subject or Complement (pp. 136–137)

PART 4

ANSWERS: 1. myself; **2.** herself; **3.** themselves; **4.** ourselves; **5.** himself; **6.** yourselves; **7.** yourself

1. Part 4 may also be used as an in-class test to assess student performance, in addition to the Assessment CD-ROM with Exam*View*®. Have students read the direction line. Collect for assessment.

2. If necessary, have students review:

   4.8 Reflexive Pronouns (pp. 132–133)

Expansion

These expansion activities provide opportunities for students to interact with one another and further develop their speaking and writing skills. Encourage students to use grammar from this lesson whenever possible.

CLASSROOM ACTIVITIES

 10-15 mins per activity

1. After the groups have discussed each question, have them report to the class. Write the nationalities and cultures represented in the class on the board. Write brief notes for each item under the country so that the class can compare.

Practice Idea: Speaking

Write nationalities represented in the class on the board. Have the class predict what each nationality would answer for each of the questions. Then ask volunteers from each nationality to say if each guess is correct or not.

2. If possible, put students from different countries and cultures together in groups to interview their married classmates.

3. If applicable, tell the students about your own wedding and whether you followed these specific traditions. Put students from different nationalities in groups to discuss traditions. Have groups share interesting traditions with the class.

4. If students don't have videos, ask them to bring in photos to share with the rest of the class.

5. Have students write the advice individually. Then put students in groups to discuss the advice.

TALK ABOUT IT

15-20 mins

Write on the board: *Married life*. Elicit ideas about being married from students and write them on the board. If necessary, ask questions such as: *What are some of the difficulties of married life?* to elicit ideas. Then have students discuss each point in pairs or groups. Have them report back to the class.

WRITE ABOUT IT

20-30 mins

1. Have students read the direction line. Elicit ideas about how to economize on a wedding. Write the students ideas on the board. Briefly model the activity with the class. Have students help you begin writing a paragraph on the board using the ideas on the board. Then have students write their own paragraph. Collect for assessment and/or have students present their paragraphs to a group.

2. Have students read the direction line and the sample paragraph. Have students brainstorm ideas about typical weddings in their country or about the specific wedding they are going to write about. Then have them tell a partner their ideas. Have them write their paragraphs individually. Encourage them to write as much as they can. Collect for assessment and/or have students present their paragraphs to a group.

Practice Idea: Writing

Have students exchange first drafts with a partner. Ask students to help their partners edit their drafts. Refer students to the Editing Advice on pages 142–143.

INTERNET ACTIVITIES

1. Tell students to do a search on bridal registry on the Internet and make a list of the types of wedding gifts couples ask for. Have them report back to the class on what the most popular gifts are.

2. Tell students to do a search on wedding planning on the Internet and find out how Americans plan for a wedding. Have students present what they found to the class orally or in writing.

Lesson 5

Lesson Overview

GRAMMAR

1. Briefly review what students learned in the previous lesson. Ask: *What did we study in Lesson 4?* (possessive forms, object pronouns, reflexive pronouns, and questions)

2. Ask: *What will we study in this lesson?* (the singular and the plural, count and noncount nouns, *there + be*, and quantity words) *Can anyone give me an example of a count and a noncount noun?* (e.g., *apple, rice*) Have students give examples. Write the examples on the board. Then ask volunteers for sentences with *there + be* (e.g., *There is a mall in our town.*).

CONTEXT

1. Ask: *What will we learn about in this lesson?* (Thanksgiving, Pilgrims, and Native Americans) Activate students' prior knowledge. Ask: *What do you know about Thanksgiving? Who or what are Pilgrims? Does anyone know the names of any Native American tribes?*

2. Have students share their knowledge and personal experiences.

Presentation Ideas

The topic for this lesson can be enhanced with the following ideas:

1. Sampling typical Thanksgiving dishes
2. Illustrations of the first Thanksgiving with Pilgrims and Native Americans
3. Books about Native American tribes
4. Native American artifacts and handicrafts

A Typical Thanksgiving
READING

1. Have students look at the photo. Ask: *Have you ever watched a Thanksgiving day parade in person or on TV?*

What kind of float do you see in this parade?

2. Have students look at the title of the reading. Ask: *What is the reading about?* Have students use the title and photo to make predictions about the reading.

3. Preteach any vocabulary words your students may not know, such as *snacks* and *diet*.

Reading Glossary

diet: a weight loss program

snack: a small amount of food, usually eaten between meals

BEFORE YOU READ

5-10 mins

1. Have students discuss the questions in pairs. Try to pair students of different cultures together.

2. Ask for a few volunteers to share their answers with the class.

Reading

CD 2 TR 11

10-15 mins

1. Have students first read the text silently. Tell them to pay special attention to singular and plural nouns. Then play the audio and have students read along silently.

2. Check students' comprehension. Ask questions such as: *When is Thanksgiving celebrated?* (the fourth Thursday of November) *When is the biggest travel day in the U.S.?* (the Sunday after Thanksgiving) *Does a typical Thanksgiving meal have a lot of calories?* (yes) *What are two activities people do on Thanksgiving?* (watch football and watch parades)

Practice Idea: Listening

To practice listening skills, have students first listen to the audio alone. Ask a few comprehension questions. Repeat the audio if necessary. Then have them open their books and read along as they listen to the audio.

Context Note

Macy's Thanksgiving Day Parade is a famous annual event that began in 1924 when an enthusiastic group of Macy's employees decided to put on the first parade. Eighty years later, the parade is considered by many Americans to be the beginning of the holiday season. The only time the parade did not take place was for three years during World War II. During those years, Macy's donated the much-needed rubber from the floats to the war effort. Now, in place of that small group of Macy's employees, more than four thousand volunteers help stage the magnificent display along two and a half miles of Manhattan streets.

5.1 Noun Plurals

 1. Copy the lists of nouns (singular and plural) from grammar chart **5.1** on the board. Keep nouns in the same groups and in the same order as in the chart in the book. For example:

10-15 mins

Singular	Plural
bee	bees
banana	bananas
church	churches
dish	dishes

2. Have students cover up grammar chart **5.1** on pages 153–154. Say: *Study these spelling changes. Can you guess what the spelling rules for adding an -s are?* If students have difficulty, give them hints. Say: *Look at the endings of these five nouns:* church, dish, box, watch, and class. *What do you add to them to make them plural?* (-es) *So what's the rule?* (When the noun ends in -ss, -sh, -ch, or -x, add -es.) Continue with the same questions for the other groups of nouns.

3. Go over the pronunciation rules for plural nouns. Say: *There are three ways to pronounce the endings of plural nouns.* Across the board, write: /s/, /z/, /əz/ and pronounce each sound. Remind students that this is about pronunciation, not spelling or writing. Then say: *Listen to each word as I say it. Tell me which sound I'm making.* Say words from the grammar chart lists on page 153 in random order. Pronounce each word carefully. Have students guess where the word belongs and write it under the sound they tell you.

4. Have students look at grammar chart **5.1**. Say: *Compare our work with the book.* Review the

rules in the grammar chart. Have students practice the pronunciation of the plural endings chorally or in pairs as needed.

5. Point out the exceptions. Nouns ending in a consonant + -o that do not add an -e are: *photos, pianos, solos, altos, sopranos, autos,* and *avocados.* Nouns that end in -f or -fe that don't change to -ves are: *beliefs, chiefs, roofs, cliffs, chefs,* and *sheriffs.*

6. Have students cover up the Irregular Noun Plurals section of the grammar chart **5.1** on page 154. Activate students' prior knowledge. Write the list of the singular nouns from the chart on the board. Ask volunteers to come up to the board and write the plural spellings.

7. Have students look at grammar chart **5.1**. Say: *Compare our nouns on the board with the plurals in the book. How many did we get right?* Review the information in the grammar chart. Explain to students that there are no rules for spelling changes with these nouns. English language learners must memorize the plural forms.

8. Demonstrate the pronunciation differences between *woman* and *women.* Say it several times and have students guess if you're saying the singular or plural. Then have students practice the pronunciation. Explain that sometimes you can use *persons* as the plural for *person* but that it's not common.

EXERCISE 1

ANSWERS: 1. holidays; **2.** turkeys; **3.** cranberries; **4.** potatoes; **5.** children; **6.** families; **7.** spices; **8.** nuts; **9.** guests; **10.** men; **11.** women; **12.** snacks; **13.** apples; **14.** peaches; **15.** tomatoes; **16.** pies; **17.** knives; **18.** deer; **19.** watches; **20.** taxes; **21.** months; **22.** geese; **23.** dishes; **24.** paths

5-10 mins

1. Have students read the direction line. Go over the example in the book. Say: *Some of the nouns in this list are regular and some are irregular.*

2. Have students complete Exercise 1 individually. Remind them to review grammar chart **5.1** on pages 153–154 if necessary. Then have them compare their answers in pairs. Tell students to practice the pronunciation of each plural. Monitor and help with pronunciation.

Practice Idea: Speaking

Have a Spelling and Pronunciation Bee. Make a list of 40 or so nouns. Divide the class into Team A and Team B. Give one team member from Team A a noun, and tell them to spell the plural form on the board. Do the same with Team B. Then give a member from Team A a plural noun to pronounce. Do the same with Team B. To make the exercise more challenging, give extra points if the team can say (or act out) what the word means.

  EXERCISE 2

CD 2
TR 12

Answers: 1. men; **2.** potatoes; **3.** children; **4.** daughters; **5.** cranberries; **6.** apples; **7.** slices; **8.** nuts; **9.** cloves; **10.** onions; **11.** mushrooms; **12.** spices; **13.** pies; **14.** dishes; **15.** men; **16.** dishes; **17.** women

⏱ 10-15 mins

1. Tell students that this exercise is about Thanksgiving dinner. Have students read the direction line. Go over the example in the book.

2. Have students complete Exercise 2 individually. Remind them to review grammar chart **5.1** on pages 153–154 if necessary. Have students compare their answers in pairs. Then play the audio and check answers as a class.

Practice Idea: Listening

To provide practice with listening skills, have students close their books and listen to the audio. Repeat the audio as needed. Ask comprehension questions, such as: *Who prepares the Thanksgiving dinner?* (The women do. The men help a little.) *What are some of the ingredients of the stuffing?* (bread, garlic cloves, onions, butter, mushrooms, and spices) *Why don't the men wash the dishes?* (They're too busy watching football.) Then have students open their books and complete Exercise 2.

Practice Idea: Speaking

Have students practice the conversation in pairs or work together to create similar conversations about special dinners for other holidays or dinners from their native countries/cultures. Ask volunteers to role-play the conversation in front of the class.

5.2 Using the Singular and Plural for Generalizations

⏱ 5-10 mins

1. Explain to students that a generalization says that something is true of all members of a group. Give an example. Say: *Students are noisy. That means that all students everywhere are noisy. Is this true?* (no)

2. Have students look at grammar chart **5.2** on page 156. Review the information. Say: *To make a generalization about a singular noun, use* a *or* an. To *make a generalization about a plural noun, don't use any article.* Go over the example sentences. Ask: *What verb tense are these sentences in?* (simple present) Point out that we use the simple present when making generalizations.

Write the following words on the board:

1. *house*
2. *cat*
3. *shark*

Ask students to write two sentences for each item. Say: *Write a generalization for a plural and for a singular.* Have volunteers write their sentences on the board (e.g., *A house is better than an apartment. Houses are expensive.*).

EXERCISE 3
Answers will vary.

⏱ 5-10 mins

1. Say: *You're going to make generalizations on all these topics.* Go over the example in the book.

2. Have students complete Exercise 3 individually. Remind them to review grammar chart **5.2** on page 156 if necessary. Then have them compare their answers in pairs.

Practice Idea: Speaking

Have students get in groups to discuss their generalizations. Did anyone have the same generalizations? Ask students to report the group's opinions to the class.

EXERCISE 4

Answers will vary.

⏱ 5-10 mins

1. Say: *You're going to make generalizations about all of these professions.* Have students read the direction line. Go over the example.

2. Have students complete Exercise 4 individually. Remind them to review grammar chart **5.2** on page 156 if necessary. Then have them compare their answers in pairs.

Practice Idea: Speaking

Have students get into groups to discuss their generalizations. Did anyone have the same generalizations? Ask students to report the group's opinions to the class.

5.3 Special Cases of Singular and Plural ≡★

⏱ 5-10 mins

1. Have students cover up the explanation side of grammar chart **5.3** on page 157. Say: *Read the first two sentences. What is the difference between the use of* million *in sentence (a) and the use of* million *in sentence (b)?* (In sentence (a), *300 million* is an exact number and is in the singular; in sentence (b), *millions* is not an exact number and is in the plural form.) After students have made their guesses, ask them to look at the explanation.

2. Ask students to look at the use of *one of* in the next set of sentences. Say: *We use the plural when we say* one of the, one of my, one of his, etc. Have volunteers make sentences using *one of* (e.g., *One of my favorite books is* Pride and Prejudice.).

3. Direct students to the next two sentences. Ask: *Is the noun singular or plural after* every? (singular) *Is the noun singular or plural after* all? (plural)

4. Point out that some words have no singular form (*pajamas, clothes, pants*, etc.). Go over the examples.

5. Say: *Some nouns may look plural, but they're actually singular, such as* news, politics, *and* economics. Remind students that adjectives do not agree in number with nouns. Go over the example.

6. Direct students to the Language Note and point out that we don't make adjectives plural.

EXERCISE 5

ANSWERS: 1. The <u>children</u> helped serve the dinner. **2.** One of her <u>daughters</u> came from New York on Thanksgiving. **3.** Ten <u>million</u> people passed through the airports that day. **4.** C; **5.** C; **6.** His pants <u>are</u> new. **7.** C; **8.** Every <u>guest</u> stayed to watch the game. **9.** Thanksgiving is one of my favorite <u>holidays</u>. **10.** C; **11.** C; **12.** C; **13.** C; **14.** Do you like <u>sweet</u> potatoes?

⏱ 5-10 mins

1. Say: *You're going to correct the mistakes in each sentence.* Have students read the direction line. Ask: *Do all sentences have mistakes?* (no) Go over the examples in the book.

2. Have students complete Exercise 5 individually. Remind them to review grammar chart **5.3** on page 157 if necessary. Go over the answers as a class.

The Origin of Thanksgiving
READING

1. Have students look at the illustration. Say: *Look at the illustration. What can you see? What are the people doing?* (Pilgrims are giving food to the Native Americans.)

2. Have students look at the title of the reading. Ask: *What is the reading about?* Have students use the title and picture to make predictions about the reading.

3. Preteach any vocabulary words your students may not know, such as *health, survive,* and *fortune.*

Reading Glossary

fortune: chance; (good or bad) luck
health: the condition of a living thing's body and mind
survive: to continue to live or exist, especially for a long time or under hard conditions

BEFORE YOU READ

1. Have students discuss the questions in pairs. Try to pair students of different cultures together.

2. Ask for a few volunteers to share their answers with the class.

Reading

CD 2
TR 13

1. Have students first read the text silently. Tell them to pay special attention to count and noncount nouns. Then play the audio and have students read along silently.

10-15 mins

2. Check students' comprehension. Ask questions such as: *Who declared Thanksgiving an official holiday?* (President Lincoln) *Why did the Pilgrims come to America?* (They wanted to be able to practice their religion.) *Why were the Pilgrims in such bad condition after their first winter?* (They did not know how to survive in the new land.) *Who helped them learn survival skills?* (Squanto and American Indians)

> ## Practice Idea: Listening
>
> To practice listening skills, have students first listen to the audio alone. Ask a few comprehension questions. Repeat the audio if necessary. Then have them open their books and read along as they listen to the audio.

Context Note

Five years before Squanto (or Tisquantum) met and helped the Pilgrims in Plymouth, he had been kidnapped in what is now known as the Plymouth Bay, by an erstwhile English colonizer and shipped off to Spain to be sold as a slave. He was freed by some Catholic priests and eventually ended up in England, where he learned the English language. Through his travels he came in contact with colonizers who eventually brought him back to his village, Patuxet, in Plymouth Bay.

5.4 Count and Noncount Nouns

10-15 mins

1. Have students cover up grammar chart **5.4** on pages 159–160. Write these five categories across the board:

    A. *Nouns that have no distinct, separate parts. We look at the whole.*

    B. *Nouns that have parts that are too small or insignificant to count.*

    C. *Nouns that are classes or categories of things. The members of the category are not the same.*

    D. *Nouns that are abstractions.*

    E. *Subjects of study.*

2. Have students go back to the reading on pages 158–159. Say: *Find the noncount nouns in the reading. Which group do the nouns in the reading belong to? Write them in your notebooks under the correct group.* Have volunteers write the words on the board.

3. Then have students look at grammar chart **5.4**. Say: *Now let's look at the chart.* Go over any errors. Review all of the words in each category.

4. Remind students that noncount nouns do not have a plural. For example, we can't say *I breathed two airs yesterday.*

EXERCISE 6

ANSWERS: 1. health; **2.** advice; **3.** corn; **4.** snow; **5.** work; **6.** friendship

5-10 mins

1. Have students read the direction line. Go over the example in the book.

2. Have students complete Exercise 6 individually. Remind them to review grammar chart **5.4** on pages 159–160 if necessary. Go over the answers as a class.

5.5 Nouns That Can Be Both Count or Noncount

5-10 mins

1. Review the example sentences in the chart. Point out that some nouns can be both count or noncount, depending on their meaning or use in a sentence.

2. Ask students to look at the list of nouns on pages 159–160. Ask them to come up with sentences using the nouns as both count or noncount nouns. Monitor responses for accuracy.

Presentation Idea

Have students go back to the reading on pages 158–159. Say: *Make two lists of words from the reading: count and noncount.* Have students compare their lists in pairs. Then go over chart **5.5** as a class.

EXERCISE 7

ANSWERS: 1. nature, trees, birds, fish; **2.** peace, friendship; **3.** food; **4.** pie; **5.** advice, corn, vegetables, knowledge; **6.** experience; **7.** meat, beans, bread, berries; **8.** fortune; **9.** plants, medicine; **10.** jewelry, rings, necklaces; **11.** information, holidays

1. Have students read the direction line. Ask: *If the noun is a count noun, what do we do?* (Write the plural form.) Go over the example.

5–10 mins

2. Have students complete Exercise 7 individually. Remind them to review grammar charts **5.4** on pages 159–160 and **5.5** on page 161 if necessary. Then check the answers as a class.

Practice Idea: Writing

Have students work in pairs to write five sentences with count nouns and five sentences with noncount nouns. If possible, have students from the same culture or country work together. Say: *Write about a historical event that happened in your native country.* Ask a few volunteers to share their sentences with the class.

Recipe for Turkey Stuffing
READING

1. Have students look at the title of the reading. Ask: *What is the reading about?* Have students use the

title and pictures to make predictions about the reading.

2. Preteach any vocabulary words your students may not know, such as *brown, sauté,* and *casserole dish.*

Reading Glossary

brown: to fry something until its color becomes brown
casserole dish: a deep dish for baking and serving mixed foods
sauté: to fry something quickly in a small amount of oil or butter

BEFORE YOU READ

 1. Have students discuss the questions in pairs. Try to pair students of different cultures together.

5–10 mins

2. Ask for a few volunteers to share their answers with the class.

Reading

CD 2 TR 14

1. Have students first read the text silently. Tell them to pay special attention to quantities. Then play the audio and have students read along silently.

10–15 mins

2. Check students' comprehension. Ask questions such as: *When do you stir in bacon bits?* (after sautéing the mushrooms and vegetables) *How long do you cook it over low heat?* (30 minutes)

Practice Idea: Listening

To practice listening skills, have students first listen to the audio alone. Ask a few comprehension questions. Repeat the audio if necessary. Then have them open their books and read along as they listen to the audio.

5.6 Quantities with Count and Noncount Nouns

1. Have students cover up grammar chart **5.6** on page 164. Say: *We can use numbers with count nouns, but we can't use numbers with noncount*

5–10 mins

nouns. We use units of measure such as a bottle, a glass, a can, etc. We can count these units of measure.

2. Write the following categories across the board in chart form:

> by container
> by portion
> by measurement
> by shape or whole piece
> other

Then write a list of ten phrases on one side of the board: *a bag of flour, a pound of meat, a work of art, a slice of pizza, a carton of milk, a piece of meat, a quart of oil, a piece of information, a roll of film, an ear of corn.*

Say: *Try to guess where these nouns and units of measure go.* Have volunteers fill in the chart on the board using the ten phrases.

3. Have students look at grammar chart **5.6**. Say: *Now compare your work with the chart.* Go over any errors. Review the example sentences in the chart and the units of measure.

Presentation Idea

Say: *Find all the quantities listed in the recipe from the reading on page 163.* Have students compare in pairs. Then go over chart **5.6** as a class.

EXERCISE 8

ANSWERS: Answers may vary. Possible answers:
1. glass of; **2.** pieces of OR cuts of OR pounds of; **3.** A gallon of; **4.** cups of; **5.** a loaf of; **6.** (x) pieces of; **7.** a bottle of; **8.** pieces of OR slices of; **9.** a piece of OR a bit of; **10.** gallons of; **11.** cloves of OR pieces of; **12.** cup of OR tablespoon of; **13.** teaspoon of OR tablespoon of

5-10 mins

1. Have students read the direction line. Ask: *Are the nouns in these sentences count or noncount?* (noncount) Go over the example.

2. Have students complete the exercise individually. Remind them to review grammar chart **5.6** on page 164 if necessary. Check the answers as a class.

Taking the Land from the Native Americans READING

1. Have students look at the map of the U.S. Explain that the darkened areas and dots show American Indian reservations. Ask: *Have you ever been on a reservation?*

2. Have students look at the title of the reading. Ask: *What is the reading about?* Have students use the title and the map to make predictions about the reading.

3. Preteach any vocabulary words your students may not know, such as *punish* and *tribe*.

Reading Glossary

punish: to discipline, to make someone pay for doing something wrong
tribe: a group of people who usually speak the same language, live in the same area, often in villages, and have many relatives within the group

BEFORE YOU READ

5-10 mins

1. Have students discuss the questions in pairs. Try to pair students of different cultures together.

2. Ask for a few volunteers to share their answers with the class.

Reading

CD 2 TR 15

10-15 mins

1. Have students first read the text silently. Tell them to pay special attention to *there + be.* Then play the audio and have students read along silently.

2. Check students' comprehension. Ask questions such as: *What or who killed so many Indians?* (settlers, directly through war and indirectly by bringing disease) *Do most of the 2 million Native Americans now live on reservations?* (no) *Why do many live off the reservations?* (There aren't many jobs, and there is a lot of poverty.)

DID YOU KNOW?

Have students read the information. Ask them if they know any other words in English that come from Indian languages. Then share this information with them:

It's been estimated that when the Europeans came to the Americas, approximately 1,000 languages were being spoken by Native Americans in North, Central, and South America. There are still about 700 languages spoken today—but by far fewer people. For example, about 200 languages are spoken in Canada and the U.S. by only 300,000 people. Many words, such as *moccasin*, *squash*, *chocolate*, *tobacco*, and *condor* in the English language today are borrowed from Indian languages.

Practice Idea: Listening

To practice listening skills, have students first listen to the audio alone. Ask a few comprehension questions. Repeat the audio if necessary. Then have them open their books and read along as they listen to the audio.

5.7 *There* + a Form of *Be*

10-15 mins

1. Have students cover up grammar chart **5.7** on page 166. Write the following sentences on the board:

   There is a reservation in Wyoming.
   There is an onion in the recipe.
   There is a lot of unemployment on some reservations.
   There is some garlic in the recipe for stuffing.
   There are 500 Indian tribes in the U.S.
   There were many deaths from diseases after the Europeans arrived.

   Say: *Underline the subject in each sentence. Then say if the subject is a count or noncount noun. If it's a count noun, say whether it's singular or plural.* Elicit the patterns for these sentences.

2. Have students look at grammar chart **5.7**. Review the example sentences in the chart. Point out the use of *there is/will be/was* with the singular subjects. Then point out the use of *a/an/one* with singular subjects.

3. Then have students look at the sentences with a noncount subject and with a plural subject. Ask: *What quantity words are they used with?* Have them compare and contrast the singular, plural, and noncount examples (*A lot of* and *some* are used with both count and noncount nouns. *Many* is used with plural count nouns.).

4. Have students look at the negative forms. Have students explain when *not* is used

and when *no* is used (With *not*, the verb is negative: *There wasn't a problem.* With *no*, the verb is affirmative: *There was no problem.* Also, we don't use *a/an/any* with *no*.). Ask: *When do you use* any? (With noncount nouns and a negative verb: *There isn't any milk.* With plural nouns and a negative verb: *There aren't any reservations.*) Go over all of the examples for negative forms.

Presentation Idea

Have students go back to the reading on page 165 to look at constructions with *there*. Ask students what kind of subject each sentence has. Ask: *Is it a count or noncount noun? If it's a count noun, is it singular or plural?*

5.8 Using *There* ≡★

10-15 mins

1. Have students cover up grammar chart **5.8** on page 167. Say: There + *a form of* be (*present, past, future*) *is used to introduce a subject into the conversation.*

2. Say: There's *is the contraction for* there is. *We do not make a contraction for* there are.

3. Write the following sentences on the board:

   There ___ one onion and three celery stalks in the recipe.
   There ___ three celery stalks and one onion in the recipe.
   There ___ dessert and coffee after the dinner.

   Say: *Fill in the blanks with* is *or* are.

4. Have students look at grammar chart **5.8**. Review the sentences with compound subjects. Go over any errors.

5. Point out that many native speakers will use the singular with a plural noun in informal speech (e.g., *There's a lot of reservations in California.*).

6. Say: There is *and* there are *are used to introduce a noun. Once it has been introduced, you use a pronoun.* Go over the examples in the chart.

7. Remind students to invert the *there is* and *there are* in questions to *is there* and *are there*. Go over the examples. Point out the short answers.

8. Explain to students that *there is* and *there are* are not used to introduce specific or unique nouns. Go over the example in the chart.

EXERCISE 9

ANSWERS: 1. are; **2.** were, are; **3.** was; **4.** were; **5.** Was there; **6.** were there; **7.** will be; **8.** will there be

10-15 mins

1. Have students read the direction line. Say: *Not all sentences are in the present tense.* Go over the example in the book.

2. Have students complete the exercise individually. Remind them to review grammar charts **5.7** on page 166 and **5.8** on page 167 if necessary. Check the answers as a class.

Practice Idea: Writing

Have students work in pairs to write eight sentences about the classroom and school with *there* + a form of *be* (e.g., *There will be a new student in our class next week.*).

EXERCISE 10

Answers will vary.

10-15 mins

1. Tell students that they are going to complete the sentences with a time or place. Have students read the direction line. Go over the example in the book.

2. Have students complete the exercise individually. Remind them to review grammar charts **5.7** on page 166 and **5.8** on page 167 if necessary. Have students compare answers in pairs. Monitor pair work. Give help as needed.

Practice Idea: Speaking

Ask: *What do you want to tell your partner about your native country? Write five sentences about your country with* there + *a form of* be. Have students exchange papers with their partners and talk about their countries. Then have volunteers report interesting things they learned from their partners.

Navajo Code Talkers ❬ READING ❭

1. Have students look at the photo. Ask: *Who do you think this man is? What do you notice about his uniform?*

2. Have students look at the title of the reading. Ask: *What is the reading about?* Have students use the title and photo to make predictions about the reading.

3. Preteach any vocabulary words your students may not know, such as *code, skillful, battleship, submarine,* and *recognition.*

Reading Glossary

battleship: a large warship with long guns
code: a way of hiding the true meaning of communication from all except those people who have the keys to understand it
recognition: credit; praise for doing something well
skillful: able to do something well
submarine: a tube-shaped ship that can travel underwater

BEFORE YOU READ

5-10 mins

1. Have students discuss the questions in pairs. Try to pair students of different cultures together.

2. Ask for a few volunteers to share their answers with the class.

 Reading

CD 2
TR 16

10-15 mins

1. Have students first read the text silently. Tell them to pay special attention to quantity words. Then play the audio and have students read along silently.

2. Check students' comprehension. Ask questions such as: *Why was Navajo a great language for a code?* (There were not many people outside of the Navajo tribe who knew it. There was no writing system for the language.) *Who created the code based on the Navajo language?* (200 Navajo Indians were recruited for the effort) *How many messages were passed in the first two days?* (more than 800)

5.9 Quantity Expressions— An Overview

5-10 mins

1. Have students look at grammar chart **5.9** on page 170. Say: *We use quantity expressions to talk about the quantity of count and noncount nouns.* Go over each example sentence. Ask students if the subject is a count or noncount noun.

2. Then ask: *Which expressions do we use with count nouns? Which expressions do we use with noncount nouns?* Make two lists. Write students' responses on the board. Tell students they will learn more about these quantity expressions in the subsequent grammar charts.

EXERCISE 11

Answers: Answers may vary. Possible answers:
1. Navajo; **2.** battleship OR general OR submarine; **3.** alphabet; **4.** 10 million; **5.** food; **6.** died; **7.** Indians; **8.** skills; **9.** food; **10.** Indians; **11.** unemployment

5-10 mins

1. Tell students that this exercise is based on the readings in this lesson. Have students read the direction line. Go over the example.

2. Have students complete the exercise individually. Remind them to review grammar chart **5.9** on page 170 if necessary. Check the answers as a class.

Context Note

The powwow is an event where Native Americans gather to celebrate their heritage with ceremonies and dancing. The dancing takes place in a round *arena*. Powwows have become so popular in the U.S. with spectators that many communities are hosting weeklong events with competitions, games, and vendors selling Native American crafts.

5.10 *Some, Any, A, No*

5-10 mins

1. Have students cover up grammar chart **5.10** on page 171. Create a fill-in exercise. On one side of the board, write the example sentences from the chart. On the other side of the board, write the explanations in random order, leaving out *some*, *any*, *a*, and *no*. For example:

    Use _____ for questions with both plural count and noncount nouns. (any)
    Use _____ or _____ with singular count nouns. (a, an)

    Say: *Study the sentences. Then fill in the explanations with* some, any, a, *or* no. Have volunteers fill in the blanks on the board.

2. Have students look at the grammar chart. Say: *Compare your work with the chart.* Go over any trouble spots.

3. Direct students to the Language Notes in the chart. Remind students that they can't use *no* and an article together. Point out that *any* used with a singular noun means *whichever*. Go over the examples.

EXERCISE 12

Answers: Answers may vary. Possible answers:
1. There's an onion in the recipe. **2.** There's a little pepper in the recipe. **3.** There's some oil in the recipe. OR There's no oil in the recipe if you use butter. **4.** There are no raisins in the recipe. **5.** There are several mushrooms in the recipe. **6.** There are no nuts in the recipe. **7.** There are no carrots in the recipe. **8.** There's no milk in the recipe.

10-15 mins

1. Tell students that this exercise is about the recipe for turkey stuffing on page 163. Have students read the direction line. Ask: *When do we delete the article in front of the noun?* (if we use *no*) Go over the examples.

2. Have students complete the exercise individually. Remind them to review grammar chart **5.10** on page 171 if necessary. Then have them compare answers in pairs. Monitor pair work. Give help as needed.

Practice Idea: Speaking

After students complete the exercise individually, have students ask and answer questions about the recipe in pairs (e.g., *Is there an onion in this recipe? Are there any mushrooms?*).

EXERCISE 13

ANSWERS: 1. any, any; **2.** any, some, any; **3.** an, no; **4.** a, no; **5.** an, some OR any, some; **6.** any OR some, any; **7.** no, any, any, no

1. Have students read the direction line. Go over the examples in the book.
2. Have students complete the exercise individually. Remind them to review grammar chart **5.10** on page 171 if necessary. Then have students check answers in pairs.

Practice Idea: Writing and Speaking

Have students write five questions for their partners using *some, any, a, an,* or *no.* Then have students take turns asking and answering questions.

5.11 *A Lot Of, Much, Many*

1. Have students cover up grammar chart **5.11** on page 173. Create a fill-in exercise. Write the sentences from the grammar chart on the board leaving out *a lot of, much,* and *many.* For example:

   _____ *American Indians served in the military.*
   It takes _____ *time to develop a code.*
   On Thanksgiving, we give thanks for the _____ *good things in our lives.*
   Today the Indians don't have _____ *land.*

   Say: *Fill in the blanks with* a lot of, much, *and* many.

2. Tell students to look at grammar chart **5.11.** Say: *Compare your work with the chart.* Review the explanations. Go over any trouble spots.

3. Direct students' attention to the Language Note. Say: *In the case of* a lot of, *when you don't*

use the noun, then just use a lot. Go over the example. Give another example: *I didn't eat a lot of bread today. I don't like to eat a lot. It's not healthy.*

EXERCISE 14

ANSWERS: 1. much OR a lot; **2.** many OR a lot of; **3.** many; **4.** a lot of OR much; **5.** many OR a lot of; **6.** a lot of OR many; **7.** much OR a lot of; **8.** a lot of; **9.** a lot of OR many; **10.** a lot of OR much; **11.** many OR a lot of

1. Have students read the direction line. Remind students that we don't use *much* in affirmative sentences. Go over the example.

2. Have students complete Exercise 14 individually. Remind them to review grammar chart **5.11** on page 173 if necessary. Have students compare answers in pairs. Then play the audio and check the answers as a class.

Practice Idea: Listening

To provide practice with listening skills, have students close their books and listen to the audio. Repeat the audio as needed. Ask comprehension questions, such as: *Is it difficult to prepare a turkey?* (no) *How long do you have to cook it for?* (many hours) *Did person B prepare all the food for the dinner?* (No. Her family helped out.) Then have students open their books and complete Exercise 14.

Practice Idea: Speaking

Have students practice the conversation in pairs. Ask volunteers to role-play all or part of the conversation in front of the class.

5.12 *A Lot Of vs. Too Much/ Too Many*

1. Tell students to look at grammar chart **5.12** on page 174. Say: *A lot of is used to describe a large quantity. It is a neutral term. But* too much

and too many *show that something is excessive.*
We use too much *with noncount nouns and*
too many *with count nouns.* Go over all the
example sentences.

2. Direct students to the Language Note. Point
out that sometimes you can use *a lot of*
in place of *too much/too many.* However,
this can only be done if there is a second
statement pointing out that the quantity was
excessive. Go over the example in the book.
Give another example (e.g., *There were a lot
of cars in the parking lot. We couldn't find any
place to park.*).

EXERCISE 15

ANSWERS: 1. too much; **2.** too much OR a lot;
3. too much; **4.** a lot of; **5.** too many; **6.** a lot of;
7. a lot of; **8.** a lot of; **9.** a lot of

5-10 mins

1. Have students read the direction line. Go over
the example in the book.

2. Have students complete the exercise
individually. Remind them to review grammar
chart **5.12** on page 174 if necessary. Then
have students check answers in pairs. Go over
possible answers as a class.

Practice Idea: Writing

Have students write five sentences about school or
work using *a lot of*, *too much*, and *too many.* Then
have students compare sentences in pairs.

**CD 2
TR 18**
EXERCISE 16

ANSWERS: 1. a lot of; **2.** a lot of; **3.** a lot of; **4.** a lot of;
5. a lot of; **6.** too many; **7.** too much

10-15 mins

1. Have students read the direction line. Go over
the example.

2. Have students complete Exercise 16
individually. Remind them to review grammar
chart **5.12** on page 174 if necessary. Have
students compare answers in pairs. Then play
the audio and check answers as a class.

Practice Idea: Listening

To provide practice with listening skills, have
students close their books and listen to the audio.
Repeat the audio as needed. Ask comprehension
questions, such as: *Who is Coleen Finn?* (a Ho-chunk
Indian) *Does she live on a reservation?* (No. She lives
in Chicago.) *Does she ever visit the reservation?*
(yes) Then have students open their books and
complete Exercise 16.

EXERCISE 17

ANSWERS: Completed statements will vary.
Correct *too* statements: 1. If I try to memorize
too <u>many</u> words…; **2.** If I make too <u>many</u> mistakes
on my homework…; **3.** If I spend too <u>much</u> money
on clothes…; **4.** If I spend too <u>much</u> time with my
friends…

10-15 mins

1. Tell students that they're going to give
information on things they do too much of.
Have students read the direction line. Go over
the example in the book. Model the example
for the class.

2. Have students complete the exercise
individually. Remind them to review grammar
chart **5.12** on page 174 if necessary. Then
have students compare answers in pairs. Have
volunteers share some of their sentences with
the class.

5.13 *A Few, Several,*
A Little

5-10 mins

Have students look at grammar chart **5.13** on
page 176. Say: A few, several, *and* a little *mean
small quantities. We use* a few *and* several *with count
nouns and* a little *with noncount nouns.* Go over
the examples.

EXERCISE 18

ANSWERS: 1. A few OR Several; **2.** a few OR several;
3. a little; **4.** A few OR Several; **5.** a little; **6.** a few
OR several; **7.** a few OR several

5-10 mins

1. Have students read the direction line. Point
out that more than one answer may be possible in
some cases. Go over the example in the book.

2. Have students complete the exercise individually. Remind them to review grammar chart **5.13** on page 176 if necessary. Then have students check answers in pairs. Go over possible answers as a class.

5.14 *A Few* vs. *Few;* *A Little* vs. *Little*

5-10 mins

1. Have students turn to the reading on page 169. Say: *Find the sentences that use* very few *and* little. *Do* very few *and* little *in these sentences mean* some *or* enough? *Or do they mean* not enough? (not enough)

2. Have students look at grammar chart **5.14**. Say: A few *and* a little *mean some or enough.* Few, very few, little, *and* very little *without the article mean* not enough. *Very* emphasizes the negative quantity.

3. Direct students to the Language Note. Explain the concept of half empty/half full. Go over the examples.

> ## Practice Idea: Speaking
>
> Take a survey. Ask students if they are a *glass is half empty* or a *glass is half full* kind of person.

EXERCISE 19

ANSWERS: 1. Few (OR Very few); **2.** a little; **3.** a little; **4.** a few; **5.** a little; **6.** (very) little; **7.** a little; **8.** (very) little; **9.** a few; **10.** a few; **11.** a little; **12.** a few; **13.** (very) few; **14.** a little; **15.** (very) few; **16.** (very) few

5-10 mins

1. Have students read the direction line. Go over the examples. Point out that more than one answer may be possible in some cases. Ask a volunteer to explain the meaning of *very little* in the example.

2. Have students complete the exercise individually. Remind them to review grammar chart **5.14** on page 177 if necessary. Then go over the answers with the class.

> ## Practice Idea: Writing
>
> Have students write eight sentences using *a little, very little, a few,* or *very few* about things they have in the house. Then have students compare sentences with a partner.

EXERCISE 20

ANSWERS: Student responses will vary. Possible answers: 1. Are there any department stores in your hometown? **2.** Are there any fast-food restaurants in your hometown? **3.** Are there any homeless people in your hometown? **4.** Are there any skyscrapers in your hometown? **5.** Are there any supermarkets in your hometown? **6.** Are there any open markets in your hometown? **7.** Are there any hospitals in your hometown? **8.** Are there any universities in your hometown? **9.** Are there any American businesses in your hometown? **10.** Are there any bridges in your hometown?

10-15 mins

1. Tell students that they're going to interview each other about their hometowns. Have students read the direction line. Remind students that in this exercise they'll be practicing count nouns. Model the example in the book for the class with a volunteer. Quickly review the quantity expressions summarized in grammar chart **5.9** on page 170.

2. Have students complete the exercise in pairs. Remind them to review grammar charts **5.10** on page 171, **5.11** on page 173, **5.12** on page 174, **5.13** on page 176, and **5.14** on page 177 if necessary. Monitor pair work. Give help as needed.

EXERCISE 21

ANSWERS: Student responses will vary. Possible answers: 1. Is there much petroleum in your native country? **2.** Is there much industry in your native country? **3.** Is there much agriculture in your native country? **4.** Is there much tourism in your native country? **5.** Is there much traffic in your hometown? **6.** Is there much rain in your hometown? **7.** Is there much pollution in your hometown? **8.** Is there much noise in your hometown?

1. Tell students that they're going to interview each other about their hometowns or native countries. Have students read the direction line. Remind students that in this exercise they'll be practicing noncount nouns. Model the example in the book for the class with a volunteer.

2. Have students complete the exercise in pairs. Remind them to review grammar charts **5.10** on page 171, **5.11** on page 173, **5.12** on page 174, **5.13** on page 176, and **5.14** on page 177 if necessary. Monitor pair work. Give help as needed.

Practice Idea: Speaking

Create two rings of students. Have half of the students stand in an outer ring around the classroom. Have the other half stand in an inner ring, facing the outer ring. Instruct students to ask and answer the questions from Exercises 20–21. Call out *turn* every minute or so. Students in the inner ring should move one space clockwise. Students now ask and answer questions with their new partners. Have students ask questions in random order. Make sure students look at each other when they're speaking.

EXERCISE 22

ANSWERS: **Student responses will vary. Possible answers: 1.** Do you have (many OR a lot of) problems in the U.S.? **2.** Do you have (many OR a lot of) friends? **3.** Do you have (many OR a lot of) relatives in New York? **4.** Do you have (much OR a lot of) time to relax? **5.** Do you have (many OR a lot of) brothers and sisters OR siblings)? **6.** Do you have (much OR a lot of) experience with small children? **7.** Do you have (many OR a lot of) questions about American customs? **8.** Do you have (much OR a lot of) trouble with English pronunciation? **9.** Do you have (much OR a lot of) information about points of interest in the city? **10.** Do you have (much OR a lot of) knowledge about computer programming?

1. Tell students that they're going to interview each other. Have students read the direction line. Say: *This time we'll use* Do you have …?

rather than Is there/are there …? Go over the examples in the book. Model the examples for the class with volunteers.

2. Have students complete the exercise in pairs. Remind them to review grammar charts **5.10** on page 171, **5.11** on page 173, **5.12** on page 174, **5.13** on page 176, and **5.14** on page 177 if necessary. Monitor pair work. Give help as needed.

Practice Idea: Speaking

Create two rings of students. Have half of the students stand in an outer ring around the classroom. Have the other half stand in an inner ring, facing the outer ring. Instruct students to ask and answer the questions from Exercise 22. Call out *turn* every minute or so. Students in the inner ring should move one space clockwise. Students now ask and answer questions with their new partners. Have students ask questions in random order. Make sure students look at each other when they're speaking.

EXERCISE 23

Answers will vary.

1. Have students read the direction line. Say: *Make sure you write about different countries, not your own.* Go over the example in the book.

2. Have students complete the statements individually. Remind them to review grammar charts **5.10** on page 171, **5.11** on page 173, **5.12** on page 174, **5.13** on page 176, and **5.14** on page 177 if necessary. Then have students compare answers in groups. Monitor group work. If possible, have students from different native countries work together in groups. Give help as needed.

Practice Idea: Speaking

Discuss the groups' findings with the class. Ask students to talk about things they learned from group members about other countries.

Summary of Lesson 5

15-20 mins

1. **Study the words that are used before count and noncount nouns.** Have students study the chart. Ask students to list the differences between the plural count and noncount columns (*many*—count/*much*—noncount; *a few*—count/*a little*—noncount; *several*—count; *how many*—count/*how much*—noncount).

   If necessary, have students review:

   5.10 *Some, Any, A, No* (p. 171)
   5.11 *A Lot Of, Much, Many* (p. 173)
   5.13 *A Few, Several, A Little* (p. 176)

2. **Sentences with *There*** Go over the sentences with count and noncount nouns. Remind students to use *there is* (singular) with noncount nouns.

   If necessary, have students review:

   5.7 *There* + a Form of *Be* (p. 166)

3. **Too Much/Too Many/A Lot Of** Go over the sentences. Remind students that *a lot of* means a large quantity. It can be used with both count and noncount nouns. It has a neutral emphasis. *Too much* (noncount nouns) and *too many* (count nouns) mean excessive.

   If necessary, have students review:

   5.12 *A Lot Of* vs. *Too Much /Too Many* (p. 174)

Editing Advice

15-20 mins

Have students close their books. Write the first few sentences without editing marks or corrections on the board. For example:

1. *She has two childrens.*
2. *Every children need love.*

Ask students to correct each sentence and provide a rule or explanation for each correction. This activity can be done individually, in pairs, or as a class. After students have corrected each sentence, tell them to turn to pages 182–183. Say: *Now compare your work with the Editing Advice in the book.* Have students read through all the advice.

Editing Quiz

ANSWERS: 1. C; **2.** children; **3.** much OR a lot of; **4.** (so) many OR a lot of; **5.** a few; **6.** C; **7.** C; **8.** C; **9.** food; **10.** One of my sisters; **11.** C; **12.** some OR ø; **13.** sugar; **14.** too; **15.** a lot of fresh fruit; **16.** bottles of soda; **17.** C; **18.** a lot of time; **19.** C; **20.** C; **21.** a lot OR a lot of time; **22.** any OR ø; **23.** homework; **24.** (very) little; **25.** C; **26.** some or ø; **27.** C; **28.** a lot of OR (so) many; **29.** C; **30.** there; **31.** C

15-20 mins

1. Tell students they are going to put the Editing Advice into practice. Have students read the direction line. Ask: *Do all the shaded words and phrases have mistakes?* (no) Go over the examples with the class. Then do #1 together.

2. Have students complete the quiz individually. Then have them compare answers with a partner before checking answers as a class.

3. For the items students had difficulties with, have them go back and find the relevant grammar chart and review it. Monitor and give help as necessary.

Lesson 5 Test/Review

50-60 mins

Use the Assessment CD-ROM with Exam*View* ®, Online Workbook, and the Web site for additional practice, review, and assessment materials.

PART 1

ANSWERS: 1. wars, people; **2.** reservations, unemployment, poverty, jobs; **3.** advice, jobs, cities; **4.** sculptures, paintings, artists, art; **5.** music, CDs

1. Part 1 may be used as an in-class test to assess student performance, in addition to the Assessment CD-ROM with Exam*View* ®. Have students read the direction line. Ask: *What do we write in the blank?* (a singular or plural form of the word in parentheses) Collect for assessment.

2. If necessary, have students review Lesson 5.

PART 2

ANSWERS: Answers may vary. Possible answers: 1. cup; **2.** glass OR cup; **3.** teaspoon OR spoonful OR a lot; **4.** gallon OR carton OR container;

5. piece OR lot; **6.** assignment; **7.** piece; **8.** bottles OR glasses OR cups; **9.** piece OR sheet; **10.** bar OR bottle OR container

1. Part 2 may also be used as an in-class test to assess student performance, in addition to the Assessment CD-ROM with Exam*View*®. Have students read the direction line. Go over the example. Ask: *What do we write in the blank?* (a measurement of quantity) Have students briefly review quantities on page 164. Collect for assessment.

2. If necessary, have students review:

   5.6 Quantities with Count and Noncount Nouns (p. 164)

PART 3

ANSWERS: 1. a; **2.** very little; **3.** a lot of; **4.** some; **5.** a; **6.** many; **7.** no; **8.** a lot of; **9.** very few; **10.** A few; **11.** A few; **12.** a lot of; **13.** a lot of

1. Part 3 may also be used as an in-class test to assess student performance, in addition to the Assessment CD-ROM with Exam*View*®. Have students read the direction line. Point out that this is a composition by an American Indian. Go over the example. Collect for assessment.

2. If necessary, have students review:

   5.10 *Some, Any, A, No* (p. 171)
   5.11 *A Lot Of, Much, Many* (p. 173)
   5.12 *A Lot Of* vs. *Too Much / Too Many* (p. 174)
   5.13 *A Few, Several, Little* (p. 176)
   5.14 *A Few* vs. *Few; A Little* vs. *Little* (p. 177)

Expansion

These expansion activities provide opportunities for students to interact with one another and further develop their speaking and writing skills. Encourage students to use grammar from this lesson whenever possible.

CLASSROOM ACTIVITIES

10-15 mins per activity

1. Have students complete the survival list with a partner. Remind students to use quantities such as *a lot of, a little, a bag of,* etc. Monitor pair work.

2. Write the location phrases on cards. Model the activity for the class. Pick a card and have students ask you questions. Encourage them to use *there is/there are*. This game can be played as a whole class or in groups.

3. Elicit vocabulary to describe the food students eat on special days and write it on the board. Have students discuss what they eat in pairs.

TALK ABOUT IT

 15-20 mins

Have students discuss each quote in pairs, in groups, or as a whole class. Say: *When you discuss these quotes, say if you agree or disagree with what's being said, what you like or don't like about it, and if it's made you change the way you think about things.*

WRITE ABOUT IT

 20-30 mins

1. Have students read the direction line. Before they begin to write, have them talk in pairs about the groups in their native countries they plan to write about. Write any helpful vocabulary on the board. Then have students write their own paragraph(s). Encourage them to write as much as they can. Collect for assessment and/or have students present their paragraphs to a group.

2. Brainstorm the advantages and disadvantages of living in a city. Write students' ideas on the board. With students help, begin writing a paragraph on the board about the advantages. Then have students write their own compositions comparing the advantages and disadvantages of city living. Collect for assessment and/or have students present their paragraphs to a group.

3. Have students read the direction line and the sample paragraph. Have students brainstorm ideas about a holiday in their country that they are going to write about. Then have them tell a partner their ideas. Have them write their paragraphs individually. Encourage them to write as much as they can. Collect for assessment and/or have students present their paragraphs to a group.

Practice Idea: Writing

Have students exchange first drafts with a partner. Ask students to help their partners edit their drafts. Refer students to the Editing Advice on pages 182–183.

OUTSIDE ACTIVITY

Assign one of the following movies to each student to ensure enough people watch all four movies: *Smoke Signals, Windtalkers, Eskimo,* or *Dances with Wolves.* Have students write a summary of the movie to share with the class orally or in writing.

INTERNET ACTIVITIES

1. Tell students to use the Internet to search for Native American Web sites. Have them find the names and locations of three tribes and any other interesting information. Have volunteers share what they found with the class.

2. Tell students to use the Internet to search for more information about the Pilgrims. Have them find out why they left England and where they went before coming to America. Have students write a short report about the Pilgrims.

Lesson 6

Lesson Overview

GRAMMAR

1. Briefly review what students learned in the previous lesson. Ask: *What did we study in Lesson 5?* (the singular and the plural, count and noncount nouns, *there + be*, and quantity words)

2. Ask: *What are we going to study in this lesson?* (adjectives, noun modifiers, adverbs, *too, enough, very, a lot of*) *Can anyone give me an example of an adjective and an adverb?* (pretty, slowly) Have students give examples. Write the examples on the board. Then ask volunteers for noun modifiers. (health club)

CONTEXT

1. Ask: *What will we learn about in this lesson?* (health) Activate students' prior knowledge. Ask: *What are common health problems? What do people need to do to be healthy?*

2. Have students share their knowledge and personal experiences.

> ### Presentation Ideas
>
> The topic for this lesson can be enhanced with the following items:
>
> 1. A flyer from a local gym
> 2. Nutritional information from fast-food restaurants

Obesity: A National Problem
READING

1. Have students look at the photo of the woman. Ask: *What is she doing?* (weighing herself)

2. Have students look at the title of the reading. Ask: *What is the reading about?* Have students use the title and the photo to make predictions about the reading.

3. Preteach any vocabulary words your students may not know, such as *average, cheap, tasty,* and *preventable.*

Reading Glossary

average: ordinary, common, neither very good nor very bad
cheap: costing very little, inexpensive
preventable: able to be prevented; avoidable
tasty: flavorful

BEFORE YOU READ

5-10 mins

1. Have students discuss the questions in pairs. Try to pair students of different cultures together.

2. Ask for a few volunteers to share their answers with the class.

Reading ═★

CD 2
TR 19

10-15 mins

1. Have students first read the text silently. Tell them to pay special attention to adjectives and noun modifiers. Then play the audio and have students read along silently.

2. Check students' comprehension. Ask questions such as: *How many Americans are overweight?* (two-thirds) *Do Americans spend millions of dollars on weight-loss products and health clubs?* (They spend billions.) *What are some diseases related to obesity?* (heart disease, high blood pressure, diabetes, arthritis, and stroke) *What type of activity is today's lifestyle missing?* (physical activity)

> ### Practice Idea: Listening
>
> To practice listening skills, have students first listen to the audio alone. Ask a few comprehension questions. Repeat the audio if necessary. Then have them open their books and read along as they listen to the audio.

DID YOU KNOW?

Have students read the information. Then ask them how children usually travel to school in their native countries.

Context Note

Dr. David Katz is the founder and director of the Yale Prevention Research Center. He is also the director of Medical Studies in Public Health at Yale University. He has written a number of books and contributes to magazines and Web sites.

Practice Idea: Speaking

Have students use the equation to calculate their body mass index (BMI) and compare with a partner (if they feel comfortable doing this).

6.1 Adjectives

10-15 mins

1. Have students cover up grammar chart **6.1** on page 192. Activate prior knowledge. Say: *I'm going to read you a statement about adjectives, and you're going to tell me* true *or* false.

   1. *Adjectives go after nouns. (F)*
   2. *We can never put two adjectives before a noun. (F)*
   3. *An adjective comes after* be, seem, *and sense-perception verbs. (T)*
   4. *An adjective can come after* it is. *(T)*
   5. *Words that end in -ed* like married, excited, *and* finished *are not adjectives. (F)*
   6. *Some -ing words are adjectives. (T)*
   7. *You can make an adjective plural. (F)*
   8. *After an adjective, we can substitute a singular noun with* one *and a plural noun with* ones. *(T)*

2. Then have students look at grammar chart **6.1**. Say: *Let's look at these examples and see if we were right or wrong.* Go over the examples and explanations.

3. Go over the *-ing* words that are adjectives.

4. Explain that the words *very, so, quite,* and *extremely* intensify the adjective. Review the conversational words that go in front of

adjectives. Go over the meanings of each word (*kind of = a little; real = very; pretty = quite*).

5. Point out that after an adjective, we can substitute a singular noun with *one* and a plural noun with *ones.*

Presentation Idea

Have students go to the reading on pages 152–153 in Lesson 5. Say: *Find as many adjectives as you can that correspond to each explanation in grammar chart* **6.1**.

EXERCISE **1**

ANSWERS: **Answers may vary. Possible answers: 1.** unhealthy OR delicious OR greasy OR tasty OR fatty; **2.** sick; **3.** one; **4.** concerned OR worried OR nervous; **5.** tired OR sleepy; **6.** tasted OR was; **7.** salty OR unhealthy OR delicious OR tasty OR fatty OR fattening; **8.** high; **9.** busy; **10.** growing OR large OR huge OR increasing

5-10 mins

1. Have students read the direction line. Go over the example.

2. Have students complete Exercise 1 individually. Remind them to review grammar chart **6.1** on page 192 if necessary. Go over the answers as a class.

EXERCISE **2**

CD 2
TR 20

ANSWERS: **1.** married; **2.** beautiful park; **3.** located; **4.** tired; **5.** a small one; **6.** a very good idea; **7.** kind of; **8.** expensive; **9.** fatty

10-15 mins

1. Have students read the direction line. Point out that this is a conversation between a husband and wife about weight. Ask: *What kind of words are in italic?* (adjectives) Go over the example.

2. Have students complete Exercise 2 individually. Remind them to review grammar chart **6.1** on page 192 if necessary. Then have students compare answers in pairs. Play the audio and check answers as class.

6.2 Noun Modifiers

 10-15 mins

1. Have students look at grammar chart **6.2** on page 194. Say: *We can use a noun to describe another noun.* Point out that when two nouns come together, the second noun is more general. The first noun describes the second noun.

2. Say: *Gerunds are nouns that end with* -ing. *Sometimes a gerund describes a noun. It shows the purpose of a noun.* Go over the example sentences.

3. Explain that when two nouns come together, the first noun is always singular. Go over the examples in the chart.

4. Point out that sometimes possessive forms act as adjectives. Go over the examples in the chart.

5. Direct students' attention to the Pronunciation Note. Point out that when a noun modifies another noun, greater stress or emphasis is placed on the first noun. Have students practice pronouncing the examples in the chart chorally. Have them continue with other examples if necessary.

EXERCISE 3

ANSWERS: **Noun modifiers in the reading:** fashion models; exercise machines; health clubs; diet colas; weight-loss products; health costs; heart disease; blood pressure; today's lifestyle; lifestyle; schoolchildren; weight problem; food commercials; snack foods; junk food; Body Mass Index

 5-10 mins

1. Have students read the direction line. Then have students go back to the reading on pages 188–189.

2. Have students complete Exercise 3 in pairs. Remind them to review grammar chart **6.2** on page 194 if necessary. Monitor pair work.

EXERCISE 4

CD 2
TR 21

ANSWERS: **1.** child seat; **2.** year-old; **3.** TV commercial; **4.** cereal box; **5.** sugar content; **6.** eyeglasses; **7.** tooth decay; **8.** toothbrush; **9.** potato chips; **10.** orange juice; **11.** health food; **12.** check-out line

10-15 mins

1. Have students read the direction line. Ask: *What are we going to write on the blanks?* (noun modifiers) Explain that this is a conversation between a mother and son while shopping at a supermarket. Point out the picture. Go over the example.

2. Have students complete Exercise 4 individually. Remind them to review grammar chart **6.2** on page 194 if necessary. Then have students compare answers in pairs. Play the audio and check answers as a class.

Obesity: The Solution READING

1. Have students look at the photo of the man. Ask: *What is he doing?* (cycling/riding a bike) Have students look at the photo on page 197. Ask: *How often do you choose to eat fruits and vegetables instead of fattening, processed foods?*

2. Have students look at the title of the reading. Ask: *What is the reading about?* Have students use the title and photos to make predictions.

3. Preteach any vocabulary words your students may not know, such as *recommendation* and *advertisers*.

Reading Glossary

advertisers: people trying to convince you to buy a product or service

recommendation: suggestion or advice about the best thing to do in a situation

BEFORE YOU READ

1. Have students discuss the questions in pairs. Try to pair students of different cultures.

2. Ask for a few volunteers to share their answers with the class.

Reading ≡★

CD 2
TR 22

1. Have students first read the text silently. Tell them to pay special attention to adverbs. Then play the audio and have students read along silently.

2. Check students' comprehension. Ask questions such as: *What ways does the reading suggest we get active?* (ride a bike or walk places instead of driving) *Do nutritionists suggest we eat alone?* (No. They suggest we eat with our families.) *How many calories do teenagers consume from soft drinks?* (10 to 15 percent) *How do experts suggest we change our living arrangements to create healthier communities?* (stores and activities should be within walking distance, build more sidewalks and bike paths)

Context Note

Many blame Americans' lack of activity on the way our living communities are developing—specifically the phenomenon known as *sprawl*. Sprawl is different from compact urban and town living. Typically, sprawl is characterized, among other things, by a lack of public spaces or community centers, a lack of varied real estate types and prices, repetitive one-story development, and extreme land consumption. Sprawl is also car-dependent. People who live in sprawl typically commute long distances to work, to shopping, and to other activities such as school. Much of a person's time is spent driving in vehicles instead of walking or carrying out other calorie-burning activities. Sprawl consumes more than 2 million acres of open space a year in the United States.

6.3 Adverbs of Manner ≡★

1. Have students cover up grammar chart **6.3** on page 198. Tell students to go back to the reading on pages 196–197. Say: *Look at all the adverbs. What do you notice about them?* (They're formed from adjectives; all except for one end with an *-ly*; most adverbs come after the verb.) Write students' responses on the board.

2. Have students look at grammar chart **6.3**. Say: *We form most adverbs by putting -ly at the end of an adjective. An adverb usually follows the verb phrase.* Point out that *-ly* adverbs of manner can come before a verb but that this is more formal. Ask students if they noticed an adverb in this position in the reading (*greatly*).

3. Direct students to the next example. Say: *Good is the adjective; well is the adverb.*

4. Point out that adverbs describe verbs, and they also describe adjectives. When adverbs describe adjectives, they go before them. Go over the examples.

5. Explain that some adverbs have the same form as the adjective. These have to be memorized. Go over the examples. Point out that *hard* is an adjective and that it also is an adverb. *Hardly* is also an adverb, but it has a completely different meaning. Go over the examples. Repeat for *late* and *lately*.

6. Point out the list of adjectives that end in *-ly*. Because these adjectives don't have an adverb form, we must use them in an adverbial phrase—*in a friendly manner; in a lively way*.

7. Words like *very*, *so*, and *real* can come before an adverb. They intensify the meaning of the adverb. Review the examples.

Practice Idea: Writing and Speaking

Have students write sentences with adverbs describing family members. Then have students talk about their family members in pairs.

EXERCISE 5

ANSWERS: **1.** constantly; **2.** quickly; **3.** regularly; **4.** poorly; **5.** well; **6.** cheaply; **7.** differently

5-10 mins
1. Have students read the direction line. Say: *You don't have to use the adverbs in the box. You can choose your own.* Go over the example in the book. Ask the class if they can think of another adverb that might work just as well in the example (*quickly, fast*).

2. Have students complete Exercise 5 individually. Remind them to review grammar chart **6.3** on page 198 if necessary. Go over the answers as a class.

EXERCISE 6

ANSWERS: **Student responses will vary. Correct adverb forms: 1.** answer every question <u>honestly</u>; **2.** walk <u>fast</u>; **3.** cook <u>well</u>; **4.** talk <u>constantly</u>; **5.** work <u>hard</u>; **6.** study <u>hard</u>; **7.** speak Spanish <u>fluently</u>;

8. type <u>fast</u>; **9.** exercise <u>regularly</u>; **10.** choose my food <u>carefully</u>

5-10 mins
1. Have students read the direction line. Ask: *What are we going to do first?* (Write the adverb on the blank.) *Then what are we going to do?* (Check what's true for me.) Go over the examples in the book.

2. Have students complete Exercise 6 individually. Remind them to review grammar chart **6.3** on page 198 if necessary. Then have students compare responses in pairs. Ask: *Do you and your partner have a lot in common?* Monitor pair work.

Practice Idea: Speaking

Create two rings of students. Have half of the students stand in an outer ring around the classroom. Have the other half stand in an inner ring, facing the outer ring. Instruct students to make questions (and answer them) from the statements in Exercise 6 (e.g., *Do you answer every question honestly?*). Call out *turn* every minute or so. Students in the inner ring should move one space clockwise. Students now ask and answer questions with their new partners. Have students ask questions in random order. Make sure students look at each other when they're speaking.

Practice Idea: Writing

Have students write five more statements with the following phrases: *sing, spend money, play soccer, read, speak English.* Tell students to use their own adverbs. Then have students ask their partners about each activity (e.g., *Do you sing well?*).

6.4 Adjective vs. Adverb

5-10 mins
1. Have students cover up grammar chart **6.4** on page 200. Write the following sentences on the board:

*Jim is **serious** about good health.*
*He takes his doctor's advice **seriously**.*
*Your composition looks **good**.*

*The teacher is looking at it **carefully**.*
*The children got **hungry**.*
*They ate lunch **hungrily**.*
*Her health is **absolutely** perfect.*
*The refrigerator is **completely** empty.*

Say: *Study the use of adjectives and adverbs in these sentences. When do we use adjectives? When do we use adverbs?* Write students' ideas on the board.

2. Have students look at grammar chart **6.4**. Go through the examples and explanations.

3. Point out that when talking about health, we use *well* (e.g., *I don't feel well today.*). But in conversational, informal English, people often use *good* (e.g., *I don't feel good today.*). Point out the different usage for *usually* vs. *as usual*.

EXERCISE 7

ANSWERS: 1. good; **2.** favorite; **3.** extremely; **4.** good; **5.** strangely; **6.** foolishly; **7.** carefully; **8.** spicy; **9.** surprised; **10.** strange; **11.** late; **12.** early; **13.** hardly

5-10 mins

1. Say: *This exercise is about a potluck dinner. A potluck dinner is a group meal where everyone brings food and shares it with each other.* Use the picture to help students understand *potluck dinner*. Have students read the direction line. Go over the example.

2. Have students complete Exercise 7 individually. Remind them to review grammar chart **6.4** on page 200 if necessary. Then have students compare answers in pairs. Play the audio and check answers as a class.

Practice Idea: Listening

To provide practice with listening skills, have students close their books and listen to the audio. Repeat the audio as needed. Ask comprehension questions, such as: *Where was the potluck dinner?* (at the math teacher's house) *When did the student come to the U.S.?* (one month ago) *What kind of dish did the student bring?* (a Mexican dish) *What kind of food do most people not like?* (spicy food) Then have students open their books and complete Exercise 7.

Sleep READING

1. Have students look at the title of the reading. Ask: *What is the reading about?* Have students use the title and the picture to make predictions about the reading.

2. Preteach any vocabulary words your students may not know, such as *nap* and *stimulated*.

Reading Glossary

nap: to sleep for a short period of time during the day
stimulated: to have increased energy or activity

BEFORE YOU READ

5-10 mins

1. Have students discuss the questions in pairs. Try to pair students of different cultures together.

2. Ask for a few volunteers to share their answers with the class.

  ### Reading ═★

CD 2
TR 23

10-15 mins

1. Have students first read the text silently. Tell them to pay special attention to *too*, *enough*, *a lot of*, and *very*. Then play the audio and have students read along silently.

2. Check students' comprehension. Ask questions such as: *How many people get enough sleep?* (35 percent) *Who causes 100,000 auto accidents a year?* (sleepy drivers) *What are some things that are keeping Americans up at night?* (24-hour Internet and TV; malls, supermarkets, and laundromats that are open late) *Should you exercise late at night?* (no)

Practice Idea: Listening

To practice listening skills, have students first listen to the audio alone. Ask a few comprehension questions. Repeat the audio if necessary. Then have them open their books and read along as they listen to the audio.

DID YOU KNOW?

Have students read the information. Then share the following information: Although Einstein may have said that he needed ten hours of sleep, other great men have said they needed very little, including Napoleon, Thomas Edison, and Winston Churchill.

6.5 *Too* and *Enough*

 1. Have students cover up grammar chart **6.5** on page 203. Create a fill-in exercise. Write the following sentences from the grammar chart on the board:

I'm too tired to drive.

She drove too fast and got a ticket.

Children eat too much food that is high in calories.

You spend too many hours watching TV.

He doesn't sleep well because he worries too much.

Five hours of sleep is not good enough.

I walked quickly enough to raise my heart rate.

Some children don't get enough exercise.

   1. *Use _____ before a count noun.*
   2. *Put _____ before nouns.*
   3. *Put _____ after adjectives and adverbs.*
   4. *_____ can come at the end of the verb phrase.*
   5. *Put _____ before adjectives and adverbs.*
   6. *Use _____ before a noncount noun.*

Say: *Study the sentences, then fill in the rules with too, too much, too many, or enough.* (**Fill-in Answers: 1.** too many; **2.** enough; **3.** enough; **4.** Too much; **5.** too; **6.** too much) Have volunteers fill in the blanks on the board.

2. Then have students look at grammar chart **6.5**. Say: *Compare your work with the grammar chart.* Go over any trouble spots.

3. Direct students to the Language Notes. Point out that an infinitive phrase can follow *too* or *enough*. Review the idiomatic expression "too good to be true" and have volunteers make their own sentences using this expression (e.g., *It didn't rain once during my vacation. It was too good to be true.*).

Context Note: Idiomatic Expressions with *Enough*

enough is enough: something is happening that is unpleasant and they want it to stop

I've had enough: had as much or more than wanted

leave well enough alone: if things are going tolerably well, leave them alone; your efforts to improve the situation may make things worse

sure enough: as expected

true enough: although something is accurate, it doesn't completely explain something

EXERCISE 8

ANSWERS: Answers may vary. Possible answers:
1. late OR much; **2.** tired OR sleepy; **3.** time; **4.** coffee OR tea; **5.** walk; **6.** much; **7.** calories OR carbohydrates; **8.** sleep OR exercise; **9.** time; **10.** late; **11.** big OR fat OR heavy OR skinny OR thin

1. Have students read the direction line. Go over the examples in the book.

2. Have students complete Exercise 8 individually. Remind them to review grammar chart **6.5** on page 203 if necessary. Go over the answers as a class.

EXERCISE 9

Answers will vary.

1. Tell students that they are going to be finishing these sentences according to what's true for them. Have students read the direction line. Ask: *What's an infinitive?* (*to* + the base form of the verb) Go over the examples.

2. Have students complete Exercise 9 individually. Remind them to review grammar chart **6.5** on page 203 if necessary. Then have students compare answers in pairs. Monitor pair work. Give help as needed.

Practice Idea: Writing

Have students write three to five more unfinished statements with *too* and *enough*. Then have students complete their partners' sentences.

EXERCISE 10

ANSWERS: 1. too much; **2.** too much; **3.** too many; **4.** too; **5.** too; **6.** too many

 5-10 mins

1. Have students read the direction line. Point out that this exercise is about a person complaining about the school cafeteria. Go over the example.

2. Have students complete Exercise 10 individually. Remind them to review grammar chart **6.5** on page 203 if necessary. Then check the answers as a class.

Practice Idea: Writing

Have students work in pairs to write complaints about their workplace, dormitory, condominium, etc.

6.6 *Too* and *Very* and *A Lot Of* ★

 5-10 mins

1. Have students scan the reading on page 202 again. Ask them to pay special attention to the use of *too* and *very*. Ask: *Which indicates that there is a problem: too or very?*

2. Have students look at grammar chart **6.6** on page 205. Read through the examples and explanations. Point out that we often use an infinitive after *too*. We don't use an infinitive after *very*.

3. Tell students not to get confused with *a lot of* and *too much/too many*. *A lot of* is a neutral expression. *Too much/too many* indicates there is a problem. Go over the examples.

🔊 EXERCISE **11** ═★

CD 2 TR 24

ANSWERS: 1. very; **2.** too much; **3.** too much; **4.** too; **5.** too; **6.** very; **7.** too; **8.** too; **9.** too; **10.** too; **11.** too; **12.** too many

10-15 mins

1. Have students read the direction line. Go over the example.

2. Have students complete Exercise 11 individually. Remind them to review grammar chart **6.6** on page 205 if necessary. Then have students compare answers in pairs. Play the audio and check answers as a class.

Practice Idea: Listening

To provide practice with listening skills, have students close their books and listen to the audio. Repeat the audio as needed. Ask comprehension questions, such as: *How much salt did the soup have?* (too much) *Did person A eat the potatoes?* (yes) *Was the cake big enough?* (No. It was too small.) Then have students open their books and complete Exercise 11.

Practice Idea: Speaking

Have students practice the conversation in pairs. Ask volunteers to role-play all or part of the conversation in front of the class.

Summary of Lesson 6

20-30 mins

1. **Adjectives and Adverbs** Have students cover up the summary of Lesson 6 on pages 206–207. Create the following exercise on the board:

   1. (quick) We ate _____.
      We had a _____ lunch.
   2. (late) We had a _____ dinner.
      We ate _____.
   3. (good) She is a _____ cook.
      She cooks _____.
   4. (serious) She looks _____.
      She is looking at the label _____.
   5. (usual) _____, he drank a cup of coffee.
      He _____ drinks coffee in the morning.

   Say: *Fill in the blanks with the correct form of adverb or adjective.*

   Then have students look at item 1 in the summary on page 206. Say: *Compare your work with the sentences.* If necessary, have students review:

   6.1 Adjectives (p. 192)
   6.3 Adverbs of Manner (p. 198)
   6.4 Adjective vs. Adverb (p. 200)

2. **Adjective Modifiers and Noun Modifiers** Have students cover up the summary of Lesson 6 on pages 206–207. Create the

following exercise on the board:

two-week, old, exercise, short, new, running, driver's, valid

1. a _____ machine (adj.)
   an _____ machine (noun)
2. _____ shoes (adj.)
   _____ shoes (noun)
3. a _____ vacation (adj.)
   a _____ vacation (noun)
4. a _____ license (adj.)
   a _____ license (noun)

Say: *Fill in the blanks with the correct form of adjective or noun modifier.* (**Exercise Answers: 1.** new, exercise; **2.** old, running; **3.** short, two-week; **4.** valid, driver's) Then have students look at item 2 in the summary on page 206. Say: *Compare your work with the sentences.* If necessary, have students review:

6.1 Adjectives (p. 192)
6.2 Noun Modifiers (p. 194)

3. ***Very/Too/Enough/Too Much/Too Many***
Have students cover up the summary of Lesson 6 on pages 206–207. Create the following exercise on the board:

very, too, enough, too much, too many

1. He's _____ healthy.
2. He's _____ young to retire.
3. I'm relaxed _____ to drive.
4. I had _____ sleep last night.
5. She doesn't eat ice cream because it has _____ fat.
6. She doesn't eat ice cream because it has _____ calories.
7. He loves coffee, but when he drinks _____, he can't sleep.

Say: *Fill in the blanks with the correct word.* (**Exercise Answers: 1.** very; **2.** too; **3.** enough; **4.** enough; **5.** too much; **6.** too many calories; **7.** too much) Then have students look at item 3 in the summary on page 207. Say: *Compare your work with the sentences.* If necessary, have students review:

6.5 *Too* and *Enough* (p. 203)
6.6 *Too* and *Very* and *A lot of* (p. 205)

Editing Advice

15-20 mins

Have students close their books. Write the first few sentences without editing marks or corrections on the board. For example:

1. *I had two importants meetings last week.*
2. *He's interest in history.*

Ask students to correct each sentence and provide a rule or explanation for each correction. This activity can be done individually, in pairs, or as a class. After students have corrected each sentence, tell them to turn to pages 207–208. Say: *Now compare your work with the Editing Advice in the book.* Have students read through all the advice.

Editing Quiz

Answers: 1. very; **2.** a lot of; **3.** C; **4.** C; **5.** C; **6.** fried chicken; **7.** too; **8.** orange juice; **9.** C; **10.** C; **11.** C; **12.** three-hour; **13.** get home late; **14.** too; **15.** tired; **16.** careful; **17.** C; **18.** C; **19.** C; **20.** his food quickly; **21.** sweet; **22.** good enough; **23.** careful; **24.** C; **25.** a very healthy diet; **26.** hard

15-20 mins

1. Tell students they are going to put the Editing Advice into practice. Have students read the direction line. Ask: *Do all the shaded words and phrases have mistakes?* (no) Go over the examples with the class. Then do #1 together.

2. Have students complete the quiz individually. Then have them compare answers with a partner before checking answers as a class.

3. For the items students had difficulties with, have them go back and find the relevant grammar chart and review it. Monitor and give help as necessary.

Lesson 6 Test/Review

30-40 mins

Use the Assessment CD-ROM with Exam*View*®, Online Workbook, and Web site for additional practice, review, and assessment materials.

PART 1

Answers: 1. running shoes; **2.** ran fast; **3.** fast enough; **4.** completely tired; **5.** arrived home late; **6.** too tired; **7.** two-hour nap

1. Part 1 may be used as an in-class test to assess student performance, in addition to the Assessment CD-ROM with Exam*View*®. Have students read the direction line. Collect for assessment.

2. If necessary, have students review:

    6.2   Noun Modifiers (p. 194)

PART 2

ANSWERS: 1. well, bad; **2.** fast, safely; **3.** slowly;
4. easily; **5.** hard, easy; **6.** usual; **7.** softly, well;
8. quickly; **9.** regularly, lazy; **10.** tired; **11.** busy;
12. hard, happy; **13.** lovely, friendly; **14.** angry,
loudly; **15.** extremely, perfect, absolutely clear

1. Part 2 may also be used as an in-class test to assess student performance, in addition to the Assessment CD-ROM with Exam*View*®. Have students read the direction line. Collect for assessment.

2. If necessary, have students review:

    6.1   Adjectives (p. 192)
    6.3   Adverbs of Manner (p. 198)
    6.4   Adjective vs. Adverb (p. 200)

Expansion

These expansion activities provide opportunities for students to interact with one another and further develop their speaking and writing skills. Encourage students to use grammar from this lesson whenever possible.

CLASSROOM ACTIVITIES

10-15
mins
per
activity

1. Have students complete the food list individually. Then have students compare lists in groups (e.g., *I used to eat a lot of potato chips. Now I eat a lot of vegetables.*).

2. Have students complete the lifestyle list individually. Then have students compare lists in pairs.

3. Have students write down all their bad habits. Then have students compare lists in pairs.

Practice Idea: Speaking

Compare answers as a class. Make a *Top Ten Bad Habits* list on the board.

4. Put students in groups. Have students think of an object in their bag or pocket. Students may take it out and keep it hidden, or write the name of the object down on a piece of paper. Remind students that they're practicing adjectives (e.g., *Is it green? Is it long?*).

5. After pairs have developed an evaluation form, discuss it as a class. Tell students that the final evaluation form will be used to evaluate your (the teacher's) class. Create a final form together on the board.

TALK ABOUT IT

Have students discuss each topic in pairs, in groups, or as a whole class.

15-20
mins

1. Ask students to decide which students come from the most healthful cultures.

2. Ask students to discuss this idea and then decide "who they are" based on what they eat.

3. Survey the class. What's the average number of hours the students sleep?

Practice Idea: Speaking

Have students share interesting dreams they have had. Then ask a few volunteers to "interpret" the meaning of their dreams.

WRITE ABOUT IT

20-30
mins

1. Have students read the direction line. Say: *Before you start writing, make two lists—one of your native culture's food and one of American food. Then write adjectives that describe the food.* Then have students write their compositions. Collect for assessment and/or have students share their compositions with the group. This can be done orally in small groups or by posting the compositions around the classroom for everyone to read.

2. Have students read the direction line and the sample paragraph. Have students describe their eating habits in a typical day to a partner. Ask questions such as *What do you usually have for breakfast? Where do you usually have lunch?* if necessary. Then have them write

their paragraphs individually. Encourage them to write as much as they can. Collect for assessment and/or have students present their paragraphs to a group.

Practice Idea: Writing

Have students exchange first drafts with a partner. Ask students to help their partners edit their drafts. Refer students to the Editing Advice on pages 207–208.

INTERNET ACTIVITIES

1. Tell students to go to the Web site for the U.S. Department of Agriculture (USDA), find an article about food and nutrition, and bring it to class. Ask: *How does your diet compare to the USDA's recommendations?* Have volunteers talk about their diets and what they learned from the USDA.

2. Tell students to use a search engine and type in *height weight* to find a copy of a height/weight chart. Have them print the chart and see if they are the right weight for their height. If appropriate, survey the class to find out what percentage of the students is at the right weight for height.

3. Tell students to use the Internet to find a conversion chart from the metric system to the English system. Have them use the chart to see how much they weigh in pounds and what their height is in feet and inches.

Lesson 7

Lesson Overview

GRAMMAR

1. Briefly review what students learned in the previous lesson. Ask: *What did we study in Lesson 6?* (adjectives, noun modifiers, adverbs, *too, enough, very, a lot of*)

2. Ask: *What are we going to study in this lesson?* (time words and time clauses; the past continuous tense) *What are some time words and time clauses?* (e.g., *when, until, before 2005*) Have students give examples. Write the examples on the board. Then ask volunteers for examples of the past continuous (e.g., *I was talking on the phone when my mother walked in.*).

CONTEXT

1. Ask: *What are we going to learn about in this lesson?* (immigrants and refugees) Activate students' prior knowledge. Ask: *Are you the first person in your family to leave your native country?*

2. Have students share their knowledge and personal experiences.

Presentation Ideas

The topic for this lesson can be enhanced with the following items:

1. A book with pictures of Ellis Island
2. Statistics on immigration from the U.S. Census Bureau

Ellis Island READING

1. Have students look at the photo. Say: *This is the Wall of Honor on Ellis Island. Whose names do you think are on it?*

2. Have students look at the title of the reading. Ask: *What is the reading about?* Have students use the title and photo to make predictions about the reading.

3. Preteach any vocabulary words your students may not know, such as *harbor, hope, registry, meet the requirements,* and *restore.*

Reading Glossary

harbor: a port
hope: desire that something will happen
meet the requirements: have or do what is necessary
registry: an office of official records
restore: to make something look like it did when it was new

BEFORE YOU READ

5-10 mins

1. Have students discuss the questions in pairs. Try to pair students of different cultures together.

2. Ask for a few volunteers to share their answers with the class.

Reading

CD 2 TR 25

10-15 mins

1. Have students first read the text silently. Tell them to pay special attention to time words. Then play the audio and have students read along silently.

2. Check students' comprehension. Ask questions such as: *When was Ellis Island being used as an immigration processing station?* (from 1892–1924) *How many immigrants were processed at Ellis Island?* (12 million) *How many people had to return to their countries?* (250,000) *When was the restoration of Ellis Island completed?* (1990)

Practice Idea: Listening

To practice listening skills, have students first listen to the audio alone. Ask a few comprehension questions. Repeat the audio if necessary. Then have them open their books and read along as they listen to the audio.

DID YOU KNOW?

Have students read the information. Ask students what other countries they think a lot of immigrants come from. Then share the following information with them:

> Many Americans like to study their genealogy, or family history. Ellis Island has become a center for genealogy. Millions of Americans try to trace their families' histories with the help of the immigration records from Ellis Island.

7.1 *When, Until, While*

⏱ **5-10 mins**

1. Have students cover up grammar chart **7.1** on page 215. Create an exercise on the board:

   1. *When immigration slowed down, Ellis Island was closed.*
   2. *Ellis Island was closed until 1990.*
   3. *While they waited, they were often tired, confused, and hungry.*

   a. _____ *means* <u>during that time</u>.
   b. _____ *means* <u>at that time</u> *or starting at that time*.
   c. _____ *means* <u>before that time</u>.

   Say: *Study the sentences. Then fill in the blanks with* when, until, *and* while *to complete the rules.*
   (**Exercise Answers: a.** While; **b.** When; **c.** Until.)

2. Then have students look at grammar chart **7.1**. Say: *Compare your answers with the chart.* Go over the examples and explanations.

3. Point out that we can sometimes also use *when* in place of *while.* Go over the example.

EXERCISE 1

ANSWERS: 1. While OR When; **2.** When; **3.** While OR When, while; **4.** until; **5.** When; **6.** until; **7.** While OR When; **8.** until; **9.** until

⏱ **5-10 mins**

1. Have students read the direction line. Go over the example. Remind students that sometimes more than one answer will be possible.

2. Have students complete Exercise 1 individually. Remind them to review grammar chart **7.1** on page 215 if necessary. Go over the answers as a class.

EXERCISE 2

Answers will vary.

⏱ **10-15 mins**

1. Have students read the direction line. Say: *Make these sentences true for you.* Go over the example. Model the example for the class. Then have a volunteer model the example.

2. Have students complete Exercise 2 individually. Remind them to review grammar chart **7.1** on page 215 if necessary. Then have students compare answers in pairs. Monitor pair work. Give help as needed.

EXERCISE 3

Answers will vary.

⏱ **10-15 mins**

1. Have students read the direction line. Say: *Make these sentences true for you.* Go over the example. Have a volunteer model the example.

2. Have students complete Exercise 3 individually. Remind them to review grammar chart **7.1** on page 215 if necessary. Then have students compare answers in pairs. Monitor pair work. Give help as needed.

Practice Idea: Writing

Have students write a paragraph about themselves using the sentences from the exercises and adding other information.

EXERCISE 4

Answers will vary.

⏱ **10-15 mins**

1. Have students read the direction line. Say: *In this exercise, you're going to name things you've never done, seen, or had. Make sentences that are true for you.* Go over the example. Model the example for the class. Then have a volunteer model the example.

2. Have students complete Exercise 4 individually. Remind them to review grammar chart **7.1** on page 215 if necessary. Then have students compare answers in pairs. Monitor pair work. Give help as needed.

7.2 *When* and *Whenever*

5-10 mins

1. Have students look at grammar chart **7.2** on page 217. Say: *We use* when *with the past to refer to a specific time.* Whenever *is used to talk about any time or every time. In the present tense,* when *and* whenever *have similar meanings.*

2. Go over the example sentences. Then point out that you can substitute *when* for *whenever* in the second example.

EXERCISE 5
Answers will vary.

10-15 mins

1. Have students read the direction line. Say: *Make sentences that are true for you.* Go over the example in the book. Model the example for the class.

2. Have students complete Exercise 5 individually. Remind them to review grammar chart **7.2** on page 217 if necessary. Have students compare answers in pairs. Monitor pair work. Give help as needed. Have a few volunteers share answers with the class.

EXERCISE 6
Answers will vary.

10-15 mins

1. Have students read the direction line. Ask: *What are some time words?* (*before, after, whenever, when*) Write the words on the board. Then say: *Make the statements true for you.* Go over the examples. Have volunteers model the examples.

2. Have students complete Exercise 6 individually. Remind them to review grammar chart **7.2** on page 217 if necessary. Then have students compare responses in pairs. Ask: *Do you and your partner have a lot in common?* Monitor pair work. Give help as needed. Have a few volunteers share answers with the class.

7.3 Time Words

5-10 mins

1. Have students cover up the examples in grammar chart **7.3**. on page 218. Then have students work in pairs. Say: *Study the explanations for the use of time words.*

Then go to the reading on page 214 and try to find examples that match the explanations. Tell students that not all the time words are used in the reading. Before having students look at the grammar chart, have volunteers explain the time words they found (*in, after, during, for, by, from…to, from…until, until*).

2. Have students look at grammar chart **7.3**. Go over the example sentences and explanations. Pay particular attention to the time words not used in the reading (*on; in,* as in after a period of time; *before;* and *ago*).

Presentation Idea

Have students scan the reading on pages 220–221 for time words. Say: *Don't read the text; just scan it for time words and circle them.* Then have students compare search results with a partner.

EXERCISE 7

ANSWERS: 1. When; **2.** For; **3.** During; **4.** Until; **5.** While; **6.** When; **7.** while; **8.** during; **9.** when; **10.** for; **11.** during; **12.** until; **13.** ago; **14.** Whenever; **15.** in; **16.** by; **17.** before; **18.** in; **19.** in; **20.** when; **21.** until; **22.** until; **23.** from, till; **24.** on

10-15 mins

1. Have students read the direction line. Ask: *What are some time words?* Have students give some examples. Then go over the example in the book.

2. Have students complete Exercise 7 individually. Remind them to review grammar chart **7.3** on page 218 if necessary. Go over the answers as a class.

Practice Idea: Writing

Have students make four statements about their past and two statements about their future using time words. Have students exchange papers with a partner to compare. Ask volunteers to share their statements.

7.4 The Past Continuous Tense—Forms

5-10 mins

1. Have students cover up grammar chart **7.4** on page 220. Ask: *How do you form the present continuous?* (*be* + verb-*ing*) *When do we use the present continuous?* (to show actions that are taking place at this moment) *Can you give an example?* (e.g., *We're studying grammar right now.*) Then ask: *How do you form the past continuous?* (*was/were* + verb-*ing*) *When do we use the past continuous?* (to show that something was in progress at a particular moment in time in the past) *Can you give an example?* (e.g., *In 1999, we were living in Colombia.*)

2. Have students look at grammar chart **7.4**. Go over the example sentences and explanations. Review how to form the negative and contractions.

Presentation Idea

Have students write affirmative and negative statements, questions, and short answers about a historical figure or about a relative, such as a grandparent.

Terence and Charlotte— Refugees   READING

1. Have students look at the photo. Ask: *What do you think these people are doing?* (waiting in line for food)

2. Have students look at the title of the reading. Ask: *What is the reading about?* Have students use the title and photo to make predictions about the reading.

3. Preteach any vocabulary words your students may not know, such as *refugee camp*, *permission*, *volunteer*, and *enroll*.

Reading Glossary

enroll: to sign up or register at a school so you can study there
permission: the right to do something

refugee camp: a temporary place for refugees to get food and shelter and be protected
volunteer: someone who works for an organization without getting paid

BEFORE YOU READ

5-10 mins

1. Have students discuss the questions in pairs. Try to pair students of different cultures together.

2. Ask for a few volunteers to share their answers with the class.

Reading

CD 2 TR 26

10-15 mins

1. Have students first read the text silently. Tell them to pay special attention to sentences with the past continuous tense. Then play the audio and have students read along silently.

2. Check students' comprehension. Ask questions such as: *Why did Terence and Charlotte have to leave Burundi?* (They were in danger because of the violence.) *Which countries did they go to before they came to the U.S.?* (Congo and Zambia) *What do they want to do when they become American citizens?* (go back to Burundi to search for their family)

Practice Idea: Listening

To practice listening skills, have students first listen to the audio alone. Ask a few comprehension questions. Repeat the audio if necessary. Then have students open their books and read along as they listen to the audio.

DID YOU KNOW?

Have students read the information. Then have them discuss difficulties refugees face when they come to the U.S.

7.5 The Past Continuous Tense—with Specific Times

5-10 mins

1. Write on the board: *Terence was working in a hospital in 1993.* Then draw the timeline. Have students say what they were doing in 1993, or some other time in the past. Write some of their sentences on the board.

2. Have students look at grammar chart **7.5** on page 221. Explain that we use the past continuous when we are talking about an action that was in progress at a specific time in the past.

EXERCISE 8
Answers will vary.

10-15 mins

1. Have students read the direction line. Say: *You're going to write about yourselves and what you were/weren't doing in January 2008.* Go over the example in the book.

2. Have students complete Exercise 8 individually. Remind them to review grammar chart **7.5** on page 221 if necessary. Then have students ask and answer questions in pairs (e.g., *Were you going to school in January 2008? No, I wasn't.*). Monitor pair work. Give help as needed. Have some students share their answers with the class.

EXERCISE 9
Answers will vary.

10-15 mins

1. Have students read the direction line. Say: *You're going to ask your partner what he or she was doing at the times listed here.* Go over the example. Have a volunteer model the example with you.

2. Have students complete Exercise 9 in pairs. Remind them to review grammar chart **7.5** on page 221 if necessary. Monitor pair work. Give help as needed.

Practice Idea: Speaking

Create two rings of students. Have half of the students stand in an outer ring around the classroom. Have the other half stand in an inner ring, facing the outer ring. Instruct students to ask each other questions from Exercises 8 and 9 (e.g., *Were you going to school in January 2008?*). Call out *turn* every minute or so. Students in the inner ring should move one space clockwise. Students now interview their new partners. Make sure students look at each other when they're asking and answering questions.

7.6 The Past Continuous Tense + a *When* Clause

10-15 mins

1. Explain that the simple past describes an action that occurred once (e.g., *heard the news, got permission*) while the continuous action was in progress. Go over the first example using the timeline: *Terence was working in a hospital when he heard the news.* Then have students plot out the next example from the grammar chart on the timeline.

2. Have students look at grammar chart **7.6** on page 222. Go over the examples and explanation.

3. Direct students to the Language Notes. Point out that if the time clause precedes the main clause, we need to separate the two clauses with a comma. Go over the examples. Point out that in questions with two clauses, only the verb in the main clause is in question form (i.e., the verb precedes the subject). Review the example.

EXERCISE 10

ANSWERS: 1. was shopping, lost; **2.** was doing, came; **3.** arrived, were waiting; **4.** knocked, were eating; **5.** was cooking, went; **6.** was shoveling, lost; **7.** was sleeping, started; **8.** got, was passing; **9.** was talking, interrupted

10-15 mins

1. Have students read the direction line. Ask: *What are we going to put in the blanks?* (simple past or past continuous) Go over the examples.

2. Have students complete Exercise 10 individually. Remind them to review grammar chart **7.6** on page 222 if necessary. Have students compare answers in pairs. Then check the answers as a class.

Albert Einstein—Refugee from Germany READING

1. Have students look at the photo of Albert Einstein. Ask: *Do you recognize this man? Who is he?* (He's the genius who developed the theory of relativity.)

2. Have students look at the title of the reading. Ask: *What is the reading about?* Have students use the

title and photo to make predictions about the reading.

3. Preteach any vocabulary words your students may not know, such as *universe*, *spare*, and *interrupt*.

Reading Glossary

interrupt: to start talking or doing something in the middle of someone's conversation or activity
spare: extra; surplus; excess
universe: the stars, planets, other heavenly bodies, and space taken together

BEFORE YOU READ

5-10 mins

1. Have students discuss the questions in pairs. Try to pair students of different cultures together.

2. Ask for a few volunteers to share their answers with the class.

Reading
CD 2
TR 27

10-15 mins

1. Have students first read the text silently. Tell them to pay special attention to the relationship of the simple past and the past continuous tenses. Then play the audio and have students read along silently.

2. Check students' comprehension. Ask questions such as: *Was Einstein successful at finding jobs when he was young?* (no) *How old was Einstein when he wrote about the structure of the universe?* (26) *What happened while he was visiting the U.S. in 1933?* (the Nazis came to power in Germany)

Practice Idea: Listening

To practice listening skills, have students first listen to the audio alone. Ask a few comprehension questions. Repeat the audio if necessary. Then have students open their books and read along as they listen to the audio.

DID YOU KNOW?

Have students read the information in the textbook. Then share the following information with them and have them discuss whether they think what Dr. Harvey did was right or wrong:

> In 1955, Dr. Thomas Harvey removed Albert Einstein's brain during an autopsy and kept it in a jar for 43 years. Over the years, Harvey gave pieces of the brain to a few select researchers. Finally, after more than four decades, he gave the brain to pathologists at Princeton University. Many people, including Einstein's family, said he should have never taken the brain. Others think he did a good job of protecting it for science.

7.7 The Past Continuous Tense in a *While* Clause

5-10 mins

1. On the board, draw a timeline similar to the timeline in grammar chart **7.5**. Go over the first example using the timeline: *While Einstein was living in Switzerland, he developed his theory of relativity.* Then have students plot out the next example from the grammar chart on the timeline.

2. Have students look at grammar chart **7.7** on page 225. Go over the examples and explanation. Compare the use of *while* and *when*.

3. Direct students to the Language Notes. Point out that you can use *while* or *when* with a continuous action, but you cannot use *while* with an action has no continuation. Go over the examples.

EXERCISE 11

ANSWERS: 1. was writing, dropped; **2.** broke, was climbing; **3.** met, was attending; **4.** was driving, ran; **5.** was riding, got; **6.** broke, was eating; **7.** met, was walking; **8.** was washing, broke

---

10-15 mins

1. Say: *In this exercise, you have to decide when to use the simple past and when to use the past continuous.* Ask: *Do we use* while *with the past continuous or with the simple past?* (past continuous) Have students read the direction line. Go over the examples.

2. Have students complete Exercise 11 individually. Remind them to review grammar chart **7.7** on page 225 if necessary. Go over the answers as a class.

CD 2
TR 28

EXERCISE 12

ANSWERS: Conversation 1: 1. was putting;
2. found; **3.** were putting; **4.** fell; **Conversation 2:**
1. was living; **2.** Were you planning OR Did you
plan; **3.** was just waiting; **4.** was living; **5.** started;
6. started; **7.** was living; **Conversation 3: 1.** was
looking; **2.** found; **3.** did you meet; **4.** was walking;
5. stopped; **6.** started; **7.** asked; **8.** dated;
9. applied; **10.** were dating; **11.** received;
12. happened; **13.** wrote; **14.** called; **15.** went;
16. were eating; **17.** asked; **18.** Did you marry;
19. returned; **20.** had; **21.** got

10-15
mins

1. Say: *There are three conversations in this exercise.*
   Have students read the direction line. Go over
   the example. Point out that Conversation 1 is
   between a wife and husband, Conversation 2
   is between two students, and Conversation 3 is
   between a granddaughter and grandmother.

2. Have students complete Exercise 12
   individually. Remind them to review grammar
   chart **7.7** on page 225 if necessary. Then have
   students compare their answers in pairs. Play
   the audio and check answers as a class.

Practice Idea: Listening

To provide practice with listening skills, have
students close their books and listen to the audio.
Repeat the audio as needed. Ask comprehension
questions, such as: *In Conversation 1, when did the
man's wife find his watch?* (when she was putting
away his socks) *In Conversation 2, where did the
student from Sudan learn English?* (in a refugee
camp in Kenya) *In Conversation 3, when did the
man ask the woman to marry him?* (while they were
eating in a beautiful restaurant) Then have students
open their books and complete Exercise 12.

Practice Idea: Speaking

Have students practice the conversations in
pairs. Ask volunteers to role-play all or part of the
conversations in front of the class.

7.8 *Was/Were Going To*

5-10
mins

Have students look at grammar chart **7.8** on
page 228. Say: *Was/were going to* + *base form
means the same thing as* was/were planning to.
Go over the examples and explanations.

CD 2
TR 29

EXERCISE 13

ANSWERS: 1. was going to go; **2.** was going to use;
3. was going to call; **4.** was going to say

10-15
mins

1. Have students read the direction line. Go over
   the example.

2. Have students complete Exercise 13
   individually. Remind them to review grammar
   chart **7.8** on page 228 if necessary. Then have
   students compare their answers in pairs. Play
   the audio and check answers as a class.

Practice Idea: Listening

To provide practice with listening skills, have
students close their books and listen to the audio.
Repeat the audio as needed. Ask comprehension
questions, such as: *Why didn't person B go to the local
library?* (because it was closed for construction) *Was
he going to use the Internet?* (Yes, but he couldn't
because his computer crashed.) Then have students
open their books and complete Exercise 13.

EXERCISE 14
Answers will vary.

10-15
mins

1. Have students read the direction line. Say:
   Complete the sentences with a logical phrase.
   Go over the example. Model the example for
   the class (e.g., *He was going to return to his
   country, but he couldn't get permission.*).

2. Have students complete Exercise 14
   individually. Remind them to review grammar
   chart **7.8** on page 228 if necessary. Then have
   students compare answers in pairs. Monitor
   pair work. Give help as needed.

7.9 Simple Past vs. Past Continuous with *When*

5-10 mins

1. Have students cover up grammar chart **7.9** on page 229. Write the following two sentences on the board:

   When Einstein graduated from college, he tried to get a job as a teacher.

   When Einstein entered college, he was living in Switzerland.

   Say: *Study the sentences. Which action happened first in sentence a? Which action was happening first in sentence b?*

2. Then have students look at grammar chart **7.9.** Say: *In sentences with* when, *the simple past in the main clause shows what happened* after *an action. Identify the main clause of each sentence* (he tried to get a job as a teacher; he was living in Switzerland). *In sentences with* when, *the past continuous in the main clause shows what was happening* at the same time *a shorter action occurred.* Go over the examples and explanations.

EXERCISE 15

ANSWERS: 1. got, was working; **2.** helped, was waiting; **3.** were living, moved; **4.** started, was working; **5.** was taking, changed; **6.** wanted, was living; **7.** became, was living

10-15 mins

1. Have students read the direction line. Go over the examples in the book.

2. Have students complete Exercise 15 individually. Remind them to review grammar chart **7.9** on page 229 if necessary. Go over the answers as a class.

Practice Idea: Writing

Have students write four sentences using the simple past and the past continuous with *when.* Say: *Write two sentences where* when *means* after. *Then write two more sentences where* when *means at the same time.*

7.10 Simple Past vs. Past Continuous

5-10 mins

1. Have students cover up grammar chart **7.10** on page 230. Create a matching exercise. Write the following on the board:

   1. *While they lived in the refugee camp, they studied English.*

   2. *While I was reading the story about Terence and Charlotte, I was underlining the verbs.*

   3. *When they got permission, they came to the U.S.*

   a. *Two past actions happened at the exact same time.*

   b. *An action happened at a specific time.*

   c. *Two past actions happened in the same time period.*

   Say: *Match the sentence to the correct description.* (**Matching Answers: 1.** c; **2.** a; **3.** b)

2. Then have students look at grammar chart **7.10.** Review the sentences and the explanations.

EXERCISE 16

ANSWERS: 1. When; **2.** While OR When; **3.** While OR When; **4.** When; **5.** when; **6.** While OR When; **7.** while

5-10 mins

1. Have students read the direction line. Say: *You have to decide whether to use* while *or* when. Go over the example in the book.

2. Have students complete Exercise 16 individually. Remind them to review grammar chart **7.10** on page 230 if necessary. Go over the answers as a class.

Practice Idea: Writing

Have students work with a partner to write a paragraph about a famous immigrant or a person they know. Tell students to write about something that happened in his or her life. Instruct them to use the simple past and the past continuous tenses.

7.11 Using the -ing Form After Time Words

5-10 mins

1. Have students look at grammar chart **7.11** on page 231. Say: *When the main clause and the time clause have the same subject, we can delete the subject of the time clause and use an* -ing *word.*

2. Go over the examples. Remind students that the clause with the time word is the time clause. Have students identify the main clauses and the time clauses in the example sentences.

EXERCISE 17

ANSWERS: 1. Einstein passed an exam before entering the university. **2.** He left high school before receiving his diploma. **3.** After developing his theory of relativity, Einstein became famous. **4.** He became interested in physics after receiving books on science. **5.** After coming to the U.S., Einstein got a job at Princeton. **6.** Before coming to the U.S., Terence and Charlotte lived in Zambia. **7.** While living in the refugee camp, the children didn't go to school. **8.** Charlotte listened to music while cleaning hotel rooms. **9.** The parents were working and going to school while raising a family.

5-10 mins

1. Have students read the direction line. Go over the example in the book. Say: *If you delete the subject in the first clause, you must use it in the following clause.*

2. Have students complete Exercise 17 individually. Remind them to review grammar chart **7.11** on page 231 if necessary. Go over the answers as a class.

Summary of Lesson 7

20-30 mins

1. **Time Words** Have students cover up the summary of Lesson 7 on page 232. Create a fill-in exercise using the chart on pages 232–233. Reproduce the sentences without the time words on a handout or on the board for students to complete. For example:

   _____ *immigrants came to America, they passed through Ellis Island.*

Then have students compare their work with the sentences in the book. If necessary, have students review:

7.3 Time Words (p. 218)

2. **Uses of the past continuous tense** Have students cover up the summary of Lesson 7 on pages 232–233. Create a matching exercise on the board:

   1. *He was sleeping at six o'clock this morning.*
   2. *Terence was living in Zambia when he got permission to come to the U.S.*
   3. *I was going to call you, but I lost your phone number.*
   a. *to show past intentions*
   b. *to describe a past action that was in progress at a specific moment*
   c. *to show the relationship of a longer past action to a shorter past action*

Say: *Match the sentence to the description.* (**Matching Answers: 1.** b; **2.** c; **3.** a) Then have students compare their work with the sentences in the book. Go over all the example sentences. If necessary, have students review:

7.4 The Past Continuous—Forms (p. 220)
7.6 The Past Continuous Tense + a *When* Clause (p. 222)
7.9 Simple Past vs. Past Continuous with *When* (p. 229)
7.10 Simple Past vs. Past Continuous (p. 230)

Editing Advice

15-20 mins

Have students close their books. Write the first few sentences without editing marks or corrections on the board. For example:

1. *When entered the teacher, the students stood up.*
2. *While she spilled the milk, she started to cry.*

Ask students to correct each sentence and provide a rule or explanation for each correction. This activity can be done individually, in pairs, or as a class. After students have corrected each sentence, tell them to turn to pages 233–234. Say: *Now compare your work with the Editing Advice in the book.* Have students read through all the advice.

Editing Quiz

10-15 mins

1. Tell students they are going to put the editing advice into practice. Have students read the direction line. Ask: *Do all the shaded words and phrases have mistakes?* (no) Go over the examples with the class. Then do #1 together.

2. Have students complete the quiz individually. Then have them compare answers with a partner before checking answers as a class.

3. For the items students had difficulties with, have them go back and find the relevant grammar chart and review it. Monitor and give help as necessary.

Lesson 7 Test/Review

30-40 mins

Use the Assessment CD-ROM with Exam*View*®, Online Workbook, and Web site for additional practice, review, and assessment materials.

PART 1

1. Part 1 may be used as an in-class test to assess student performance, in addition to the Assessment CD-ROM with Exam*View*®. Have students read the direction line. Collect for assessment.

2. If necessary, have students review:

   7.6 The Past Continuous Tense + a *When* Clause (p. 222)

   7.9 Simple Past vs. Past Continuous with *When* (p. 229)

   7.10 Simple Past vs. Past Continuous (p. 230)

PART 2

1. Part 2 may also be used as an in-class test to assess student performance, in addition to the Assessment CD-ROM with Exam*View*®. Have students read the direction line. Point out that in some cases, more than one answer is possible. Collect for assessment.

2. If necessary, have students review:

   7.1 *When, Until, While* (p. 215)

   7.2 *When* and *Whenever* (p. 217)

   7.3 Time Words (p. 218)

   7.9 Simple Past vs. Past Continuous with *When* (p. 229)

   7.11 Using the *-ing* Form After Time Words (p. 231)

Expansion

These expansion activities provide opportunities for students to interact with one another and further develop their speaking and writing skills. Encourage students to use grammar from this lesson whenever possible.

CLASSROOM ACTIVITIES

10-15 mins per activity

1. Have students complete the event chart individually. Then have students compare charts in pairs or groups (e.g., *Before I came to the U.S., I was living with relatives in Belize.*).

Practice Idea: Speaking

Have students ask and answer questions about an event that happened to them. Tell students to fill out the chart. Say: *Tell your partner the event you're going to talk about. For example:* I moved to the U.S. *Ask your partner questions about the event. For example:* What happened before you moved to the U.S.? Before I moved to the U.S., I was living with relatives in Belize.

2. Before the groups begin, model the activity with a few students. Have students go around the circle clockwise. After the person answers the question, he or she turns to the person on the left and says a year or specific time of the year.

TALK ABOUT IT

15-20 mins

1. Put students in groups to discuss the quotes by Einstein. Tell students to try and rephrase the quotes.

2. Ask students if they know of any other famous geniuses. Write them on the board.

   Some famous geniuses:

   Charles Darwin (1809–1882): Naturalist

   Galileo Galilei (1564–1642): Physicist/Astronomer

   George Eliot (Mary Ann Evans) (1819–1880): Writer

   Leonardo da Vinci (1452–1519): Renaissance artist

   Marie Curie (1867–1934): Physicist

   Rembrandt (1606–1669): Artist

   Wolfgang Amadeus Mozart (1756–1791): Composer

Practice Idea: Speaking

Have students create presentations about famous geniuses or immigrants. Ask students to include pictures or illustrations. Have students discuss their presentations in groups. Display presentations around the classroom.

3. Have students discuss their experiences with immigration in small groups. Tell students that they should talk about what happened or was happening before they came to the U.S., as well as what happened during and after the immigration process.

WRITE ABOUT IT

20-30 mins

1. Have students read the direction line. Then have students brainstorm ideas about a major historical event in their country or somewhere else in the world. Suggest to students that they can also write about natural disasters

that affected their country or region, such as earthquakes, tsunamis, floods, and volcanoes. Have students share their ideas with a partner and discuss the event and the changes that happened. Then have them write their compositions. Collect for assessment and/or have students share their compositions with the group. This can be done orally in small groups or by posting the compositions around the classroom for everyone to read.

2. Ask: *What are some of the reasons people emigrate to another country from their home country?* Write students ideas on the board. Then have students read the direction line and write their compositions. Collect for assessment and/or have students share their compositions with a partner.

3. Have students read the direction line and the sample paragraph. Have students describe their arrival in the U.S. to a partner. Then have them write their compositions individually. Encourage them to write as much as they can. Collect for assessment and/or have students present their compositions to a group.

Practice Idea: Writing

Have students exchange first drafts with a partner. Ask students to help their partners edit their drafts. Refer students to the Editing Advice on pages 233–234.

OUTSIDE ACTIVITIES

1. Say: *Most people remember what they were doing when they heard shocking news.* Ask students: *Do you remember what you were doing when you heard about the terrorist attacks in the U.S. on September 11, 2001?* Have students ask another classmate or a friend or neighbor, *What were you doing when you heard about the attack on September 11?* and report this information to the class.

2. Have students think of other famous events that most people remember well. Make a list with the class of possible. Then have students choose one and ask people what they were doing when this event happened and report their findings to the class.

3. Tell students to ask an American about his or her cultural background. Then have them report to the class how he or she answered this question.

4. Tell students to find the book *An Immigrant Class* by Jeff Libman. Have them read an immigrant story and then report on it to the class orally or in writing.

1. Tell students to look for the Ellis Island Web site and find out what time the museum is open. Have them look at what names are on the wall of the museum and find out if their family's name is on the wall.

2. Have students use a search engine and type in famous immigrants. Have them find information about an immigrant that they find interesting and report this information to the class orally or in writing.

Lesson 8

Lesson Overview

GRAMMAR

1. Briefly review what students learned in the previous lesson. Ask: *What did we study in Lesson 7?* (time words and time clauses; the past continuous)

2. Ask: *What are we going to study in this lesson?* (modals and related expressions) *Can anyone give me an example of a modal?* (e.g., *can, could, would*) Have students give examples. Write the examples on the board.

CONTEXT

1. Ask: *What are we going to learn about in this lesson?* (renting an apartment) Activate students' prior knowledge. Ask: *Do you rent an apartment?*

2. Have students share their knowledge and personal experiences.

Presentation Ideas

The topic for this lesson can be enhanced with the following items:

1. Classified section of newspapers

2. Real estate magazines or circulars advertising apartments for rent

3. A copy of a lease

8.1 Modals and Related Expressions—An Overview

1. Have students look at grammar chart **8.1** on page 240. Say: *Modals are followed by the base form of a verb. Modals never have an -s, -ed, or -ing ending.* Go over the list of modals and the example sentences.

5-10 mins

2. Say: *There are some related expressions with verbs that act as modals and have the same meanings.* Go over the list of expressions and the examples.

An Apartment Lease READING

1. Have students look at the lease on page 240. Ask: *Do you have a lease that looks something like this?* Point out the photo on page 241, and ask: *Who do you think this man is? What is he doing?*

2. Have students look at the title of the reading and the photos. Ask: *What is the reading about?* Have students make predictions about the reading.

3. Preteach any vocabulary words your students may not know, such as *damage, repair, wear and tear,* and *terms.*

Reading Glossary

damage: harm
repair: to fix something; make something work again
terms: items in a contract or agreement
wear and tear: use that causes damage

BEFORE YOU READ

1. Have students discuss the questions in pairs.

5-10 mins

2. Ask for a few volunteers to share their answers with the class.

Reading

CD 3
TR 01

1. Have students first read the text silently. Tell them to pay special attention to modals and related expressions. Then play the audio and have students read along silently.

10-15 mins

2. Check students' comprehension. Ask questions such as: *What do people have to sign when they rent an apartment?* (a lease) *What does the lease contain?* (rules for the landlord and the tenant) *What is a security deposit?* (It's money paid in advance to the landlord in case there is damage.)

8.2 Negatives with Modals

5-10 mins

1. Have students cover up grammar chart **8.2** on page 242. Say: *Find all the negative modals in the reading (must not, may not, can't).* Ask: *How do you form the negative with modals?* (Put *not* after a modal.)

2. Have students look at grammar chart **8.2**. Say: *You can make a contraction with some modals.* Review the list of modals and their negative forms. Point out that the negative of *can* is *cannot. Can't* is the contraction. The negative of *will* is *will not.* The contraction is *won't.* And the negative of *may* is *may not,* and the negative of *might* is *might not.* There are no contractions for *may not* and *might not.*

EXERCISE 1

ANSWERS: 1. can't; **2.** shouldn't; **3.** mustn't; **4.** may not; **5.** can't; **6.** might not

5-10 mins

1. Have students read the direction line. Ask: *What do we write on the blanks?* (the negative of the underlined word) Go over the example.

2. Have students complete Exercise 1 individually. Remind them to review grammar chart **8.2** on page 242 if necessary. Go over the answers as a class.

8.3 Statements and Questions with Modals

5-10 mins

1. Have students cover up grammar chart **8.3** on page 243. Write the following statement on the board:

    He can have a cat in his apartment.

    Say: *Write a yes/no question, a negative short answer, an information question with* what, *and a question about the subject.*

    Then write the negative statement from the chart on the board:

    He shouldn't pay his rent late.

    Say: *Write a negative question for this statement.*

2. Have students look at grammar chart **8.3**. Say: *Now compare your work with the chart.* Go over any trouble spots with the class.

EXERCISE 2

ANSWERS: 1. can't I have; **2.** must we pay; **3.** can install; **4.** can't the landlord refuse; **5.** shouldn't they (OR the tenants) make; **6.** May I; **7.** Can the landlord

10-15 mins

1. Have students read the direction line. Go over the example.

2. Have students complete Exercise 2 individually. Remind them to review grammar chart **8.3** on page 243 if necessary. Go over the answers as a class.

8.4 Must, Have To, Have Got To

10-15 mins

1. Go over grammar chart **8.4** on page 244. Say: *Must, have to, and have got to all have the same meaning. However,* must *is very formal. Use* have to *or* have got to *in more informal settings.*

2. Go over the examples and explanations. Point out that *must*, *have to*, and *have got to* as imperatives all express the same sense of urgency.

3. Explain that *must* should not be used to express personal obligation. Point out that *must* doesn't have its own past form. The past of both *have to* and *must* is *had to*.

4. Direct students to the Language Note and Pronunciation Note. Point out that we don't usually use *have got to* for questions or negatives. Explain that native speakers often pronounce *have to* as *hafta* and *got to* as *gotta*. Model the pronunciation for the class.

EXERCISE 3

Answers: 1. sign; **2.** return; **3.** notify; **4.** be

5-10 mins

1. Have students read the direction line. Go over the example.

2. Have students complete Exercise 3 individually. Remind them to review grammar chart **8.4** on page 244 if necessary. Then go over the answers as a class.

EXERCISE 4

Answers will vary.

10-15 mins

1. Ask: *What do you have to do on a regular basis? Car maintenance? House maintenance? Get your hair cut? Go grocery shopping?* Have students read the direction line. Go over the example. Model the example for the class.

2. Have students complete Exercise 4 individually. Remind them to review grammar chart **8.4** on page 244 if necessary. Then have students compare answers in pairs. Monitor pair work. Give help as needed.

Practice Idea: Speaking

Do a class survey. Find out what everyone's number one item is on the "have to do" list.

EXERCISE 5

Answers will vary.

10-15 mins

1. Say: *In this exercise, you're going to write about the things you had to do last weekend. Write sentences that are true for you.* Have students read the direction line. Go over the example. Model the activity. Then have a volunteer give an example.

2. Have students complete Exercise 5 individually. Remind them to review grammar chart **8.4** on page 244 if necessary. Then have students compare answers in pairs. Circulate to observe pair work. Give help as needed.

EXERCISE 6

Answers will vary.

10-15 mins

1. Have students read the direction line. Ask: *Which modal or expression are we going to use?* (have got to) Go over the example. Model the example.

2. Have students complete Exercise 6 individually. Remind them to review grammar chart **8.4** on page 244 if necessary. Then have students compare answers in pairs. Monitor pair work. Give help as needed.

Practice Idea: Writing

Have students write three more sentence starters for their partners to finish using *have got to*.

8.5 Obligation with *Must* or *Be Supposed To*

5-10 mins

1. Have students look at grammar chart **8.5** on page 246. Say: *If you are not in a position of authority, avoid using* must. *Instead, use* be supposed to.

2. Explain that when you report on a law that was broken or a task that was not carried out, we use *be supposed to*.

3. Direct students to the Pronunciation Note. Explain that the *d* in *supposed to* is not pronounced. Model the pronunciation. Do a choral practice of the pronunciation with the class.

EXERCISE 7

ANSWERS: 1. You're supposed to carry your driver's license with you when you drive.
2. You're supposed to stop at a red light.
3. We're supposed to put money in the parking meter during business hours. **4.** Your landlord is supposed to notify you if he wants you to leave.
5. The landlord is supposed to give me a smoke detector. **6.** The teacher is supposed to give a final grade at the end of the semester. **7.** We're supposed to write five compositions in this course.
8. We're supposed to bring our books to class.

5-10 mins

1. Have students read the direction line. Ask: *When do we use* be supposed to? (when we're not in a position of authority) Go over the example.

2. Have students complete Exercise 7 in pairs. Remind them to review grammar chart **8.5** on page 246 if necessary. Go over the answers as a class.

EXERCISE 8

ANSWERS: Answers may vary. Possible answers:
1. I'm not supposed to have; **2.** is supposed to provide (OR give); **3.** are supposed to clean (the apartment); **4.** is supposed to install;
5. was supposed to pay; **6.** is supposed to fix;
7. is supposed to return; **8.** is supposed to take out; **9.** is supposed to clean; **10.** are supposed to use

10-15 mins

1. Have students read the direction line. Say: *Remember. We also use* be supposed to *when we're reporting on a law or rule.* Go over the example in the book.

2. Have students complete Exercise 8 individually. Remind them to review grammar chart **8.5** on page 246 if necessary. Go over the answers as a class.

Practice Idea: Writing and Speaking

Have students write statements about their apartments and lease agreements. Ask: *What are you and the landlord supposed to do?* Then have students compare information in pairs. Ask volunteers to describe their rental agreements to the class.

EXERCISE 9
Answers will vary.

10-15 mins

1. Have students read the direction line. Go over the example. Then have a volunteer model the example.

2. Have students complete Exercise 9 in pairs. Remind them to review grammar chart **8.5** on page 246 if necessary. Monitor pair work. Give help as needed. Have volunteers write some of their sentences on the board.

Practice Idea: Speaking

Have students ask and answer questions in pairs about things they're supposed to do at home, at work, and at school this week (e.g., *What are you supposed to do at work this week? I'm supposed to organize the files in my office.*).

8.6 *Can, May, Could,* and Alternate Expressions

10-15 mins

1. Have students cover up grammar chart **8.6** on page 248. Create a matching exercise. Write the following on the board:

   1. *I can clean the apartment by Friday.* _____
   2. *I can't understand the lease.* _____
   3. *I can't have a pet in my apartment.* _____
   4. *The landlord may not keep my deposit if my apartment is clean and in good condition.* _____
   5. *I couldn't speak English five years ago, but I can now.* _____

6. *I could have a dog in my last apartment, but I can't have one in my present apartment.* _____
   a. *ability*
   b. *possibility*
   c. *permission*

Say: *Decide if each sentence is an example of ability, possibility, or permission. Write a, b, or c.* (**Matching Answers: 1.** b; **2.** a; **3.** c; **4.** c; **5.** a; **6.** c)

2. Then have students look at grammar chart **8.6**. Go over the examples and explanations. Point out that *could* is the past of *can.*

3. Review all of the alternate expressions.

4. Direct students to the Pronunciation Note. Go over the pronunciation of *can* and *can't.* Tell students that they must listen for the sound of the vowel and not the ending because the final *t* in *can't* is difficult to hear. Tell students that this is often confusing for native speakers as well. Point out that in short answers, *can* may sound like /kæn/. But tell students that in a short answer, they can easily distinguish between the two by listening for *yes* or *no.* Demonstrate the pronunciation with the sentences in the grammar chart. Direct students to the Language Note. Go over the meaning of the expression *can't afford.* Go around the room and ask students to tell you things they can't afford. Model the exercise (e.g., *I can't afford a Mercedes.*).

Presentation Idea

Prepare between 10 and 20 sentences with *can* and *can't.* After students have gone through chart **8.6**, read the sentences and ask students to raise their hands if they hear *can* and to keep their hands down if they hear *can't.*

EXERCISE 10 =★
Answers will vary.

5-10 mins

1. Have students read the direction line. Explain that this exercise is about things that are permitted or not permitted at your school.

Say: *There may be several ways to complete each statement correctly.* Go over the examples. Ask volunteers to give alternate expressions for the examples.

2. Have students complete Exercise 10 individually. Remind them to review grammar chart **8.6** on page 248 if necessary. Have students compare their answers in pairs. Then go over the answers as a class.

Practice Idea: Writing

Have students complete the statements from Exercise 10 in as many correct ways as possible.

EXERCISE 11

ANSWERS: 1. change; **2.** park; **3.** talk; **4.** leave; **5.** use a cell phone; **6.** leave

5-10 mins

1. Have students read the direction line. Go over the example. Remind students that answers will vary.

2. Have students complete Exercise 11 individually. Remind them to review grammar chart **8.6** on page 248 if necessary. Have students compare their answers in pairs. Then go over the answers as a class.

EXERCISE 12
Answers will vary.

10-15 mins

1. Have students read the direction line. Say: *Write four statements or questions about the rules of the class, school, library, cafeteria, and so on.* Go over the examples. Model an example for the class (e.g., *You can't use your books during a test.*). Encourage students to write some questions as well.

2. Have students complete Exercise 12 in pairs. Remind them to review grammar chart **8.6** on page 248 if necessary. Monitor pair work. Give help as needed.

Practice Idea: Speaking

Have students talk about school rules in groups. What can't they do that they would like to do? (e.g., *We're not permitted to eat in class. They should change this rule. I work all day and don't have time to eat before class.*)

EXERCISE 13
Answers will vary.

1. Have students read the direction line. Say: *Write three statements about what you could not do in your last school or class, and compare them with what you can do in this school or class.* Go over the example. Have a volunteer model an example for the class.

2. Have students complete Exercise 13 individually. Remind them to review grammar chart **8.6** on page 248 if necessary. Then have students compare statements in pairs. Monitor pair work.

EXERCISE 14
Answers will vary.

1. Have students read the direction line. Say: *Write three statements about what you could not do in your native country, and compare them with what you can do here in the U.S.* Go over the example. Have a volunteer model an example for the class.

2. Have students complete Exercise 14 individually. Remind them to review grammar chart **8.6** on page 248 if necessary. Then have students compare statements in pairs. Monitor pair work.

Practice Idea: Speaking

Have students talk about what they could and couldn't do in their native countries. If possible, put students from different countries in groups together.

Tenants' Rights

1. Have students look at the photo. Say: *This girl has a problem with her apartment. What do you think the problem is?* (e.g., *The apartment is cold.*)

2. Have students look at the title of the reading. Ask: *What is the reading about?* Have students use the title and photo to make predictions about the reading.

3. Preteach any vocabulary words your students may not know, such as *mayor*.

Reading Glossary

mayor: the elected head of a city's government

BEFORE YOU READ

1. Have students discuss the questions in pairs. Try to pair students of different cultures together.

2. Ask for a few volunteers to share their answers with the class.

Reading

CD 3
TR 02

1. Have students first read the text silently. Tell them to pay special attention to *should* and *had better*. Then play the audio and have students read along silently.

2. Check students' comprehension. Ask questions such as: *Why is person A unhappy about the apartment?* (It's cold. There's not enough heat in the winter.) *Did person A talk to the landlord?* (Yes, twice.) *What does person B suggest?* (Call the mayor's office for information about tenants' rights.) *Does person A want to report the problem to the mayor's office?* (no)

Practice Idea: Listening

To practice listening skills, have students first listen to the audio alone. Ask a few comprehension questions. Repeat the audio if necessary. Then have them open their books and read along as they listen to the audio.

Context Note

If you're renting an apartment, you should always be aware of your rights as a tenant. States usually have laws on tenants' rights in the following areas: apartment sharing, heating season, eviction, security deposits, and pets.

8.7 Should; Had Better

5-10 mins
1. Have students cover up grammar chart **8.7** on page 252. Create a fill-in exercise. Write the following on the board:

   1. *Your landlord _____ give you a smoke detector; it's the law.*
   2. *You _____ talk to the landlord about the problems.*
   3. *The landlord _____ give me heat, or I'm going to move.*

   a. *Use* should *for advice.*
   b. *Use* must *for rules and laws.*
   c. *Use* had better *for warnings.*

   Say: *Study the three rules for* should, must, *and* had better. *Then fill in the blanks with the correct word.*

2. Go over the answers with the class (**Matching Answers: 1.** b; **2.** a; **3.** c).

3. Then have students look at grammar chart **8.7**. Go over the examples and explanations.

4. Direct students to the Pronunciation Note. Explain that native speakers often don't say the *had* in *had better*. Demonstrate the pronunciation.

EXERCISE 15

ANSWERS: Answers may vary. Possible answers:
1. You should get a roommate. **2.** You should ask them to be quieter. **3.** You should replace the battery. **4.** You should ask the landlord for permission. **5.** You should pay it now. **6.** You should talk to her about the problem. **7.** You should ask the landlord to explain it. **8.** You should replace it. **9.** You should write him a letter. OR You should go to court. **10.** You should move.

10-15 mins
1. Have students read the direction line. Go over the example in the book. Have a volunteer model #1.

2. Have students complete Exercise 15 individually. Remind them to review grammar chart **8.7** on page 252 if necessary. Then have students compare answers in pairs. Monitor pair work. Give help as needed.

Practice Idea: Writing

Say to students: *Write down three to five problems you need advice for.* Have students exchange problems with a partner. Then have each partner write advice. Survey the class to find out if students were happy with the advice. Ask volunteers to read the problems and the advice.

Practice Idea: Writing

Have students write to an advice columnist seeking advice for a problem they have. Ask students not to put their names on the letters. If necessary, show students examples of advice columns such as *Dear Abby*. Collect the letters and read them out loud. Ask the class to give advice.

EXERCISE 16

CD 3 TR 03

ANSWERS: Answers may vary. Possible answers:
1. take (OR bring) an umbrella OR bring (OR take) a raincoat; **2.** drive slowly; **3.** come home early OR not stay out so late; **4.** read too much OR read in dim light; **5.** take off OR remove; **6.** be quiet; **7.** unplug the TV OR leave the TV off; **8.** read; **9.** take (OR bring OR have OR carry) your cell phone; **10.** move

10-15 mins
1. Say: *In this conversation, a woman is talking about her mother, who worries a lot.* Have students read the direction line. Go over the example.

2. Have students complete Exercise 16 individually. Remind them to review grammar chart **8.7** on page 252 if necessary. Have students compare their answers in pars. Then play the audio and check answers as a class.

Using Craigslist.org to Find a Roommate READING

1. Have students look at the photo. Say: *What do you think this man is doing?* (e.g., *Using a computer/ searching on the Internet/looking for an apartment on the Internet*)

2. Have students look at the title of the reading. Ask: *What is the reading about?* Have students use the title and photo to make predictions about the reading.

3. Preteach any vocabulary words your students may not know, such as *ad*, *mess*, and *lie*.

Reading Glossary

ad: abbreviation of advertisement
lie: to not tell the truth
mess: an untidy state

BEFORE YOU READ

1. Have students discuss the questions in pairs.
2. Ask for a few volunteers to share their answers with the class.

5–10 mins

CD 3
TR 04

10–15 mins

Reading

1. Have students first read the text silently. Tell them to pay special attention to the negative of modals and related expressions. Then play the audio and have students read along silently.

2. Check students' comprehension. Ask questions such as: *Why is person A looking for a new roommate?* (His roommate moved out./He can't pay the rent by himself.) *What advice does person B give him?* (put an ad on Craigslist) *What does person B suggest he does before he takes pictures of his apartment?* (clean it up) *Why can't person B's cousin be his roommate?* (because she has a dog/because in his country men and women aren't supposed to live together)

8.8 Negatives of Modals ≡★

10–15 mins

1. Have students cover up grammar chart **8.8** on page 256. Create a chart on the board with the following headers: *against the law/rules (formal), against the law/rules (informal), no permission, not necessary, not advisable,* and *warning.*

   Then write the following sentences from the chart on the board in random order:

   1. *You <u>don't have to</u> tell your parents.*
   2. *You'd <u>better not</u> take pictures now. Your apartment is a mess.*
   3. *You'<u>re not supposed</u> to have a dog in your apartment.*
   4. *Renters <u>must not</u> change the locks without the owner's permission.*
   5. *You <u>shouldn't</u> include your phone number in the ad.*
   6. *I <u>can't</u> have a dog in my apartment.*

Lesson 8   **109**

Say: *Put the underlined modal or expression in the correct category.*

2. Then have students look at grammar chart **8.8**. Say: *Let's go through the examples and explanations and see if we were right.* (**Answers: 1.** not necessary; **2.** warning; **3.** against the law/rules (informal); **4.** against the law/rules (formal); **5.** not advisable; **6.** no permission)

3. Direct students to the comparisons. Say: *Although* must *and* have to *have similar meanings in the affirmative, they mean completely different things in the negative.* Don't have to *means that it's not necessary;* must not *means it's prohibited.* Read the examples.

4. Say: Must not *and* not supposed to *both mean that something is prohibited, although* must not *is more formal than* not supposed to*. Should not *expresses that something is a bad idea. It does not express prohibition.*

EXERCISE 17
Answers will vary.

10-15 mins

1. Have students read the direction line. Say: *When you say something that's addressed to every one in general, you use the pronoun* you. Go over the example in the book.

2. Have students complete Exercise 17 in pairs. Remind them to review grammar chart **8.8** on page 256 if necessary. Monitor pair work. Give help as needed. Go over the answers as a class.

Practice Idea: Speaking

Survey the class. Find out what students answered for some of the items in Exercise 17.

EXERCISE 18
Answers will vary.

10-15 mins

1. Have students read the direction line. Say: *Make statements with* have to *and* don't have to *that are true for you.* Go over the examples in the book.

2. Have students complete Exercise 18 individually. Remind them to review grammar

chart **8.8** on page 256 if necessary. Then have students compare their answers in pairs. Monitor pair work. Give help as needed. Have students share some of their answers with the class.

Practice Idea: Speaking

Create two rings of students. Have half of the students stand in an outer ring around the classroom. Have the other half stand in an inner ring, facing the outer ring. Instruct students to ask and answer questions based on the items from Exercise 18. Tell students to answer questions with a short answer (e.g., *Do you have to speak English every day? Yes, I have to/No, I don't have to.*). Call out *turn* every minute or so. Students in the inner ring should move one space clockwise. Students now interview their new partners. Make sure students look at each other when they're speaking.

EXERCISE 19
Answers will vary.

10-15 mins

1. Have students read the direction line. Say: *You're going to interview a classmate who is not from the same country you're from.* Model #1 with a volunteer.

2. Have students complete Exercise 19 in pairs. Remind them to review grammar chart **8.8** on page 256 if necessary. Monitor work. Give help as needed.

Practice Idea: Speaking

Discuss the questions as a class. Make a chart on the board. Write the countries represented in the class across the top. Write the number of the questions down the side. Poll the class, using a check for *yes* answers and an *X* for *no* answers.

EXERCISE 20

CD 3
TR 05

Answers: 1. 're not supposed to; **2.** don't have to;
3. don't have to; **4.** 're not supposed to;
5. don't have to; **6.** 're not supposed to;
7. 're not supposed to

10-15 mins

1. Say: *In this conversation, one student is showing another student his apartment.* Have students read the direction line. Go over the example in the book.

2. Have students complete Exercise 20 individually. Remind them to review grammar chart **8.8** on page 256 if necessary. Then have students compare answers in pairs. Play the audio and check answers as a class.

Practice Idea: Listening

To provide practice with listening skills, have students close their books and listen to the audio. Repeat the audio as needed. Ask comprehension questions, such as: *Where does person A keep his bike?* (in his apartment) *Is the apartment expensive?* (yes) *Is he allowed to hang up pictures in his apartment?* (yes) Then have students open their books and complete Exercise 20.

 EXERCISE 21

CD 3
TR 06

Answers: Answers may vary. Possible answers:
1. mustn't OR can't OR 're not supposed to OR may not; **2.** can't OR 're not supposed to; **3.** had better not OR shouldn't; **4.** shouldn't; **5.** don't have to; **6.** don't have to; **7.** shouldn't; **8.** can't OR 're not supposed to OR may not; **9.** don't have to

10-15 mins

1. Say: *In this conversation, students are asking the teacher questions about an exam.* Have students read the direction line. Go over the example in the book. Say: *Remember, all the answers should be in the negative.*

2. Have students complete Exercise 21 individually. Remind them to review grammar chart **8.8** on page 256 if necessary. Then have students compare answers in pairs. Play the audio and check answers as a class.

Practice Idea: Listening

To provide practice with listening skills, have students close their books and listen to the audio. Repeat the audio as needed. Ask comprehension questions, such as: *Do students have to sit in a specific seat for the exam?* (no) *Can they use their books during the exam?* (no) *Do they have to bring paper?* (no) Then have students open their books and complete Exercise 21.

Practice Idea: Speaking

Have students practice the conversation in pairs. Then ask volunteers to act out the conversation for the class.

The New Neighbors   READING

1. Have students look at the illustration. Ask: *What's going on in this picture?* (A neighbor is bringing cookies to someone who just moved in. The new neighbor is unpacking her things in the new apartment.)

2. Have students look at the title of the reading. Ask: *What is the reading about?* Have students use the title and picture to make predictions about the reading.

3. Preteach any vocabulary words your students may not know, such as *crib, worry,* and *whisper.*

Reading Glossary

crib: a small bed with high sides where a baby sleeps
whisper: soft, quiet talking
worry: fear that something bad may happen; anxiety

BEFORE YOU READ

5-10 mins

1. Have students discuss the questions in pairs.

2. Ask for a few volunteers to share their answers with the class.

Reading

CD 3
TR 07

10-15 mins

1. Have students first read the text silently. Tell them to pay special attention to *must*. Then play the audio and have students read along silently.

2. Check students' comprehension. Ask questions such as: *Where does Lisa live?* (downstairs) *Does the new neighbor have kids?* (Yes. She has a 10-month-old son.) *How does Lisa know that Paula has a baby?* (She saw a crib.) *What does Lisa's daughter spend a lot of time doing?* (talking on the phone)

Practice Idea: Listening

To practice listening skills, have students first listen to the audio alone. Ask a few comprehension questions. Repeat the audio if necessary. Then have them open their books and read along as they listen to the audio.

Context Note

Many towns and cities in the U.S. have newcomer clubs that provide new residents with the opportunity to meet people. They usually have events such as barbecues, potluck dinners, book clubs, and playgroups for kids. Many groups have general meetings as well as meetings for special interests and hobbies. Some newcomer clubs even have newsletters and Web sites.

8.9 *Must* for Conclusions

5-10 mins

1. Have students cover up grammar chart **8.9** on page 261. Ask students: *What does* must *mean?* (It's a formal way to say that something is necessary.) Have students go back to the reading on page 261. Say: *There is another use for* must. *Read through the text again. What does* must *mean in this reading?* Discuss students' ideas.

2. Have students look at grammar chart **8.9**. Read through the explanation at the top of the chart. Go over the example sentences and the explanations. Review the negative *must not*.

EXERCISE 22

ANSWERS: Answers may vary. Possible answers:
1. She must be divorced (OR widowed). OR She must not have a husband. **2.** She must be a nurse. **3.** She must like coffee. **4.** She must like classical music. **5.** She must know how to sew. (OR She must sew.) **6.** She must enjoy cooking. **7.** She must play the piano. **8.** She must like modern art. **9.** She must be busy. **10.** She must love cats.

10-15 mins

1. Have students read the direction line. Say: *Read each statement about Lisa's apartment, and make a logical deduction about Lisa's life.* Go over the example.

2. Have students complete Exercise 22 individually. Remind them to review grammar chart **8.9** on page 261 if necessary. Go over the answers as a class.

Practice Idea: Speaking

Have students work in pairs. Ask students to take three to five things out of their bags or pockets. Have students make logical conclusions about their partners' lives based on their personal items (e.g., a mystery novel—*You must like to read mysteries.*).

Practice Idea: Writing

Have students try to make negative deductions about Lisa's life from each statement (e.g., *Lisa must not have a husband.*).

EXERCISE 23

CD 3
TR 08

ANSWERS: 1. be; **2.** speak; **3.** know; **4.** be; **5.** be; **6.** be

10-15 mins

1. Say: *In this conversation, Alma introduces herself to her new neighbor, Eva.* Have students read the direction line. Go over the example in the book.

112 Grammar in Context 2 • Teacher's Edition

2. Have students complete Exercise 23 individually. Remind them to review grammar chart **8.9** on page 261 if necessary. Then have students compare answers in pairs. Play the audio and check answers as a class.

Practice Idea: Listening

To provide practice with listening skills, have students close their books and listen to the audio. Repeat the audio as needed. Ask comprehension questions, such as: *When did Eva move in?* (last week) *How did Alma guess that Eva was from Bosnia?* (from her last name; Alma is from Bosnia, too) *Who is in Eva's class?* (Alma's husband) Then have students open their books and complete Exercise 23.

Practice Idea: Speaking

Have students practice the conversation in pairs. Then have volunteers role-play all or part of the conversation in front of the class.

Practice Idea: Speaking

Have students work in pairs to create a conversation between new neighbors. Tell students to make the conversation as true for them as possible. Then ask volunteers to role-play the conversations in front of the class.

8.10 *Will* and *May/Might* ☰★

10-15 mins

1. Have students look at grammar chart **8.10** on page 264. Say: Will *and* may/might *are used to express certainty, uncertainty, and possibility.* Review the example sentences and explanations for *will.* Point out that the contraction for *will not* is *won't.* Explain that *will* is used for certainty in the future. Go around the room and ask volunteers to make statements about their futures using *will* and *won't* (e.g., *I will register for English class next semester.*).

2. Say: May *and* might *both have the same meaning. They can express uncertainty or possibility about the future and about the present.* Review the example sentences and explanations. Point out that there are no contractions for *may not* and *might not.*

3. Say: Maybe *is an adverb. It means* possibly *or* perhaps. *It can mean the same thing as* may *and* might. *It usually comes at the beginning of the sentence.* Go over the example sentences.

4. Direct students to the wrong examples with *maybe.* Ask: *What's wrong with these sentences? Correct them* (**Corrected Sentences:** Maybe I'll move. Maybe he doesn't understand. Maybe the apartment is cold in winter.). Review word order with *may* and *might* (subject + *may/ might* + verb).

EXERCISE 24

ANSWERS: 1. My sister may (OR might) come to live with me. **2.** She may (OR might) find a job in this city. **3.** My landlord may (OR might) raise my rent. **4.** I may (OR might) get a dog. **5.** My landlord may (OR might) not allow me to have a dog. **6.** I may (OR might) move next year. **7.** I may (OR might) buy a house soon. **8.** I may (OR might) not stay in this city. **9.** I may (OR might) not come to class tomorrow. **10.** The teacher may (OR might) review modals if we need more help.

5-10 mins

1. Have students read the direction line. Go over the example.

2. Have students complete Exercise 24 in pairs. Remind them to review grammar chart **8.10** on page 264 if necessary. Go over the answers as a class.

Practice Idea: Speaking

Have students discuss each statement with a partner. Ask: *Which statements are a possibility for you? Change the information when necessary* (e.g., My brother might come to live with me.).

EXERCISE 25

Answers will vary.

10-15 mins

1. Say: *Complete these sentences with information that is true for you.* Have students read the direction line. Go over the examples.

2. Have students complete Exercise 25 individually. Remind them to review grammar chart **8.10** on page 264 if necessary. Then have students compare answers in pairs. Monitor pair work. Give help as needed.

EXERCISE 26

CD 3
TR 09

ANSWERS: Answers may vary. Possible answers:
1. be; **2.** have, be; **3.** know (it), be; **4.** allow; **5.** rain; **6.** move OR leave OR not, raise; **7.** be, have, be

10-15 mins

1. Have students read the direction line. Go over the example in the book.

2. Have students complete Exercise 26 individually. Remind them to review grammar chart **8.10** on page 264 if necessary. Then have students compare answers in pairs. Play the audio and check possible answers as a class.

Practice Idea: Listening

To provide practice with listening skills, have students close their books and listen to the audio. Repeat the audio as needed. Ask some comprehension questions, such as: *In conversation 1, who is Terry Karson?* (person A's next-door neighbor) *Has person A ever seen Terry?* (no) *Is Terry a man or a woman?* (We don't know.) Then have students open their books and complete Exercise 26.

Practice Idea: Speaking

Have students create short dialogues in pairs using *maybe, may,* and *might.* Then have volunteers role-play their dialogues in front of the class.

At a Garage Sale

1. Have students look at the photo on page 267. Ask: *What's going on in the photo?* (People are at a garage sale.)

2. Have students look at the title of the reading. Ask: *What is the reading about?* Have students use the title and photo to make predictions about the reading.

3. Preteach any vocabulary words your students may not know, such as *deposit.* Direct students to the footnotes on bargaining at the bottom of page 267.

Reading Glossary

deposit: a partial payment to hold goods or property until the buyer makes complete payment

BEFORE YOU READ

5-10 mins

1. Have students discuss the questions in pairs.

2. Ask for a few volunteers to share their answers with the class.

Reading

CD 3
TR 10

10-15 mins

1. Have students first read the text silently. Explain that this is a conversation between a seller and buyer at a garage sale. Tell students to pay special attention to modals and related expressions. Then play the audio and have students read along silently.

2. Check students' comprehension. Ask questions such as: *What item is the buyer interested in?* (a microwave) *How are they going to see if it's working well?* (They're going to plug it in and boil a cup of water.) *Why is the seller selling it?* (He's moving.) *How much is the seller asking for it?* ($40)

Practice Idea: Listening

To practice listening skills, have students first listen to the audio alone. Ask a few comprehension questions. Repeat the audio if necessary. Then have them open their books and read along as they listen to the audio.

Context Note

Garage sales, also known as yard sales or tag sales, are usually held when the weather is good—in the spring or early fall in colder states. They are usually held on weekends. Unlike most transactions in the U.S., it's acceptable to bargain for a lower price at a garage sale.

8.11 Using Modals and Questions for Politeness

10-15 mins

1. Have students cover up grammar chart **8.11** on page 268. Create a matching exercise on the board:

   1. *May I write you a check?*
   2. *Could you plug it in?*
   3. *I'd like to boil a cup of water.*
   4. *I'd rather pay by check.*
   5. *Why don't we boil a cup of water?*

   a. *to express preference*
   b. *to ask permission*
   c. *to offer a suggestion*
   d. *to request that someone do something*
   e. *to express want or desire*

   Say: *Match the use with the example.*

2. Have students look at grammar chart **8.11**. Say: *Compare your work with the chart.* (**Matching Answers: 1.** b; **2.** d; **3.** e; **4.** a; **5.** c) Then review the modals for politeness. Explain that *can* for permission is not considered as polite as *may* or *could*. Point out that *could* and *would* for requests sound softer than *can* and *will*.

3. Review questions for politeness. Explain that *would you like* has the same meaning as *do you want*. However *would you like* is softer sounding and is considered more polite. Remind students that the contraction for *would* after pronouns is *'d*.

4. To ask for and express preferences, *would rather* is used. Go over the examples.

5. To make a suggestion more polite, English speakers often make a negative question using *why don't*. Go over the examples.

6. Direct students to the Language Note. Look at the examples and point out that the question makes the instruction more polite.

EXERCISE 27

ANSWERS: 1. May I help you? OR Can I help you? OR Could I help you? **2.** May I close the door? OR Can I close the door? OR Could I close the door? **3.** May I leave the room? OR Can I leave the room? OR Could I leave the room? **4.** May I write you a check? OR Can I write you a check? OR Could I write you a check?

5-10 mins

1. Say: *In this exercise, you're going to practice* may, can, *and* could + I. Have students read the direction line. Go over the examples.

2. Have students complete Exercise 27 in pairs. Remind them to review grammar chart **8.11** on page 268 if necessary. Go over the answers as a class.

EXERCISE 28

ANSWERS: 1. Can you repeat the sentence? OR Could you repeat the sentence? OR Will you repeat the sentence? OR Would you repeat the sentence? **2.** Can you give me your paper? OR Could you give me your paper? OR Will you give me your paper? OR Would you give me your paper? **3.** Can you spell your name? OR Could you spell your name? OR Will you spell your name? OR Would you spell your name? **4.** Can you tell me your phone number? OR Could you tell me your phone number? OR Will you tell me your phone number? OR Would you tell me your phone number?

5-10 mins

1. Have students read the direction line. Say: *Now you're going to be asking someone to do something for you.* Go over the examples.

2. Have students complete Exercise 28 in pairs. Remind them to review grammar chart **8.11** on page 268 if necessary. Monitor pair work. Go over the answers as a class.

EXERCISE 29

ANSWERS: 1. I would OR I'd like to ask you a question. **2.** The teacher would like to speak with you. **3.** Would you like to try out the oven? **4.** Yes. I would (OR I'd) like to see if it works.

5-10 mins

1. Say: *Now we're going to practice* would like. Have students read the direction line. Go over the example.

2. Have students complete Exercise 29 in pairs. Remind them to review grammar chart **8.11** on page 268 if necessary. Monitor pair work. Go over the answers as a class.

EXERCISE 30

ANSWERS: 1. Why don't you take a sweater? **2.** Why don't we turn off the light? **3.** Why don't you turn left here? **4.** Why don't we leave early?

5-10 mins

1. Say: *Now practice negative questions.* Have students read the direction line. Go over the examples.

2. Have students complete Exercise 30 in pairs. Remind them to review grammar chart **8.11** on page 268 if necessary. Monitor pair work. Go over the answers as a class.

Practice Idea: Speaking

Play a game. Have the class sit in a circle. Toss a ball to one student and make a request or polite command such as *Could I borrow a dollar?* The student answers, tosses the ball to another student, and asks another question with a different modal or related expression. Tell students that they can't repeat a modal or expression that the last two or three students have used. Remind students that they can use negative questions. If necessary, write all of the modals and related expressions on the board before beginning the game.

EXERCISE 31
Answers will vary.

10-15 mins

1. Say: *In this exercise, you're going to talk about what you prefer.* Have students read the direction line. Go over the example. Have a volunteer model #1.

2. Have students complete Exercise 31 by asking and answering questions in pairs (e.g., *Would you rather live in the U.S. or in another country?*). Remind them to review grammar chart **8.11** on page 268 if necessary. Monitor pair work. Give help as needed.

Practice Idea: Speaking

Do a class survey. Find out how students answered each question. Write the results for the class on the board.

EXERCISE 32

ANSWERS: Student responses will vary. Correct question constructions: 1. Would you rather read fact or fiction? **2.** Would you rather watch funny movies or serious movies? **3.** Would you rather listen to classical music or popular music? **4.** Would you rather visit Europe or Africa? **5.** Would you rather own a large luxury car or a small sports car? **6.** Would you rather watch a soccer game or take part in a soccer game? **7.** Would you rather write a letter or receive a letter? **8.** Would you rather cook or eat in a restaurant?

10-15 mins

1. Have students read the direction line. Say: *Now you're going to be asking someone what he or she prefers.* Go over the example. Model the example with a volunteer.

2. Have students complete Exercise 32 in pairs. Tell students to take turns asking and answering each question. Remind them to review grammar chart **8.11** on page 268 if necessary. Monitor pair work. Give help as needed.

Practice Idea: Speaking

Create two rings of students. Have half of the students stand in an outer ring around the classroom. Have the other half stand in an inner ring, facing the outer ring. Instruct students to ask and answer questions from Exercise 32. Call out *turn* every minute or so. Students in the inner ring should move one space clockwise. Students now ask and answer questions with their new partners. Make sure students look at each other when they're talking.

EXERCISE 33 ≡★

CD 3
TR 11

ANSWERS: 1. Could you show it to me? **2.** Would you wait a minute? **3.** Could you plug it in? **4.** I'd rather sell; **5.** Would you give them both to me for $15? **6.** I'd rather; **7.** Can you show me some identification? **8.** Would you spell your name for me?

10-15 mins

1. Say: *We're going to make a conversation more polite.* Have students read the direction line. Explain that this is a conversation between a seller and a buyer at a garage sale. Go over the example in the book.

2. Have students complete Exercise 33 individually. Remind them to review grammar chart **8.11** on page 268 if necessary. Then have students compare answers in pairs. Play the audio and check possible answers as a class.

Practice Idea: Listening

To provide practice with listening skills, have students close their books and listen to the audio. Repeat the audio as needed. Ask some comprehension questions such as: *What is the buyer interested in?* (a lamp) *How many lamps does the seller have?* (two) *Does the seller want to sell only one?* (No. The seller prefers to sell both together.) Then have students open their books and complete Exercise 33.

Practice Idea: Speaking

Have students practice the conversation in pairs. Then ask volunteers to role-play the conversation in front of the class.

Summary of Lesson 8

20-30 mins

1. **Modals** Have students cover up the example column of the chart on page 271. Have students work in pairs to write a sentence for each use of the modal. Then ask volunteers to write their sentences on the board. Go over

the chart and review trouble spots with the class. If necessary, have students review:

2. **Related Expressions** Have students cover up the example column of the chart on page 272. Have students work in pairs to write a sentence for each use of the expression. Then ask volunteers to write their sentences on the board. Go over the chart and review trouble spots with the class. If necessary, have students review:

Editing Advice

10-15 mins

Have students close their books. Write the first few sentences without editing marks or corrections on the board. For example:

1. *I must to study.*
   I can helping you now.

2. *He cans cook.*

Ask students to correct each sentence and provide a rule or an explanation for each correction. This activity can be done individually, in pairs, or as a class. After students have corrected each sentence, tell them to turn to pages 272–273. Say: *Now compare your work with the Editing Advice in the book.* Have students read through all the advice.

Editing Quiz

ANSWERS: 1. we're not permitted; **2.** C; **3.** C; **4.** 're supposed to; **5.** allowed; **6.** might OR may; **7.** permitted; **8.** C; **9.** can't you; **10.** I would (OR I'd) rather; **11.** C; **12.** couldn't agree; **13.** I had (OR I'd) better not; **14.** ø

10-15 mins

1. Tell students they are going to put the editing advice into practice. Have students read the direction line. Ask: *Do all the shaded words and phrases have mistakes?* (no) Go over the examples with the class. Then do #1 together.

2. Have students complete the quiz individually. Then have them compare answers with a partner before checking answers as a class.

3. For the items students had difficulties with, have them go back and find the relevant grammar chart and review it. Monitor and give help as necessary.

Lesson 8 Test/Review

20-30 mins

Use the Assessment CD-ROM with Exam*View*®, Online Workbook, and Web site for additional practice, review, and assessment materials.

PART 1

ANSWERS: 1. would; **2.** shouldn't; **3.** Can; **4.** Would; **5.** have to; **6.** had; **7.** couldn't go; **8.** must; **9.** Can; **10.** have to; **11.** don't have to; **12.** 've got to; **13.** might; **14.** has to; **15.** 'm not supposed to; **16.** may; **17.** would

1. Part 1 may be used as an in-class test to assess student performance, in addition to the Assessment CD-ROM with Exam*View*®. Have students read the direction line. Explain that this is a conversation between two friends. Collect for assessment.

2. If necessary, have students review Lesson 8.

PART 2

ANSWERS: Answers may vary. Possible answers:
1. can't, must; **2.** supposed OR permitted OR allowed; **3.** better, might OR may; **4.** rather, than; **5.** must, should; **6.** may not OR must; **7.** got; **8.** 've got to OR have; **9.** have; **10.** allowed OR permitted OR supposed

1. Part 2 may also be used as an in-class test to assess student performance, in addition to the Assessment CD-ROM with Exam*View*®. Have students read the direction line. Point out that more than one answer may be possible. Collect for assessment.

2. If necessary, have students review Lesson 8.

Expansion

These expansion activities provide opportunities for students to interact with one another and further develop their speaking and writing skills. Encourage students to use grammar from this lesson whenever possible.

CLASSROOM ACTIVITIES

10-15 mins per activity

1. If the class is large, do this activity in groups. Ask volunteers to present one of the problems to the class or group or to create their own problems.

2. Put students from the same country in pairs. Have them present information about laws in their countries and how they compare to laws in the U.S. to the class.

TALK ABOUT IT

15-20 mins

1. Put students in groups to discuss the procedures for renting an apartment in another country or city. Have each group write a list of differences between the city or country they choose and the city where they live. Have groups present their lists to the class.

2. Elicit different ways of finding apartments or houses to rent. Write the students' ideas on the board. Then ask students to tell their groups how they found the apartment they're living in now.

3. Have students discuss in pairs or small groups what they like and what they dislike about where they live.

WRITE ABOUT IT

20-30
mins

1. Have students read the direction line. Then tell students to make a list of the rules in their apartment buildings in the U.S. and another list with rules in their native country. Write their ideas on the board. Then have them write their compositions. Collect for assessment and/or have students share their compositions with the group. This can be done orally in small groups or by posting the compositions around the classroom for everyone to read.

2. Have students read the direction line. Have students write a list of steps a student must take to register for classes at the school. Then ask them to write an explanation of the steps for a student interested in registering. Collect for assessment and/or have students share their compositions with the group.

Practice Idea: Writing

Have students create a brochure for new students. Have them write down the procedure for registering, along with other rules, regulations, and tips that might be useful for new students. Display the brochures in the classroom.

3. Have students read the direction line and the sample paragraph. Tell students to make a list of the rules in this school. Then have them compare their lists with a partner and discuss how they are different from rules in another school they attended. Then have them write their compositions individually. Encourage them to write as much as they can. Collect for assessment and/or have students present their compositions to a group.

Practice Idea: Writing

Have students exchange first drafts with a partner. Ask students to help their partners edit their drafts. Refer students to the Editing Advice on pages 272–273.

OUTSIDE ACTIVITIES

1. Tell students to look at the Sunday newspaper for notices about garage sales or apartment sales. Ask them to find out what kind of items are going to be sold. Suggest that if they have time, they go to a sale. Have them report on the items for sale and about their experience to the class.

2. Tell students to get a newspaper and look for the advice column. Have them read the problems and the advice and circle the modals. Ask them to decide if they agree with the advice. Have them bring the advice columns to class and discuss the modals used and the advice given in groups.

3. Have students bring their leases to class and compare them in pairs. Ask: *Can you understand what the rules are in your apartment? Are their differences in your leases? Who has a better lease?*

INTERNET ACTIVITIES

1. Tell students to use the Internet to find information about tenants' rights in the city where they live. Have them print the page and circle the modals. Have students bring their pages to class to compare in pairs or small groups.

2. Tell students to find a phone directory online and look up the names and addresses of moving companies in their city. Ask them to call a company to find out the price of a move. Have them report back to the class on the price.

3. Tell students to find apartments for rent online. Have them print a page and bring it to class to discuss with their classmates the price of apartments and what is included.

Lesson 9

Lesson Overview

GRAMMAR

1. Briefly review what students learned in the previous lesson. Ask: *What did we study in Lesson 8?* (modals and related expressions)

2. Ask: *What are we going to study in this lesson?* (the present perfect and the present perfect continuous) *Can anyone give me an example of the present perfect?* (e.g., *I have seen* Star Wars *ten times.*) Have students give examples. Write the examples on the board. Then ask for examples of the present perfect continuous.

CONTEXT

1. Ask: *What will we learn about in this lesson?* (the Internet) Activate students' prior knowledge. Ask: *Do you use the Internet a lot? What do you use it for?*

2. Have students share their knowledge and personal experiences.

Presentation Ideas

The topic for this lesson can be enhanced with the following items:

1. Articles about the Internet and its use

2. Statistics about the number of people who use the Internet and what they use it for

3. Information from a genealogy Web site

9.1 The Present Perfect Tense—An Overview ═★

⏱ 5-10 mins

1. Have students look at grammar chart **9.1** on page 280. Write on the board: have/has + *past participle*. Say: *We form the present perfect tense for* I, you, we, they, *and plural nouns with the auxiliary* have *plus the past participle. For* he,

she, it, *and singular nouns, we use* has *plus the past participle.* Review the example sentences in the chart.

2. Say: *We can also use the present perfect with* there. *If a plural noun follows* there, *then we use* have. *If a singular noun follows* there, *then we use* has. Go over the examples.

Presentation Idea

Write the following sentences on the board:

I have been in the U.S. for three years.

We have written a job résumé.

She has found a job as a programmer.

There has been a problem with my computer all day.

Say: *Here are some sentences in the present perfect tense. Can you tell me the rules for forming this tense?* Have volunteers explain the rules for forming the present perfect. Then go over chart **9.1**.

Google READING

1. Have students look at the photo of the Google Web site. Ask: *Do you use Google? What is it?* (an Internet search engine) *Who do you think these two men are?* (the two founders of Google) For those who are not familiar with Google, point to the image of the Web page on page 281.

2. Have students look at the title of the reading. Ask: *What is the reading about?* Have students use the title and photo to make predictions about the reading.

3. Preteach any vocabulary words your students may not know, such as *expert, banner,* and *worth.*

Reading Glossary

banner: a graphic on a Web page that's often used as an advertisement
expert: a master at something; an authority
worth: value

BEFORE YOU READ

1. Have students discuss the questions in pairs.
2. Ask for a few volunteers to share their answers with the class.

Reading

CD 3
TR 12

1. Have students first read the text silently. Tell them to pay special attention to the present perfect tense. Then play the audio and have students read along silently.
2. Check students' comprehension. Ask questions such as: *When did Page and Brin begin their business?* (when they were graduate students in California) *Where they both born in the U.S.?* (No. Brin was born in Russia.) *What's different about the look of Google compared to the look of other search sites.* (It's very clean. There are no advertisements.)

DID YOU KNOW?

Have students read the information. Then ask them if they know where the word *Google* comes from. Share the following information with them: The name of the search engine Google was derived from the word *googol*, which is the number 1 followed by 100 zeros. The word *googol* was coined by a nine-year-old boy—the nephew of an important American mathematician—Edward Kasner.

> ### Practice Idea: Listening
>
> To practice listening skills, have students first listen to the audio alone. Ask a few comprehension questions. Repeat the audio if necessary. Then have them open their books and read along as they listen to the audio.

EXERCISE 1

ANSWERS: 1. Google <u>has grown</u> over the years. **T**;
2. Sergey Brin <u>has lived</u> in the U.S. all his life. **F**;
3. Larry Page and Sergey Brin <u>have known</u> each

other since they were children. **F**; **4.** Larry Page <u>has been interested</u> in computers since he was a child. **T**; **5.** Brin and Page <u>have returned</u> to college to finish their degrees. **F**; **6.** Brin and Page <u>have become</u> rich. **T**; **7.** The noun "Google" <u>has become</u> a verb. **T**

---

1. Have students read the direction line. Go over the example.
2. Have students complete Exercise 1 individually. Remind them to review grammar chart **9.1** on page 280 if necessary. Go over the answers as a class.

9.2 The Past Participle

1. Have students cover up grammar chart **9.2** on pages 282–283. Write the following list of past forms and past participles on the board:

Past Form	Past Participle
walked	walked
talked	talked
studied	studied
cooked	cooked

Say: *These are regular verbs. What do you notice about the past form and the past participle?* (They're the same.)

2. Have students look at grammar chart **9.2**. Say: *Irregular verbs have irregular past participles. These participles have to be memorized. Some are the same as the past tense form, and some are completely different. Look at grammar chart 9.2 on pages 282–283.*

3. Go over the list of irregular verbs on the chart. Model the pronunciation of the past participles.

4. Have students try to identify spelling patterns. Give them a hint. Say: *Sometimes the past participle is more closely related to the base form, and sometimes it resembles the past form. Sometimes a vowel is changed or a consonant added.* Review students' findings, and write them on the board. There are eight categories in the irregular verbs chart:

   1. Past participle = base form
   2. Add *-n* to the base form (for *fly*, change *y* to *o* and add *w*)
   3. Remove final *-e*, add *-n* to the past form
   4. Add *-n* to the past form
   5. Change vowel from *a* in past form to *u*

6. Add -n to base form, double consonant if last vowel sound is /d/ or /t/
7. Add -en to base form
8. Miscellaneous changes

Presentation Idea

After students have gone through chart **9.2**, have them go through the reading on page 281 and circle the irregular past participles.

EXERCISE 2

ANSWERS: 1. gone; **2.** seen; **3.** looked; **4.** studied; **5.** brought; **6.** taken; **7.** said; **8.** been; **9.** found; **10.** left; **11.** lived; **12.** known; **13.** liked; **14.** fallen; **15.** felt; **16.** come; **17.** broken; **18.** worn; **19.** chosen; **20.** driven; **21.** written; **22.** put; **23.** begun; **24.** wanted; **25.** gotten; **26.** flown; **27.** sat; **28.** drunk; **29.** grown; **30.** given

5-10 mins
1. Have students read the direction line. Go over the example.
2. Have students complete Exercise 2 individually. Remind them to review grammar chart **9.2** on pages 282–283 if necessary. Go over the answers as a class.

Practice Idea: Speaking

Have students practice the pronunciation of each past participle in pairs. Circulate to observe pronunciation. Give help as needed.

9.3 The Present Perfect— Contractions and Negatives =★

5-10 mins
1. Have students cover up grammar chart **9.3** on page 284. Write the following sentences from the chart on the board:

I've had a lot of experience with computers.
He's been interested in computers since he was a child.

I haven't studied programming.
Brin hasn't returned to college.

Say: *Explain how to form the affirmative and negative contractions with the present perfect.* Have volunteers explain.

2. Go over the examples and explanations in the chart. Point out that most singular nouns can contract with *has*.

3. Direct students to the Language Note. Explain that an *'s* can mean *has* or *is*. Say: *The word following the contraction will tell you what the contraction means.* Go over the examples.

EXERCISE 3 =★

ANSWERS: 1. 've; **2.** 've; **3.** 's; **4.** haven't; **5.** 's; **6.** 've; **7.** haven't

---

5-10 mins
1. Have students read the direction line. Go over the example. Remind students to use contractions whenever possible.

2. Have students complete Exercise 3 individually. Remind them to review grammar chart **9.3** on page 284 if necessary. Then go over the answers as a class.

9.4 Adding an Adverb =★

5-10 mins
1. Have students cover up grammar chart **9.4** on page 285. Then have students go back to the reading on page 281. Say: *Find where adverbs have been used with the present perfect (They have never returned … Have you ever noticed …).* Then ask: *Where do you put the adverb?* (between *have/has* and the past participle)

2. Then have students look at grammar chart **9.4**. Go over the examples.

3. Direct students to the Language Note. Explain that *already* often comes at the end of the verb phrase.

EXERCISE 4 =★

ANSWERS: 1. The teacher has given a test on Lesson 8 already OR The teacher has already give a test on Lesson 8. **2.** We have never heard of Page and Brin. **3.** They have always been interested in search technology. **4.** You have probably used Google. **5.** Brin hasn't even finished his degree.

6. Brin and Page have already become billionaires. OR Brin and Page have become billionaires already.

---

1. Have students read the direction line. Go over the example. Ask: *What kind of word is in the parentheses?* (an adverb)

2. Have students complete Exercise 4 individually. Remind them to review grammar chart **9.4** on page 285 if necessary. Then have students compare answers in pairs. Then go over the answers as a class.

(5-10 mins)

⬭ **Practice Idea: Writing**

Have students write three to five sentences about their experiences with the Internet (e.g., *I have never used Google.*).

9.5 The Present Perfect— Statements and Questions

1. Have students cover up grammar chart **9.5** on page 286. Write the following on the board:

   Larry has lived in the U.S. all his life.

   Say: *Write a yes/no question, a short answer, and then ask a question with* how long.

   Then write the following on the board:

   They haven't finished their degrees.

   Say: *Write a negative question based on this statement.*

2. Then have students look at grammar chart **9.5**. Say: *Compare your work with the chart.* Go over the examples and explanations.

3. Direct students to the Language Note. Point out that we can't make a contraction with a short affirmative answer. Go over the example.

(5-10 mins)

EXERCISE 5

ANSWERS: 1. Which ones have you used? **2.** Why haven't they finished their degrees? **3.** How much money have they made? **4.** How long has he been in the U.S.? **5.** How many people have they hired to work for Google? **6.** How many times have you

---

used the computer lab this semester? **7.** Why have the memory and speed of computers increased? **8.** How have they become part of our daily lives?

---

1. Say: *Ask a question about the statement.* Have students read the direction line. Go over the example. Have a volunteer do #1.

2. Have students complete Exercise 5 individually. Remind them to review grammar chart **9.5** on page 286 if necessary. Then have students compare answers in pairs. Then go over the answers as a class.

(10-15 mins)

9.6 Continuation from Past to Present ≡★

1. Have students cover up grammar chart **9.6** on page 287. Write the following sentence from the reading on the board: *Since its start in 1998, Google has become one of the most popular search engines.*

   Ask: *When did Google start to become popular?* (in 1998) *Correct. In the past. Is Google still popular?* (yes) *So, today, in the present, it is still popular.*

2. Have students look at grammar chart **9.6**. Say: *We use the present perfect tense to show that an action or a state that started in the past and continues to the present.* Point out the timeline.

3. Go over the examples and explanations in the chart. Explain the use of the following with the present perfect:
   a. *for +* an amount of time
   b. *since* with dates
   c. *since* with a verb
   d. *how long*
   e. *always*
   f. *never*

(10-15 mins)

■ **Presentation Idea**

After students have gone through chart **9.6**, have them write statements and questions about themselves and their families using *for, since, how long, always,* and *never.*

EXERCISE 6

5-10 mins

1. Have students read the direction line. Go over the example.

2. Have students complete Exercise 6 individually. Remind them to review grammar chart **9.6** on page 287 if necessary. Then go over the answers with the class.

EXERCISE 7

Answers will vary.

10-15 mins

1. Say: *In this exercise, you're going to write true statements about yourselves.* Have students read the direction line. Go over the examples. Model the examples for the class.

2. Have students complete Exercise 7 individually. Remind them to review grammar chart **9.6** on page 287 if necessary. Then have students compare answers in pairs. Monitor pair work. Give help as needed. Have volunteers share some of their sentences with the class.

EXERCISE 8

Answers will vary.

10-15 mins

1. Have students read the direction line. Go over the example in the book. Model the example for the class.

2. Have students complete Exercise 8 in pairs. Remind them to review grammar chart **9.6** on page 287 if necessary. Monitor pair work. Give help as needed. Have volunteers share some of their sentences with the class.

EXERCISE 9

Answers will vary.

10-15 mins

1. Have students read the direction line. Go over the example in the book. Model the example for the class.

2. Have students complete Exercise 9 in pairs. Remind them to review grammar chart **9.6** on page 287 if necessary. Monitor pair work.

Give help as needed. Have volunteers share some of their sentences with the class.

Practice Idea: Speaking

Create two rings of students. Have half of the students stand in an outer ring around the classroom. Have the other half stand in an inner ring, facing the outer ring. Instruct students to ask and answer questions from Exercises 8 and 9 (e.g., *What have you always thought about? I've always thought about my future.*). Call out *turn* every minute or so. Students in the inner ring should move one space clockwise. Students now interview their new partners. Make sure students look at each other when they're talking.

EXERCISE 10

Answers will vary.

10-15 mins

1. Have students read the direction line. Go over the examples. Ask a volunteer to model the exercise.

2. Have students complete Exercise 10 individually. Remind them to review grammar chart **9.6** on page 287 if necessary. Monitor pair work. Give help as needed. Have volunteers share some of their sentences with the class.

EXERCISE 11

Answers will vary.

10-15 mins

1. Say: *Now talk about what you've never done or been.* Have students read the direction line. Go over the examples. Ask a volunteer to model the exercise.

2. Have students complete Exercise 11 individually. Remind them to review grammar chart **9.6** on page 287 if necessary. Monitor pair work. Give help as needed. Have volunteers share some of their sentences with the class.

9.7 The Simple Present vs. the Present Perfect ≡★

5-10 mins

1. Have students look at grammar chart **9.7** on page 290. Review the examples and explanations.

2. Ask students to circle words and expressions that accompany the present perfect (e.g., *since*, *always*, etc.).

EXERCISE 12

ANSWERS: 1. always been an English teacher OR always taught English; **2.** always worked at this college/school; **3.** always thought about grammar; **4.** always been easy for you; **5.** always been (*teacher's name*); **6.** always been interested in languages; **7.** always lived in this city

10-15 mins

1. Have students read the direction line. Say: *You're going to ask me questions about my life and my job.* Go over the example.

2. Complete Exercise 12 as a class. Remind students to review grammar chart **9.7** on page 290 if necessary as they formulate the questions.

EXERCISE 13

CD 3 TR 13

ANSWERS: 1. haven't; **2.** long; **3.** have; **4.** 've; **5.** been; **6.** 've; **7.** heard; **8.** learned; **9.** has had; **10.** 've; **11.** been; **12.** 've; **13.** heard; **14.** 've; **15.** spoken; **16.** 've; **17.** heard; **18.** 've; **19.** lived; **20.** 've; **21.** lived; **22.** 've; **23.** learned

10-15 mins

1. Say: *In this conversation, two students are talking about their homes in Burundi and North Dakota.* Have students read the direction line. Go over the example.

2. Have students complete Exercise 13 individually. Remind them to review grammar chart **9.7** on page 290 if necessary. Have students compare their answers in pairs. Then play the audio and go over the answers as a class.

Practice Idea: Listening

To provide practice with listening skills, have students close their books and listen to the audio. Repeat the audio as needed. Ask comprehension questions, such as: *How long has student B been in the U.S.?* (about a year) *Where is student B from?* (Burundi) *Did student B use computers in Africa?* (no) Then have students open their books and complete Exercise 13.

Practice Idea: Speaking

Have students practice the conversation in pairs. Ask volunteers to role-play all or part of the conversation in front of the class.

Practice Idea: Speaking

Have students work in pairs to create a similar conversation that is true for them. Then have volunteers role-play all or part of the conversation in front of the class.

9.8 The Present Perfect vs. the Simple Past

5-10 mins

1. Have students look at grammar chart **9.8** on page 292. Review the examples and explanations. Point out that the simple past shows a single action that happened in the past. The action did not continue. The present perfect describes an action that began in the past and continues into the present.

2. Explain that *when* is used with the simple present and *how long* is used with the present perfect.

Presentation Idea

Have students go back to the reading on page 281. Say: *Circle the verbs in the simple past.* Ask: *When do we use the simple past? When do we use the present perfect?* Then have students look at chart **9.8**.

EXERCISE 14

CD 3 TR 14

ANSWERS: 1. bought; **2.** changed; **3.** 've always wanted; **4.** made; **5.** found; **6.** 've downloaded; **7.** 've made; **8.** didn't have; **9.** Did you sell; **10.** removed; **11.** left; **12.** passed; **13.** took; **14.** got; **15.** 've had

10-15 mins

1. Have students read the direction line. Go over the example.

2. Have students complete Exercise 14 individually. Remind them to review grammar charts **9.7** on page 290 and **9.8** on page 292 if necessary. Have students compare their answers in pairs. Then play the audio and go over the answers as a class.

Practice Idea: Listening

To provide practice with listening skills, have students close their books and listen to the audio. Repeat the audio as needed. Ask comprehension questions, such as: *How long has person B had an Internet connection?* (since 1999) *Does person B buy things online?* (yes) *Did person B use to have a CD burner?* (No, but person B does now.) *What did person B do with his old computer?* (He left it on top of a dumpster.) Then have students open their books and complete Exercise 14.

Practice Idea: Speaking

Have students practice the conversation in pairs. Ask volunteers to role-play all or part of the conversation in front of the class.

9.9 The Present Perfect Continuous—An Overview

5-10 mins Have students look at grammar chart **9.9** on page 294. Say: *We use the present perfect continuous to talk about an action that started in the past and continues to the present.* Review the examples.

Genealogy READING

1. Have students look at the photo. Ask: *What is the photo of?* (the children in a family) *What do you notice about the photo?* (It's old.)

2. Have students look at the title of the reading. Ask: *What is the reading about? What is genealogy?* (the names and history of one's family) Have students

use the title and photo to make predictions about the reading.

3. Preteach any vocabulary words your students may not know, such as *ancestors*, *amateur*, and *census*.

Reading Glossary

amateur: a person who does activities, such as sports, for pleasure and without pay
ancestors: the persons from whom one is descended
census: a count by the government of the people in a country

BEFORE YOU READ

5-10 mins

1. Have students discuss the questions in pairs. Try to pair students of different cultures together.

2. Ask for a few volunteers to share their answers with the class.

Reading ═★
CD 3 TR 15

10-15 mins

1. Have students first read the text silently. Tell them to pay special attention to the present perfect and the present perfect continuous tenses. Then play the audio and have students read along silently.

2. Check students' comprehension. Ask questions such as: *Is genealogy a popular hobby?* (yes) *Why is the popularity of genealogy increasing?* (probably because the Internet has made searching much easier) *How old are most family historians?* (over 40) *What did Cyndi Howells do so that she could work on her family history more?* (She quit her job.)

Practice Idea: Listening

To practice listening skills, have students first listen to the audio alone. Ask a few comprehension questions. Repeat the audio if necessary. Then have them open their books and read along as they listen to the audio.

9.10 The Present Perfect Continuous—Forms

10-15 mins

1. Have students cover up grammar chart **9.10** on pages 295–296. Say: *Go back to the reading on pages 294–295. Find some examples of the present perfect continuous, and try to figure out the rule for forming it.* Then ask a volunteer to tell you how to form the present perfect continuous (*have/has + been + present participle*). Write it on the board. Ask students to say how they might form the negative (*have/has + not + been + present participle*). Then ask students to make questions from the reading (e.g., *Has Cyndi been giving lectures all over the country?*).

2. Write the following on the board: *Cyndi has been working on her family history.*

   Say: *Write a yes/no question, a short answer, and an information question with how long.* Have volunteers write their statements and questions on the board. Then write this negative statement on the board: *They haven't been using the public library.* Say: *Write a negative question for this statement.* Have a volunteer write the negative question on the board.

3. Then have students look at grammar chart **9.10**. Say: *Compare your work with the chart.* Go over any trouble spots with the class.

4. Direct students to the short answers. Explain that only the auxiliary *have* or *has* is used with short answers. Also, words like *since* and *for* can be used alone with the date or time period (e.g., *Since 1992. For 12 years.*).

EXERCISE 15 =⭐

ANSWERS: 1. has been growing; **2.** has been working; **3.** has been lecturing; **4.** has been increasing; **5.** has, been keeping; **6.** Have, been working; **7.** have been using; **8.** has not been living

10-15 mins

1. Have students read the direction line. Go over the example in the book.

2. Have students complete Exercise 15 individually. Remind them to review grammar chart **9.10** on pages 295–296 if necessary. Go over the answers as a class.

Practice Idea: Writing

Ask: *What have you been working on lately? Write five to ten sentences about a hobby or pastime you enjoy. Use the present perfect continuous tense to describe what you've been doing* (e.g., I have been gardening since 1999. I have been working on creating a perennial garden in the back of the house. I have been planting bulbs every fall. I have been fertilizing the soil and watering the beds.).

9.11 The Present Perfect Continuous—Use =⭐

10-15 mins

1. Have students cover up grammar chart **9.11** on page 297. Write the following sentence on the board along with the timeline: *He has been living in the U.S. since 1979.*

   Ask: *When did he start living in the U.S.?* (in 1979) *Correct. In the past. Is he still living here?* (yes) *So, today, he is still living in the U.S.*

2. Have students look at grammar chart **9.11**. Say: *We use the present perfect continuous tense to show that an action or state started in the past and continues to the present.* Point out the timeline.

3. Go over the examples and explanations in the chart. Explain the use of the following with the present perfect continuous:

   1. *for* + an amount of time
   2. *since* with dates
   3. some verbs (*live, work, study, teach, wear*) can be used for both
   4. if the action is still happening, use continuous
   5. don't use with *always* or *never*
   6. *think about* (action)
   7. expressions with *have*

4. Remind students that the present perfect continuous is used with action verbs. Point out the list of nonaction verbs in the chart.

EXERCISE 16

Answers will vary.

5-10 mins

1. Say: *You're going to write true statements about your life.* Have students read the direction line. Go over the example. Say: *Remember, use* for *or* since *in your sentences.* Model the example for the class.

2. Have students complete Exercise 16 individually. Remind them to review grammar chart **9.11** on page 297 if necessary. Then have students compare answers in pairs. Monitor pair work. Give help as needed. Have volunteers share their sentences with the class.

Practice Idea: Speaking

Have students think of three to five more questions they would like to ask their partners. Then have students take turns asking and answering questions in pairs.

EXERCISE 17

Answers will vary.

10-15 mins

1. Say: *Now you're going to find out some information about your partner.* Have students read the direction line. Go over the example. Ask: *When do we ask a question with* how long? (when the answer to the first question is *yes*) Model the example with a volunteer.

2. Have students complete Exercise 17 in pairs. Remind them to review grammar chart **9.11** on page 297 if necessary. Monitor pair work. Give help as needed.

EXERCISE 18

ANSWERS: Answers may vary. Correct question constructions: 1. How long have you been teaching English? **2.** How long have you been working at this school? **3.** How long have you been living in this city? **4.** How long have you been using this book? **5.** How long have you been living at your present address?

10-15 mins

1. Say: *Now you're going to ask me some questions.* Have students read the direction line. Go over the example.

2. Complete Exercise 18 as a class. Remind them to review grammar chart **9.11** on page 297 if necessary as they formulate their questions.

Practice Idea: Speaking

If possible, bring in other teachers for students to interview in groups. Have students prepare extra questions ahead of time.

EXERCISE 19

ANSWERS: Answers may vary. Possible answers:
1. have, been working, 've been working; **2.** is, has, been; **3.** does, has, living, 's been living, was; **4.** am, have you been studying, (answers will vary); **5.** is, How, has s/he been teaching, (answers will vary); **6.** they are, have they been using, Since; **7.** Are, am, long have you been using the Internet, I've been using the Internet; **8.** Do, do, long have they been living, were; **9.** is, has she been studying her family history, (answers will vary)

10-15 mins

1. Say: *In this exercise, you're going to read to nine mini-conversations.* Have students read the direction line. Go over the example.

2. Have students complete Exercise 19 individually. Remind them to review grammar chart **9.11** on page 297 if necessary. Then have students compare answers in pairs or go over the answers as a class.

Practice Idea: Speaking

Have students practice the mini-conversations in pairs. Ask volunteers to role-play the conversations in front of the class.

E-Books READING

1. Have students look at the photo. Ask: *What is the photo of?* (an e-book)

2. Have students look at the title of the reading. Ask: *What is the reading about? What are e-books?* Have students use the title and photo to make predictions about the reading.

3. Preteach any vocabulary words your students may not know, such as *hobby* and *electronic device*.

Reading Glossary

electronic device: electronic apparatus, piece of electronic equipment

hobby: activity you do in your free or leisure time

BEFORE YOU READ

5-10 mins

1. Have students discuss the questions in pairs. Try to pair students of different cultures together.

2. Ask for a few volunteers to share their answers with the class.

Reading

CD 3
TR 16

10-15 mins

1. Have students first read the text silently. Tell them to pay special attention to the present perfect tense. Then play the audio and have students read along silently.

2. Check students' comprehension. Ask questions such as: *Did person B take ten books to the beach?* (no, only one, the e-book) *How many books has person B downloaded?* (about a hundred) *Do you need a computer to download books?* (no)

Practice Idea: Listening

To practice listening skills, have students first listen to the audio alone. Ask a few comprehension questions. Repeat the audio if necessary. Then have them open their books and read along as they listen to the audio.

9.12 The Present Perfect with Repetition from Past to Present ≡★

10-15 mins

1. Have students cover up grammar chart **9.12** on page 302. Write the following sentence on

the board along with the timeline:
I have read five books this year.

Ask: *Do you think I might read more books this year?* (Yes, the possibility that I'll read more is high.)

2. Have students look at grammar chart **9.12**. Say: *We use the present perfect to talk about the repetition of an action in a time period that includes the present. There is a probability that this action will occur again.* Point out the timeline.

3. Go over the examples and explanations in the chart. Point out that the expressions *so far* and *up to now* hint at the action continuing into the future. Questions about repetition are asked with *how many* and *how much*. The use of *at all* also indicates that an action may happen in the future (e.g., *I haven't checked my e-mail at all today (but I will check it at some point).*). Review the examples from the chart.

4. Explain to students that the simple past is used with closed time periods (e.g., *in 1998*). The present perfect is used with time periods that remain open (e.g., *since 1998*).

5. Direct students to the Language Note. Explain to students that we don't use the present perfect continuous for repetition. Go over the example sentences.

EXERCISE 20

ANSWERS: Student responses will vary. Correct questions: 1. Have we had any tests so far (OR up to now)? **2.** Has this lesson been difficult so far (OR up to now)? **3.** Has the teacher given a lot of homework so far (OR up to now)? **4.** Have you understood all the explanations so far (OR up to now)? **5.** Have you had any questions about this lesson so far (OR up to now)?

10-15 mins

1. Have students read the direction line. Go over the example in the book. Model the example with a volunteer, using *up to now*.

2. Have students complete Exercise 20 in pairs. Remind them to review grammar chart **9.12** on page 302 if necessary. Monitor pair work. Give help as needed.

EXERCISE 21

ANSWERS: Student responses will vary. Correct questions: 1. How many letters have you written this month? **2.** How many times have you eaten in a restaurant this month? **3.** How many times have you gotten paid this month? **4.** How many international calls have you made this month? **5.** How many books have you bought this month? **6.** How many times have you gone to the movies this month? **7.** How many movies have you rented this month? **8.** How many times have you cooked this month?

10-15 mins

1. Have students read the direction line. Go over the example in the book.

2. Have students complete Exercise 21 in pairs. Remind them to review grammar chart **9.12** on page 302 if necessary. Monitor pair work. Give help as needed.

EXERCISE 22
Answers will vary.

10-15 mins

1. Say: *You're going to write questions for your classmates or me* (the teacher). Have students read the direction line. Go over the examples in the book. Ask: *What words can we use for repetition?* (so far *and* up to now)

2. Have students write the questions individually. Remind them to review grammar chart **9.12** on page 302 if necessary. Then have students mingle in the classroom asking and answering questions. Give help as needed.

Practice Idea: Speaking

Create two rings of students. Have half of the students stand in an outer ring around the classroom. Have the other half stand in an inner ring, facing the outer ring. Instruct students to ask and answer questions from Exercises 20 and 21. Tell students to answer questions with a short answer. Call out *turn* every minute or so. Students in the inner ring should move one space clockwise. Students now interview their new partners. Make sure students look at each other when they're talking.

9.13 The Simple Past vs. the Present Perfect with Repetition

5-10 mins

1. Have students look at grammar chart **9.13** on page 304. Say: *We can use both the simple past and the present perfect to express repetition. However, with the simple past, the repetition of the action happened in a time period in the past and won't be repeated again in the future.*

2. Go over the examples and explanations in the chart. Point out that the expressions *so far, today,* and *this semester* used with the present perfect indicate that the number may not be final. To show that the number is final, we use the simple past with a past time expression such as *yesterday, last week,* or *last semester.*

3. Explain to students that sometimes you can use either the simple past or the present perfect with a present time expression to mean the same thing. Go over the examples.

Presentation Idea

Have students go back to the reading on pages 294–295. Ask students to underline the verbs in the simple past, circle the verbs in the present perfect, and put a box around verbs in the present perfect continuous. Ask students to discuss the tense of each verb with a partner. Then have students go through chart **9.13**.

EXERCISE 23

ANSWERS: 1. did you live in; **2.** have you lived in; **3.** did you attend; **4.** have you attended; **5.** have you had; **6.** did you have

5-10 mins

1. Say: *In this exercise, you're going to complete the question and then respond with an answer that's true for you.* Have students read the direction line. Go over the examples.

2. Have students complete Exercise 23 in pairs. Remind them to review grammar chart **9.13** on page 304 if necessary. Monitor pair work. Give help as needed.

9.14 The Present Perfect with Indefinite Past Time

5-10 mins

1. Have students look at grammar chart **9.14** on page 305. Say: *We use the present perfect to refer to an action that occurred at an indefinite time in the past (that is, there was no specified time or date for the beginning of the action). Words that show indefinite time are:* ever, yet, *and* already.

   Point out the example on the timeline in the grammar chart: *Have you ever seen an e-book?* Say: *This question is not concerned with a specific time.*

2. Go over the examples and explanations in the chart. Point out that a question with *ever* asks about any time between the past and the present.

3. Say: Yet *and* already *refer to an indefinite time in the recent past.* Review the questions and short answers with *yet* and *already*.

4. Then say: *We can also use the present perfect with no reference to time at all.* Go over the examples.

EXERCISE 24
Answers will vary.

5-10 mins

1. Have students read the direction line. Say: *Give short answers to the following questions.* Ask: *Is there a difference between* No, I haven't *and* No, I never have? (no)

2. Have students ask and answer the questions in pairs. Remind them to review grammar chart **9.14** on page 305 if necessary. Monitor pair work. Give help as needed.

EXERCISE 25
Answers will vary.

5-10 mins

1. Have students read the direction line. Say: *Give short answers to the following questions.*

Ask: *Is there a difference between* Yes, I have *and* Yes, I already have? (There's a slight difference. With *already,* there's an expectation that it just happened.) *No, not yet* means that you expect to do the action soon.

2. Have students ask and answer the questions in pairs. Remind them to review grammar chart **9.14** on page 305 if necessary. Monitor pair work. Give help as needed.

9.15 Answering a Present Perfect Question

5-10 mins

1. Have students cover up grammar chart **9.15** on page 307. Write the following sentence from the grammar chart on the board: *Have you ever used Google?* Go around the class and ask random students that question. Write their responses on the board.

2. Then have students look at grammar chart **9.15**. Say: *We can answer a present perfect question with the present perfect OR with the simple past.* If possible, point to several examples from students on the board. Say: *If the response does not have a specific time or number of times, use the present perfect. If the response has a specific time or number of times, use the simple past.* Go over the examples in the chart.

EXERCISE 26
ANSWERS: Student responses will vary. Correct question constructions: 1. Have you ever worked in a factory? **2.** Have you ever lost a glove?

3. Have you ever seen an e-book? **4.** Have you ever fallen out of bed? **5.** Have you ever made a mistake in English grammar? **6.** Have you ever told a lie? **7.** Have you ever eaten raw fish? **8.** Have you ever studied calculus? **9.** Have you ever met a famous person? **10.** Have you ever gone to an art museum? **11.** Have you ever downloaded a book? **12.** Have you ever broken a window? **13.** Have you ever bought a book online? **14.** Have you ever downloaded music? **15.** Have you ever gone to Las Vegas? **16.** Have you ever traveled by ship? **17.** Have you ever been in love? **18.** Have you ever written a poem? **19.** Have you ever sent a text message?

10-15 mins

1. Say: *Your partner is going to ask questions in the present perfect.* Have students read the direction line. Ask: *When do you use the simple past in the answer?* (when you give a specific time or number of times) Go over the examples in the book.

2. Have students ask and answer the questions in pairs. Remind them to review grammar chart **9.15** on page 307 if necessary. Monitor pair work. Give help as needed.

Practice Idea: Speaking

Survey the class on some of the information from Exercise 26 (e.g., *Have you ever met a famous person?*). And ask students to expand on the topic (e.g., *Who[m] did you meet? Where did you meet him or her?*).

EXERCISE 27
Answers will vary.

10-15 mins

1. Say: *Now you get to ask me some questions.* Have students read the direction line. Go over the examples. Answer the questions.

2. Have students complete Exercise 27 in pairs. Remind them to review grammar chart **9.15** on page 307 if necessary. Monitor pair work. Give help as needed.

3. Have students ask you their questions and answer them.

EXERCISE 28

ANSWERS: Student responses will vary. Correct questions: 1. Has your country ever had a civil war? **2.** Has your country's leader ever visited the U.S.? **3.** Has an American president ever visited your country? **4.** Has your country ever had a woman president? **5.** Have you ever gone back to visit your country? **6.** Has there ever been an earthquake in your hometown?

10-15 mins

1. Say: *Ask your partner questions about his or her native country.* Have students read the direction line. Go over the example.

2. Have students complete Exercise 28 in pairs. Remind them to review grammar chart **9.15** on page 307 if necessary. Monitor pair work. Give help as needed.

Practice Idea: Speaking

Have students from different countries discuss their answers to the questions from Exercise 28 in groups (e.g., *Has your country ever had a civil war? Yes, my country has had many civil wars. My country is still going through a civil war.*).

EXERCISE 29

ANSWERS: Student responses will vary. Correct questions are: 1. Have you found a doctor yet? **2.** Have you made any new friends yet? **3.** Have you opened a bank account yet? **4.** Have you saved any money yet? **5.** Have you thought about your future yet? **6.** Have you written to your family yet? **7.** Have you gotten a credit card yet? **8.** Have you bought a computer yet? **9.** Have you gotten a telephone yet? **10.** Have you gotten a Social Security card yet?

10-15 mins

1. Say: *Now ask your partner questions about things he or she has done in the U.S.* Have students read the direction line. Go over the example.

2. Have students complete Exercise 29 in pairs. Remind them to review grammar chart **9.15** on page 307 if necessary. Monitor pair work. Give help as needed.

Practice Idea: Speaking

Create two rings of students. Have half of the students stand in an outer ring around the classroom. Have the other half stand in an inner ring, facing the outer ring. Instruct students to ask and answer questions from Exercise 29 in random order. Call out *turn* every minute or so. Students in the inner ring should move one space clockwise. Students now ask and answer questions with their new partners. Make sure students look at each other when they're talking.

Practice Idea: Speaking

Have students practice the conversation in pairs. Ask volunteers to role-play all or part of the conversation in front of the class.

Practice Idea: Speaking

Have students work in pairs to create their own conversations about their family histories. Have volunteers role-play all or part of their conversations in front of the class.

 EXERCISE 30

CD 3
TR 17

ANSWERS: 1. 've only been; **2.** left; **3.** was; **4.** 've read; **5.** 've been; **6.** for; **7.** 've been working; **8.** did you start; **9.** started; **10.** was; **11.** 've found; **12.** did you find; **13.** used; **14.** 've also gone; **15.** Have you ever gone; **16.** went; **17.** found; **18.** have you found; **19.** far; **20.** 've found

10-15
mins

Say: *You're going to have to choose what tense to use. Answers may vary.* Have students read the direction line. Go over the examples in the book.

Have students complete Exercise 30 individually. Remind them to review grammar chart **9.15** on page 307 if necessary. Then have them compare answers in pairs. Play the audio and go over answers as a class.

Practice Idea: Listening

To provide practice with listening skills, have students close their books and listen to the audio. Tell students: *You're going to hear a conversation between two students. They're talking about their family histories.* Repeat the audio as needed. Ask comprehension questions, such as: *Where are the two students from?* (Guatemala and Cuba) *Are they both interested in family history?* (yes) Then have students open their books and complete Exercise 30.

Summary of Lesson 9

20-30
mins

1. **Compare the present perfect and the simple past.** Have students cover up the summary on page 310. Create a matching exercise on the board.

   1. *We have had four tests so far.*
   2. *She used the Internet three times yesterday.*
   3. *I've done the homework already.*
   4. *Did you visit the art museum last month?*
   5. *My father came to the U.S. in 2002.*
   6. *My father has had his job in the U.S. for many years.*

   a. *The action of the sentence began in the past and includes the present.*
   b. *The action of the sentence is completely past.*
   c. *Repetition from past to present*
   d. *Repetition in a past time period*
   e. *The action took place at an indefinite time between the past and the present.*
   f. *The action took place at a definite time in the past.*

   Say: *First match the sentences with the description. Then identify each sentence as simple past or present perfect.* (**Matching Answers: 1.** c; **2.** d; **3.** e; **4.** f; **5.** b; **6.** a) Have students look at the chart on page 310. Say: *Compare your work with the chart.*

Review all the examples. Go over any trouble spots with the class. If necessary, have students review:

9.1 The Present Perfect Tense—An Overview (p. 280)

9.6 Continuation from Past to Present (p. 287)

9.8 The Present Perfect vs. the Simple Past (p. 292)

9.12 The Present Perfect with Repetition from Past to Present (p. 302)

9.13 The Simple Past vs. the Present Perfect with Repetition (p. 304)

9.14 The Present Perfect with Indefinite Past Time (p. 305)

2. **Compare the present perfect and the present perfect continuous.** Have students cover up the summary on page 311. Create a matching exercise. On the board, write:

   1. *continuous action (nonaction verbs)*
   2. *continuous action (action verbs)*
   3. *repeated action*
   4. *nonstop action*
   5. *question with* how many
   6. *question with* how long
   7. *action that is at an indefinite time, completely in the past*
   8. *action that started in the past and is still happening*

   Then write the example sentences from the chart for each use.

   Say: *First match the sentences with the use. Then identify each sentence as present perfect or present perfect continuous.* (**Matching Answers: 1.** continuous action (nonaction verbs): I have had my car for five years. **2.** continuous action (action verbs): I've been driving a car for 20 years. **3.** repeated action: Cyndi's Web site has won several awards. **4.** nonstop action: The U.S. Census has been keeping records since the 1880s. **5.** question with *how many*: How many times have you gone to New York? **6.** questions with how long: *How long* has he been living in New York? **7.** action that is at an indefinite time, completely in the past: Cyndi has created a Web site. **8.** action that started in the past and is still happening: Cyndi has been working on her family history since 1992.)

Have students look at the chart on page 311. Say: *Compare your work with the chart.*
Review all the examples. Go over any trouble spots with the class. If necessary, have students review:

9.1 The Present Perfect Tense—An Overview (p. 280)

9.9 The Present Perfect Continuous—An Overview (p. 294)

9.11 The Present Perfect Continuous—Use (p. 297)

9.12 The Present Perfect with Repetition from Past to Present (p. 302)

9.14 The Present Perfect with Indefinite Past Time (p. 305)

Editing Advice

15-20 mins

Have students close their books. Write the first few sentences without editing marks or corrections on the board. For example:

She has been taken a test for two hours.
She has giving him a present.

Ask students to correct each sentence and provide a rule or an explanation for each correction. This activity can be done individually, in pairs, or as a class. After students have corrected each sentence, tell them to turn to pages 311–312. Say: *Now compare your work with the Editing Advice in the book.* Have students read through all the advice.

Editing Quiz

ANSWERS: 1. came; **2.** have been changing OR have changed; **3.** I came; **4.** For; **5.** have been studying; **6.** C; **7.** C; **8.** improved OR been improving; **9.** haven't taken; **10.** C; **11.** yet; **12.** been eating (OR eaten); **13.** C; **14.** 've been gaining; **15.** C; **16.** C; **17.** started; **18.** haven't had; **19.** C; **20.** 've never taken; **21.** C; **22.** C; **23.** I've lived; **24.** C; **25.** C; **26.** How long; **27.** have you

15-20 mins

1. Tell students that they are going to put the Editing Advice into practice. Have students read the direction line. Ask: *Do all the shaded words and phrases have mistakes?* (no) Go over the examples with the class. Then do #1 together.

2. Have students complete the quiz individually. Then have them compare answers with a partner before checking answers as a class.

3. For the items students had difficulties with, have them go back and find the relevant grammar chart and review it. Monitor and give help as necessary.

Lesson 9 Test/Review

 Use the Assessment CD-ROM with Exam*View*®, Online Workbook, and Web site for additional practice, review, and assessment materials.

20-30 mins

PART 1

ANSWERS: Conversation 1: 1. studied; **2.** 've been working OR 've been working; **3.** Have, thought; **4.** was; **5.** 've always wanted; **6.** was; **7.** graduated; **8.** haven't had; **Conversation 2: 1.** have you been; **2.** Has your life changed; **3.** came; **4.** came; **5.** lived; **6.** 've lived OR 've been living; **7.** Have you always lived; **8.** 've moved; **9.** haven't found

1. Part 1 may be used as an in-class test to assess student performance, in addition to the Assessment CD-ROM with Exam*View*®. Have students read the direction line. Collect for assessment.

2. If necessary, have students review Lesson 9.

PART 2

ANSWERS: Paragraph 1: 1. use; **2.** 've used OR 've been using; **3.** started; **4.** became; **5.** have been working; **6.** found; **7.** is living OR lives; **8.** was; **9.** came; **10.** has lived OR has been living; **11.** haven't found; **Paragraph 2: 1.** came; **2.** broke; **3.** 've lived OR 've been living; **4.** was; **5.** didn't know; **6.** arrived; **7.** 've studied OR 've been studying; **8.** speak; **9.** haven't started

1. Part 2 may also be used as an in-class test to assess student performance, in addition to the Assessment CD-ROM with Exam*View*®. Have students read the direction line. Collect for assessment.

2. If necessary, have students review Lesson 9.

Expansion

These expansion activities provide opportunities for students to interact with one another and further develop their speaking and writing skills.

Encourage students to use grammar from this lesson whenever possible.

CLASSROOM ACTIVITIES

 1. Rather than having students check off the things they've done first, encourage students to read through the list together as a group.

10-15 mins per activity

2. Model the activity. Make a presentation of your family tree on the board or on handouts for your students.

Practice Idea: Speaking

Have students create visual presentations of their family tree. Encourage students to be creative. Display the family trees around the room. Ask volunteers to talk about their families.

TALK ABOUT IT

 1. Put students in groups to discuss the questions. Then have groups report back to the class on what they discussed.

15-20 mins

2. Elicit a few advantages of e-books and write them on the board. Then put students in groups to discuss the advantages and disadvantages. Have each group come up with two lists. Then have groups compare lists and decide on a final list as a class. Write the list on the board.

3. Have students discuss the question in pairs. Then put pairs together to make groups of four and have them share their opinions, encourage them to explain and justify their arguments.

WRITE ABOUT IT

 1. Have students read the direction line. Brainstorm new technology and write a list on the board. Have students choose one of the items on the list and say how it has changed people's lives. Write their ideas on the board. Then have students choose another item from the list and write their paragraphs individually. Collect for assessment and/or have students share their paragraphs with the group.

20-30 mins

2. Have students read the direction line and the sample paragraph. Then tell students to choose a topic to write about and make a list of the things that have changed in their lives. Have students talk about how their life has changed with a partner. Then have them write their compositions. Collect for assessment and/or have students share their compositions with the group.

Practice Idea: Writing

Have students exchange first drafts with a partner. Ask students to help their partners edit their drafts. Refer students to the Editing Advice on pages 311–312.

OUTSIDE ACTIVITIES

1. Tell students to interview an American about his or her family history. Ask them to find out if this person knows the stories of his or her ancestors and their native countries. Have students prepare for the interview with the American by brainstorming a list of questions (e.g., *Do you know which ancestors first came to the U.S.? When did they come?*). Ask students to report back to the class on something interesting they discovered from the interview.

2. Tell students to ask at their public library or the school library if they have any e-books available for them to read on the computer. Have students report back on what books are available. Encourage them to choose a book to read and tell the class something about it.

INTERNET ACTIVITIES

1. Tell students to go to a search engine and type in *Larry Page* and *Sergey Brin*. Have them find an interesting fact about one of them that they didn't know and share it with the class.

2. Tell students to type the word *genealogy* into a search engine and see how many Web sites they find.

3. Tell students to find Cyndi Howell's genealogy Web site on the Internet and find out about people who have the same last name as theirs. Have them report back to the class on what they found.

4. Tell students to go to an online bookstore like Amazon.com or barnesandnoble.com and look for a book they are interested in. Have them find out how much the book costs and how much they have to pay for shipping. Tell them to find out if they can find e-books there as well. Have students report back to the class with their findings.

Lesson 10

Lesson Overview

GRAMMAR

1. Briefly review what students learned in the previous lesson. Ask: *What did we study in Lesson 9?* (the present perfect and present perfect continuous)

2. Ask: *What are we going to study in this lesson?* (gerunds and infinitives) *Can anyone give me an example of a gerund?* (e.g., *I like **walking**.*) Have students give examples. Write the examples on the board. Then ask for examples of infinitives (e.g., *I like **to walk**.*).

CONTEXT

1. Ask: *What will we learn about in this lesson?* (finding a job) Activate students' prior knowledge. Ask: *Do you have a job? How did you find it? Did you need to write a résumé?*

2. Have students share their knowledge and personal experiences.

Presentation Ideas

The topic for this lesson can be enhanced with the following items:

1. The classified section of a newspaper
2. Samples of résumés and cover letters

10.1 Gerunds—An Overview

⏱ 5-10 mins
1. Have students cover up grammar chart **10.1** on page 320. Create a matching exercise. Write the following on the board:

   1. *Finding a job is hard.*
   2. *I don't enjoy talking about myself.*
   3. *I thought about changing my career.*
   4. *I got help by talking with my counselor.*

   a. *object of the preposition*
   b. *object*
   c. *part of an adverbial phrase*
   d. *subject*

   Ask: *What role does the gerund play in each of the sentences?*

   Review the example sentences in the chart. (**Matching Answers: 1.** d; **2.** b; **3.** a; **4.** c)

2. Then have students look at grammar chart **10.1**. Say: *Now compare your answers with the chart.* Go over the examples. Point out that gerunds are often in many expressions with *go*.

3. Explain that we put *not* in front of a gerund to make it negative. Go over the examples.

Finding a Job   READING

1. Have students look at the photo. Ask: *What do you think is going on in the photo?* (a job interview)

2. Have students look at the title of the reading. Ask: *What is the reading about?* Have students use the title and photo to make predictions about the reading.

3. Preteach any vocabulary words your students may not know, such as *résumé* and *in charge*.

Reading Glossary

in charge: to be in control or command
résumé: a short statement of one's work history and education used to get a new job

BEFORE YOU READ

⏱ 5-10 mins
1. Have students discuss the questions in pairs.

2. Ask for a few volunteers to share their answers with the class.

CD 3
TR 18

10-15 mins

Reading ═⭐

1. Have students first read the text silently. Tell them to pay special attention to gerunds. Then play the audio and have students read along silently.

2. Check students' comprehension. Ask questions such as: *How long should your résumé be?* (one page) *What does* networking *mean?* (exchanging information with anyone you know) *If you're prepared for an interview, how will you feel?* (relaxed) *Do Americans change jobs frequently?* (yes)

Practice Idea: Listening

To practice listening skills, have students first listen to the audio alone. Ask a few comprehension questions. Repeat the audio if necessary. Then have them open their books and read along as they listen to the audio.

DID YOU KNOW?

Have students read the information. Then ask them what other occupations they think are growing. Share the following information with them: According to the Bureau of Labor Statistics, the ten fastest growing occupations are:

1. medical assistants
2. network systems and data communications analysts
3. physician assistants
4. social and human service assistants
5. home health aids
6. medical records and health information technicians
7. physical therapist aids
8. computer software engineers, applications
9. computer software engineers, systems software
10. physical therapist assistants

10.2 Gerund as Subject

⏱ 5-10 mins
Have students look at grammar chart **10.2** on page 323. Go over the examples and explanations. Explain that gerunds can be used as the subject of a sentence. When used as a subject, they take a singular verb. Put *not* in front of a gerund to make it negative.

EXERCISE 1
Answers will vary.

⏱ 10-15 mins
1. Have students read the direction line. Say: *Make a logical sentence using the gerund as the subject.* Remind students that answers will vary. Go over the example.
2. Have students complete Exercise 1 individually. Remind them to review grammar chart **10.2** on page 323 if necessary. Go over the answers as a class.

Practice Idea: Writing

Have students work in pairs to make a flyer giving advice to students going on a job interview. Display the flyers around the class.

EXERCISE 2
Answers will vary.

⏱ 10-15 mins
1. Have students read the direction line. Go over the example. Have a volunteer model the example.
2. Have students complete Exercise 2 individually. Remind them to review grammar chart **10.2** on page 323 if necessary. Then have students compare answers in pairs. Monitor pair work. Give help as needed.

Practice Idea: Speaking

Do Exercise 2 as a class survey. How did students complete each statement?

EXERCISE 3
Answers will vary.

⏱ 10-15 mins
1. Say: *The questions in this next exercise will help you prepare for an interview.* Have students read the direction line. Say: *Remember, you don't have to try to use a gerund in every answer.* Go over the examples.

2. Have students complete Exercise 2 individually. Remind them to review grammar chart **10.2** on page 323 if necessary. Then have students compare answers in pairs. Monitor pair work. Give help as needed.

> ### Practice Idea: Speaking
>
> Have students carry out mock interviews. Tell students to find a new partner. One student plays the interviewer and the other is the job applicant. Students may also perform the interview in front of a group of students.

EXERCISE 4
Answers will vary.

10-15 mins

1. Have students read the direction line. Go over the examples.

2. Have students complete Exercise 4 in groups. Remind them to review grammar chart **10.2** on page 323 if necessary. Monitor group work. Give help as needed.

> ### Practice Idea: Speaking
>
> Have groups report to the class about behaviors that might hurt your chances of getting a job.

10.3 Gerund after Verb

10-15 mins

1. Have students cover up grammar chart **10.3** on page 325. Have students go back to the reading on pages 320–322. Say: *In the reading, there is one verb that is immediately followed by a gerund; circle it* (avoid).

2. Have students look at grammar chart **10.3**. Explain that some verbs can be followed by a gerund. Review the list with the class. Go over the examples.

3. Say: *Go + gerund is used in many expressions.* Review the list of gerunds with *go*. Go over the example sentences.

4. Review the expressions *mind, put off,* and *can't help.*

EXERCISE 5
Answers will vary.

10-15 mins

1. Have students read the direction line. Go over the example. Say: *If you can't think of a gerund, you can also use just a noun.* Have a volunteer model the example.

2. Have students complete Exercise 5 individually. Remind them to review grammar chart **10.3** on page 325 if necessary. Then have students compare answers in pairs. Monitor pair work. Give help as needed. Have volunteers share some of their sentences.

EXERCISE 6
Answers will vary.

10-15 mins

1. Ask: *What advice do you have for tourists visiting your native country?* Have students read the direction line. Go over the examples.

2. Have students complete Exercise 6 individually. Remind them to review grammar chart **10.3** on page 325 if necessary. Then have students compare answers in pairs. Monitor pair work. Give help as needed. Have volunteers share their advice with the class.

> ### Practice Idea: Writing
>
> Have students make brochures about their hometowns. Tell them to include their recommendations from Exercise 6.

EXERCISE 7
Answers will vary.

10-15 mins

1. Have students read the direction line. Go over the examples. Say: *You have to give a reason why you do or don't like something. Use* because.

2. Have students complete Exercise 7 in pairs. Remind them to review grammar chart **10.3** on page 325 if necessary. Monitor pair work. Give help as needed.

Create two rings of students. Have half of the students stand in an outer ring around the classroom. Have the other half stand in an inner ring, facing the outer ring. Instruct students to ask and answer questions from Exercise 7 in random order (e.g., *Do you like to go shopping? I like to go shopping for clothes because I like to try new styles.*). Call out *turn* every minute or so. Students in the inner ring should move one space clockwise. Students now interview their new partners. Make sure students look at each other when they're talking.

10.4 Gerund after Preposition

 10-15 mins

1. Have students cover up grammar chart **10.4** on pages 327–328. Have students go back to the reading on pages 320–322. Say: *Try to find gerunds that follow prepositions. Underline the preposition and the gerund* (e.g., *succeed in finding, worried about saying or doing,* etc.).

2. Then have students look at grammar chart **10.4**. Say: *A gerund can follow a preposition. It's important to choose the correct preposition after a verb or an adjective.*

3. Review the verb + preposition combinations. Go over the common combinations. Check that students understand the meanings of the expressions.

4. Review the adjective + preposition combinations. Go over the common combinations. Check that students understand the meanings of the expressions.

5. Direct students to the Language Notes. Review the verbs that can also be followed by an infinitive. Tell students that the sentences have the same meaning. Point out that *to* does not always indicate an infinitive. Sometimes *to* is a preposition preceding a gerund. Compare the sentences.

6. Remind students to look at Appendix H for a list of verbs and adjectives followed by a preposition.

Presentation Idea

After students have gone through the chart, have them write four sentences with prepositions and gerunds. Say: *Write two sentences with an adjective followed by a preposition and gerund, and two sentences with a verb followed by a preposition and gerund.*

EXERCISE 8
Answers will vary.

10-15 mins

1. Say: *You're going to ask your partner some questions.* Have students read the direction line. Go over the example. Have two volunteers model the example.

2. First have students complete the questions. Remind them to review grammar chart **10.4** on pages 327–328 if necessary. Then have students take turns asking and answering the questions in pairs. Monitor pair work. Give help as needed.

Practice Idea: Speaking

Have students discuss their statements as a class. Do many students have the same interests or fears?

EXERCISE 9
Answers will vary.

10-15 mins

1. Say: *Complete these statements and make them true for you.* Have students read the direction line. Go over the example. Have a volunteer model the example.

2. Have students complete Exercise 9 individually. Remind them to review grammar chart **10.4** on pages 327–328 if necessary. Then have students compare answers in pairs. Monitor pair work. Give help as needed.

EXERCISE 10

Answers will vary.

10-15
mins

1. Ask: *How have things changed for you since coming to live in the U.S.? Do you have the same dreams and worries? Or have things changed a lot for you?* Have students read the direction line. Go over the examples in the book.

2. Have students complete Exercise 10 individually. Remind them to review grammar chart **10.4** on pages 327–328 if necessary. Then have students compare answers in pairs. Monitor pair work. Give help as needed. Have volunteers share some of their sentences with the class.

> **Practice Idea: Speaking**
>
> Do a class survey. How many students feel they have changed a lot? Ask volunteers to explain.

10.5 Gerund in Adverbial Phrase ≡★

5-10
mins

1. Have students look at grammar chart **10.5** on page 330. Say: *We can use a gerund in an adverbial phrase that begins with a preposition:* before, by, after, without, *etc.* Review the example sentences.

2. Ask: *How can you tell the difference between a gerund in an adverbial phrase and a gerund after a preposition?* (The preposition in an adverbial phrase is not preceded by a verb or an adjective.)

3. Have students go back to the reading on pages 320–322. Ask students to find all of the gerunds and adverbial phrases. Have them compare that construction with the gerunds after a preposition.

EXERCISE 11 ≡★

Answers will vary.

5-10
mins

1. Have students read the direction line. Go over the example. Ask: *What kind of words are we going to put on the blanks?* (gerunds)

---

2. Have students complete Exercise 11 individually. Remind them to review grammar chart **10.5** on page 330 if necessary. Then go over the answers as a class.

CD 3
TR 19

EXERCISE 12

ANSWERS: Answers may vary. Possible answers:
1. making OR scheduling; **2.** about; **3.** giving OR leaving OR making; **4.** answering; **5.** working; **6.** working; **7.** at; **8.** working; **9.** talking; **10.** about; **11.** improving; **12.** taking; **13.** of; **14.** looking OR searching; **15.** looking OR searching; **16.** in; **17.** finding OR locating

5-10
mins

1. Have students read the direction line. Go over the example in the book. Ask: *What are we going to write on the blanks?* (gerunds) *What are we going to write if there are two blanks?* (a preposition and a gerund)

2. Have students complete Exercise 12 individually. Remind them to review grammar chart **10.5** on page 330 if necessary. Then have students compare answers in pairs. Play the audio and go over the answers as a class.

> **Practice Idea: Listening**
>
> To provide practice with listening skills, have students close their books and listen to the audio. Repeat the audio as needed. Say: *You're going to hear two friends talking about searching for jobs in the U.S.* Ask comprehension questions, such as: *Who does his friend suggest he talk to about finding a job?* (a job counselor) *What is the job counselor going to help him with?* (preparing for job interviews) *What does he dislike doing?* (talking about himself) Then have students open their books and complete Exercise 12.

> **Practice Idea: Speaking**
>
> Have students practice the conversation in pairs. Ask volunteers to role-play all or part of the conversation in front of the class.

10.6 Infinitives—An Overview

5-10 mins

1. Have students cover up grammar chart **10.6** on page 332. Create a matching exercise on the board:

   1. *I want to find a job.*
   2. *I want you to help me.*
   3. *I'm happy to help you.*
   4. *It's important to write a good résumé.*
   5. *He went to a counselor to get good advice.*

   a. *An infinitive follows certain expressions with it.*
   b. *An object can be added before an infinitive.*
   c. *An infinitive is used after certain verbs.*
   d. *An infinitive is used to show purpose.*
   e. *An infinitive can follow certain adjectives.*

   Say: *Match the explanation to the sentence.*
   (**Matching Answers: 1.** c; **2.** b; **3.** e; **4.** a; **5.** d)

2. Then have students look at grammar chart **10.6**. Say: *Compare your work with the chart.* Go over any trouble spots with the class.

Tips on Writing a Résumé

READING

1. Have students look briefly at the résumé. Ask: *Do you have a résumé? Does it look like this résumé? How is it different? What are résumés like in your native country?*

2. Have students look at the title of the reading. Ask: *What is the reading about?* Have students use the title and the résumé to make predictions about the reading.

3. Preteach any vocabulary words your students may not know, such as *relevant*, *hire*, and *liar*.

Reading Glossary

hire: to pay for the services of; employ
liar: a person who doesn't tell the truth
relevant: loosely connected; appropriate

BEFORE YOU READ

 5-10 mins

1. Have students discuss the questions in pairs.
2. Ask for a few volunteers to share their answers with the class.

Reading

 CD 3 TR 20

10-15 mins

1. Have students first read the text silently. Tell them to pay special attention to infinitives. Then play the audio and have students read along silently.

2. Check students' comprehension. Ask questions such as: *Do employers want to see every job you've ever had on a résumé?* (Not necessarily. They want to see only relevant work.) *What kind of verbs should you use in a résumé?* (action verbs) *What should you check your résumé for?* (errors) *Should you put personal information about yourself or your family in the résumé?* (no)

Practice Idea: Listening

To practice listening skills, have students first listen to the audio alone. Ask a few comprehension questions. Repeat the audio if necessary. Then have them open their books and read along as they listen to the audio.

Context Note

The American résumé is different from the European CV or *curriculum vitae*. The résumé is a brief marketing tool that summarizes a person's professional career and educational background. It's usually a one-page or two-page document. The CV is a formal package that describes in detail a person's professional and educational background. It is often printed on high-quality paper and bound. Supporting documents (such as publications) are often included in the package. The résumé does not contain any personal information (e.g., marital status) about the applicant, whereas the CV will often include personal information and a photo of the applicant.

10.7 Infinitive as Subject ⚊★

10-15 mins

1. Have students look at grammar chart **10.7** on page 334. Say: *Like gerunds, infinitives can also be used as the subject of a sentence.* Go over the example sentences.

2. Review the list of adjectives you can use before the infinitive as a subject.

3. Review the list of nouns you can use before the infinitive as a subject.

4. Say: *To make a statement that is true for a particular person, use* for + *noun/object pronoun.* Go over the example sentences.

5. Point out that there is no difference in meaning between an infinitive and a gerund when used as a subject.

Presentation Idea

Have students go back to the reading on pages 332–333. Say: *Underline the* it *expressions and all the infinitives used as subjects.*

EXERCISE 13

ANSWERS: Answers may vary. Possible answers:
1. to write OR to list; **2.** to check; **3.** to practice; **4.** to look; **5.** to include OR to put; **6.** to describe; **7.** to write OR prepare

10-15 mins

1. Have students read the direction line. Go over the example in the book.

2. Have students complete Exercise 13 individually. Remind them to review grammar chart **10.7** on page 334 if necessary. Then have students compare answers in pairs. Monitor pair work. Give help as needed. Have volunteers share some of their sentences.

EXERCISE 14
Answers will vary.

10-15 mins

1. Have students read the direction line. Go over the examples in the book. Ask a volunteer to identify the object in one of the example sentences.

2. Have students complete Exercise 14 individually. Remind them to review grammar chart **10.7** on page 334 if necessary. Then have students compare answers in pairs. Monitor pair work. Give help as needed. Have volunteers share some of their sentences.

Practice Idea: Speaking

Have students discuss their statements in groups. Ask: *What statements does everyone agree with? What statements does everyone disagree with?*

EXERCISE 15

ANSWERS: 1. It's (not) important for me to get a college degree. **2.** It's (not) important for me to find an interesting job. **3.** It's (not) important for me to have a car. **4.** It's (not) important for me to speak English well. **5.** It's (not) important for me to read and write English well. **6.** It's (not) important for me to study American history. **7.** It's (not) important for me to become and American citizen. **8.** It's (not) important for me to own a computer. **9.** It's (not) important for me to have a cell phone. **10.** It's (not) important for me to make a lot of money.

10-15 mins

1. Say: *In this exercise, you're going to say what's important for you to do or have.* Go over the example in the book. Ask a volunteer to model the example.

2. Have students complete Exercise 15 in pairs. Remind them to review grammar chart **10.7** on page 334 if necessary. Monitor pair work. Give help as needed. Have volunteers share some of their sentences.

Practice Idea: Speaking

Use the items from Exercise 15 and do a class survey. What's important to the majority of the students? What's not important?

EXERCISE 16
Answers will vary.

10-15 mins

1. Have students read the direction line. Go over the example in the book. Ask a volunteer to model the example.

2. Have students complete Exercise 16 individually. Remind them to review grammar chart **10.7** on page 334 if necessary. Then have students compare answers in pairs. Monitor pair work. Give help as needed.

Practice Idea: Speaking

Have students discuss their answers to Exercise 16 in groups.

EXERCISE 17
Answers will vary.

10-15 mins

1. Have students read the direction line. Go over the examples in the book. Say: *In this exercise, try to use both infinitives and gerunds.* Ask: *Is there a gerund in one of the example sentences?* (Yes, learning.)

2. Have students complete Exercise 17 individually. Remind them to review grammar chart **10.7** on page 334 if necessary. Then have students compare answers in pairs. Monitor pair work. Give help as needed. Have volunteers share some of their sentences.

Practice Idea: Writing

Have students work in pairs to create a pamphlet for new students. Ask students to use infinitives and gerunds as subjects. Display pamphlets around the room.

10.8 Infinitive after Adjective

5-10 mins

Have students look at grammar chart **10.8** on page 336. Say: *Some adjectives can be followed by an infinitive.* Go over the example sentences and the list of adjectives. Remind students that these infinitives are not subjects with *it* expressions.

EXERCISE 18
CD 3
TR 21

ANSWERS: 1. to go; **2.** to have; **3.** to have OR to get; **4.** to help; **5.** to have

10-15 mins

1. Say: *In this conversation, two women are talking about an upcoming job interview.* Have students read the direction line. Go over the example.

2. Have students complete Exercise 18 individually. Remind them to review grammar chart **10.8** on page 336 if necessary. Then have students compare answers in pairs. Play the audio and go over the answers as a class.

Practice Idea: Listening

To provide practice with listening skills, have students close their books and listen to the audio. Repeat the audio as needed. Say: *In this conversation, two women are talking about an upcoming job interview.* Ask comprehension questions, such as: *Is person A nervous about the job interview?* (yes) *Is person B going to go into the interview with her?* (No. She said that she'll wait in the car.) *Is person A going to see a job counselor?* (No. She doesn't have time.) Then have students open their books and complete Exercise 18.

Practice Idea: Speaking

Have students practice the conversation in pairs. Ask volunteers to role-play the conversation in front of the class.

EXERCISE 19
Answers will vary.

10-15 mins

1. Say: *Make statements that are true for you.* Go over the example. Have a volunteer model the example.

2. Have students complete Exercise 19 individually. Remind them to review grammar chart **10.8** on page 336 if necessary. Then have students compare answers in pairs. Monitor pair work. Give help as needed.

Practice Idea: Speaking

Have volunteers share some of their answers from Exercise 19 with the class.

10.9 Infinitive after Verb

5-10 mins

1. Have students cover up grammar chart **10.9** on page 338. Then have students go back to the reading on pages 332–333. Ask: *What verbs are followed by an infinitive? Make a list.*

2. Have students look at grammar chart **10.9**. Ask: *Are the verbs from the reading on the list in the chart?* Go over the examples.

3. Direct students to the Pronunciation Note. Model the pronunciation of the *to (ta)* in infinitives. Model the pronunciation of *want to (wanna)*. Have students listen as you pronounce all the sentences in the chart.

EXERCISE 20

ANSWERS: 1. Do you plan to look for a job?
2. Do you expect to make a lot of money at your next job? **3.** Do you like to work with computers?
4. Do you prefer to work the second shift?
5. Do you need to see a job counselor? **6.** Do you hope to become rich some day? **7.** Do you like to work with people? **8.** Do you try to keep up with changes in technology? **9.** Do you want to learn another language?

10-15 mins

1. Have students read the direction line. Go over the example in the book. Say: *Give a short answer to the questions.*

2. Have students complete Exercise 20 in pairs. Remind them to review grammar chart **10.9** on page 338 if necessary. Monitor pair work. Give help as needed.

Practice Idea: Speaking

Create two rings of students. Have half of the students stand in an outer ring around the classroom. Have the other half stand in an inner ring, facing the outer ring. Instruct students to ask and answer questions from Exercise 20. Tell students to answer questions with a short answer. Call out *turn* every minute or so. Students in the inner ring should move one space clockwise. Students now interview their new partners. Make sure students look at each other when they're talking.

Context Note

Job interviews are stressful, which is why it's best to be prepared and to practice beforehand. There are many books with lists of possible questions an interviewer might ask and helpful hints on how to best answer the questions. Here are some typical interview questions:

What are your strengths and weaknesses?

Why did you go into this field?

What is success and how do you measure it?

Tell me about a situation at your last job that you feel you handled well.

Tell me about a situation at your last job that you feel you handled badly.

Why do you want to work here?

Why should we hire you?

EXERCISE 21
Answers will vary.

10-15 mins

1. Have students read the direction line. Go over the examples in the book. Ask: *What tenses are these sentences in?* (The first is in the simple present. The second is in the present continuous.) *You can write these sentences in any tense.*

2. Have students complete Exercise 21 individually. Remind them to review grammar chart **10.9** on page 338 if necessary. Then have students compare sentences in pairs. Monitor pair work. Have volunteers share some of their sentences with the class.

EXERCISE 22
Answers will vary.

10-15 mins

1. Have students read the direction line. Model #1 for the students (e.g., *I like to stay home on the weekends because I'm never home during the week. I'm always at work.*).

2. Have students complete Exercise 22 individually. Remind them to review grammar chart **10.9** on page 338 if necessary. Then have students discuss their answers in groups or as a class.

10.10 Gerund or Infinitive after Verb ≡★

5-10 mins

1. Have students look at grammar chart **10.10** on page 340. Say: *Some verbs can take an infinitive or a gerund without changing meaning.* Review the list of verbs and go over the example sentences.

2. Direct students to the Language Notes. Say: *Try has different meanings when used with an infinitive or with a gerund. With an infinitive, try means to make an effort. With a gerund, it means to use a different technique when what you're presently doing isn't working.* Go over the examples in the chart.

EXERCISE 23 ≡★
Answers will vary.

5-10 mins

1. Have students read the direction line. Go over the examples. Say: *Complete some sentences with a gerund and others with an infinitive.*

2. Have students complete Exercise 23 individually. Remind them to review grammar chart **10.10** on page 340 if necessary. Go over the answers as a class.

10.11 Object before Infinitive ≡★

5-10 mins

1. Have students look at grammar chart **10.11** on page 341. Say: *We can use an object after*

the verb and before the infinitive. Go over the example sentences. Review object pronouns if necessary.

2. Say: *We often use objects after the verbs on the list.* Go over the verbs.

3. Point out that the verb *help* can be followed by an object + base form or an object + infinitive. Go over the example sentences.

EXERCISE 24 ≡★
CD 3 TR 22

ANSWERS: 1. him; **2.** to give; **3.** us; **4.** to go; **5.** us; **6.** to eat; **7.** you; **8.** to eat; **9.** her; **10.** to say; **11.** you; **12.** to ask; **13.** them; **14.** to work; **15.** them; **16.** to come; **17.** (to) leave; **18.** us; **19.** to do

10-15 mins

1. Say: *In this conversation, two friends are talking about their jobs.* Have students read the direction line. Go over the examples.

2. Have students complete Exercise 24 individually. Remind them to review grammar chart **10.11** on page 341 if necessary. Then have students compare answers in pairs. Play the audio and go over the answers as a class.

EXERCISE 25

ANSWERS: 1. The teacher (wants us/doesn't want us) to talk to another student during a test. **2.** The teacher (wants us/doesn't want us) to study before a test. **3.** The teacher (wants us/doesn't want us) to copy another student's homework in class. **4.** The teacher (wants us/doesn't want us) to learn English. **5.** The teacher (wants us/doesn't want us) to speak our native language in class. **6.** The teacher (wants us/doesn't want us) to improve our pronunciation. **7.** The teacher (wants us/doesn't want us) to talk about our native countries in class. **8.** The teacher (wants us/doesn't want us) to sit in rows.

10-15 mins

1. Have students read the direction line. Go over the examples.

2. Have students complete Exercise 25 individually. Remind them to review grammar chart **10.11** on page 341 if necessary. Have students compare answers in pairs. Monitor pair work. Have volunteers share some of their sentences.

EXERCISE 26

ANSWERS: 1. I (don't) expect him/her to correct my homework. **2.** I (don't) expect him/her to give tests. **3.** I (don't) expect him/her to speak my native language. **4.** I (don't) expect him/her to help me after class. **5.** I (don't) expect him/her to come to class on time. **6.** I (don't) expect him/her to pass all students. **7.** I (don't) expect him/her to know a lot about my native country. **8.** I (don't) expect him/her to answer my questions in class. **9.** I (don't) expect him/her to teach us American history. **10.** I (don't) expect him/her to pronounce my name correctly.

10-15 mins

1. Have students read the direction line. Go over the examples.

2. Have students complete Exercise 26 in pairs. Remind them to review grammar chart **10.11** on page 341 if necessary. Monitor pair work. Have volunteers share some of their sentences.

EXERCISE 27
Answers will vary.

10-15 mins

1. Have students read the direction line. Go over the examples. Have a volunteer model the activity.

2. Have students complete Exercise 27 individually. Remind them to review grammar chart **10.11** on page 341 if necessary. Then have students compare answers in pairs. Monitor pair work.

10.12 Infinitive to Show Purpose ≡★

5-10 mins

Have students look at grammar chart **10.12** on page 343. Say: *We use the infinitive to show purpose.* Go over the example sentences. Explain that you can also say *in order to* to show purpose. Go over the example sentences.

EXERCISE 28

ANSWERS: Answers may vary. Possible answers: 1. to make OR to schedule OR to set up; **2.** to earn more money; **3.** to look for OR to search for; **4.** to write OR to help you with; **5.** to get to OR go to; **6.** to send; **7.** to get OR to find, to get experience; **8.** to talk OR to chat, to make OR to receive; **9.** to mail; **10.** to request OR to receive OR to obtain OR to get; **11.** to say

10-15 mins

1. Have students read the direction line. Go over the example. Have a volunteer do #1.

2. Have students complete Exercise 28 individually. Remind them to review grammar

chart **10.12** on page 343 if necessary. Then have students compare answers in pairs. Monitor pair work.

Rita's Story **READING**

1. Have students look at the illustrations. Ask: *What's going on in these pictures?* (In the first picture, a woman is wearing traditional Indian clothing. She's sitting in a comfortable chair. She looks happy. In the second picture, the same woman is vacuuming. It looks like she has a name tag on her shirt. This might mean that she works in the cleaning business.)

2. Have students look at the title of the reading. Ask: *What is the reading about?* Have students use the title and pictures to make predictions about the reading.

3. Preteach any vocabulary words your students may not know, such as *shift* and *impolite.*

Reading Glossary

impolite: showing bad manners; rude
shift: a segment of work time

BEFORE YOU READ

5-10 mins

1. Have students discuss the questions in pairs. If possible put students from different cultures together.

2. Ask for a few volunteers to share their answers with the class.

Reading

CD 3
TR 23

10-15 mins

1. Have students first read the text silently. Tell them to pay special attention to *used to, be used to,* and *get used to.* Then play the audio and have students read along silently.

2. Check students' comprehension. Ask questions such as: *Did Rita learn English before she came to the U.S.?* (Yes. But she studied British English.) *What did she use to do in India?* (She was an elementary school teacher.) *What is she doing now?* (She cleans rooms in a hotel.) *Who prepares dinner at her house?* (her husband) *Does Rita like wearing a uniform?* (No. In India, she liked to wear traditional clothes.)

Practice Idea: Listening

To practice listening skills, have students first listen to the audio alone. Ask a few comprehension questions. Repeat the audio if necessary. Then have them open their books and read along as they listen to the audio.

Context Note

Over the years, workplace attire has become more and more casual. However, some fields, such as law or finance, still maintain a more formal, conservative dress code. In corporate New York, for example, employees are expected to wear dark, conservative suits. Some companies may relax the code one day of the week, such as Fridays, and allow employees to wear very casual attire. Often, these days are known as "casual Fridays" or "dress-down days."

10.13 *Used To vs. Be Used To*

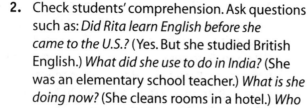
10-15 mins

1. Have students cover up grammar chart **10.13** on page 346. Write the following on the board:

   1. *Rita used to be an elementary school teacher.*
   2. *I'm used to working in the day, not at night.*
   3. *If you emigrate to the U.S., you have to get used to many new things.*

   Ask: *Which sentence means* to be accustomed to (sentence 2), *which means* to become accustomed to (sentence 3), *and which sentence means that something was a past habit or custom* (sentence 1)?

2. Have students look at grammar chart **10.13**. Say: Used to + *the base form means that an activity was a habit or custom in the past.* Be used to + *a gerund or a noun means that you're comfortable with that thing or activity.* Get used to + *a gerund or a noun means* become accustomed to something.

3. Review how to form the negative of each expression.

EXERCISE 29

Answers will vary.

10-15 mins

1. Have students read the direction line. Ask: *Are we going to use* be used to + *gerund or noun, or are we going to use* used to + *the base form?* (*used to* + base form) Go over the examples in the book. Model the exercise for the class.

2. Have students complete Exercise 29 individually. Remind them to review grammar chart **10.13** on page 346 if necessary. Then have students compare statements in pairs. Monitor pair work. Have a few volunteers share some of their statements with the class.

EXERCISE 30

Answers will vary.

10-15 mins

1. Ask: *How did you use to do things in your native country?* Have students read the direction line. Go over the example in the book. Have a volunteer model the exercise.

2. Have students complete Exercise 30 individually. Remind them to review grammar chart **10.13** on page 346 if necessary. Then have students compare sentences in pairs. Monitor pair work. Give help as needed. Have a few volunteers share some of their statements with the class.

EXERCISE 31

ANSWERS: 1. sitting; **2.** calling; **3.** writing; **4.** wearing; **5.** working; **6.** paying OR spending; **7.** sitting OR remaining seated

10-15 mins

1. Have students read the direction line. Go over the example in the book. Explain that this is about a student who wrote about things that are new for her in an American classroom. Ask: *In the example, is the person comfortable or uncomfortable taking multiple-choice tests?* (not comfortable) Say: *Now you say what you're used to—essay tests or multiple-choice tests.* Have a volunteer say what he or she is used to.

2. Have students complete the exercise individually. Remind them to review grammar chart **10.13** on page 346 if necessary. Then have students tell their partners what they're used to. Monitor pair work. Give help as needed.

EXERCISE 32

Answers will vary.

10-15 mins

1. Say: *In this exercise, you're going to write about what you've had to become accustomed to—or what you've had to get comfortable with—in the U.S., or in a new town or school.* Have students read the direction line. Go over the examples. Model the exercise for the class.

2. Have students complete Exercise 32 individually. Remind them to review grammar chart **10.13** on page 346 if necessary. Then have students compare sentences with a partner. Monitor pair work. Give help as needed.

EXERCISE 33

Answers will vary.

10-15 mins

1. Ask: *What are you used to doing?* Have students read the direction line. Go over the example. Model the activity for the class.

2. Have students complete Exercise 33 by asking and answering questions in pairs (e.g., *What kind of work are you used to? I'm used to restaurant work. I've worked in a lot of restaurants.*). Remind them to review grammar chart **10.13** on page 346 if necessary. Monitor pair work. Give help as needed.

EXERCISE 34

CD 3
TR 24

ANSWERS: 1. work; **2.** speak; **3.** I'm; **4.** get; **5.** live; **6.** used; **7.** used to; **8.** used to; **9.** work; **11.** think

10-15 mins

1. Say: *In this conversation, two friends are talking about what they're used to and not used to.* Have students read the direction line. Go over the example. Have a volunteer do the first item.

2. Have students complete Exercise 34 individually. Remind them to review grammar chart **10.13** on page 346 if necessary. Then have students compare answers in pairs. Play the audio and go over the answers as a class.

Practice Idea: Listening

To provide practice with listening skills, have students close their books and listen to the audio. Tell students: *In this conversation, two friends are talking about what they're used to and not used to.* Repeat the audio as needed. Ask comprehension questions, such as: *What does person B do during the day?* (sleep) *What does person B do during the night?* (work) *Does person B like working the night shift?* (no) Then have students open their books and complete Exercise 34.

Summary of Lesson 10

20-30 mins

1. **Gerunds** Have students cover up the summary on page 350. Create a matching exercise on the board. On one side, write the example sentences. On the other side, write the explanations in random order. Ask students to match the sentences with the explanations. If necessary, have students review:

   10.1 Gerunds—An Overview (p. 320)
   10.2 Gerund as Subject (p. 323)
   10.3 Gerund after Verb (p. 325)
   10.4 Gerund after Preposition (pp. 327–328)
   10.5 Gerund in Adverbial Phrase (p. 330)

2. **Infinitives** Have students cover up the summary on page 350. Create a matching exercise on the board. On one side, write the example sentences. On the other side, write the explanations in random order. Ask students to match the sentences with the explanations.

   Say: *Now look at the summary on page 350. Compare your work with the chart on infinitives.* Go over any trouble spots. If necessary, have students review:

   10.6 Infinitives—An Overview (p. 332)
   10.7 Infinitive as Subject (p. 334)
   10.8 Infinitive after Adjective (p. 336)
   10.9 Infinitive after Verb (p. 338)
   10.10 Gerund or Infinitive after Verb (p. 340)
   10.11 Object before Infinitive (p. 341)
   10.12 Infinitive to Show Purpose (p. 343)

3. **Gerund or Infinitive—No Difference in Meaning** Have students look at the summary on page 350. Remind students that some verbs can take an infinitive and a gerund with no change in meaning. Ask students to try to list some of the verbs that take both. Go over the example sentences. If necessary, have students review:

   10.10 Gerund or Infinitive after Verb (p. 340)

4. **Gerund or Infinitive—Difference in Meaning** Have students look at the summary on page 350. Review *used to* + base form; *be used to* + gerund or noun; and *get used to* + gerund or noun. If necessary, have students review:

   10.13 *Used To* vs. *Be Used To* (p. 346)

Editing Advice

15-20 mins

Have students close their books. Write the first few sentences without editing marks or corrections on the board. For example:

1. *He read the whole book without use a dictionary.*
2. *She insisted in driving me home.*

Ask students to correct each sentence and provide a rule or an explanation for each correction. This activity can be done individually, in pairs, or as a class. After students have corrected each sentence, tell them to turn to pages 351–352. Say: *Now compare your work with the Editing Advice in the book.* Have students read through all the advice.

Editing Quiz

ANSWERS: 1. want to be; **2.** me to study; **3.** C; **4.** starting; **5.** Studying; **6.** to become; **7.** C; **8.** C; **9.** advised me to take; **10.** for; **11.** I used to; **12.** helping; **13.** to come; **14.** it's; **15.** C; **16.** C; **17.** C

10-15 mins

1. Tell students they are going to put the editing advice into practice. Have students read the direction line. Ask: *Do all the shaded words and phrases have mistakes?* (no) Go over the examples with the class. Then do #1 together.

2. Have students complete the quiz individually. Then have them compare answers with a partner before checking answers as a class.

3. For the items students had difficulties with, have them go back and find the relevant grammar chart and review it. Monitor and give help as necessary.

Lesson 10 Test/Review

20-30 mins

Use the Assessment CD-ROM with Exam*View*®, Online Workbook, and Web site for additional practice, review, and assessment materials.

PART 1

ANSWERS: Answers may vary. Possible answers: 1. doing; **2.** being; **3.** to work; **4.** to be OR to spend time; **5.** to take OR to bring; **6.** to help; **7.** doing;

8. going OR to go; **9.** to take; **10.** working; **11.** working; **12.** helping; **13.** to help; **14.** to have OR to work at; **15.** to be; **16.** returning OR going back; **17.** talking; **18.** watching; **19.** reading; **20.** to learn; **21.** hearing OR saying; **22.** making; **23.** dancing; **24.** shopping OR to shop

1. Part 1 may be used as an in-class test to assess student performance, in addition to the Assessment CD-ROM with Exam*View*®. Have students read the direction line. Explain that this is a conversation between Molly and her friend about Molly's work situation. Collect for assessment.

2. If necessary, have students review Lesson 10.

PART 2

ANSWERS: 1. of OR about; **2.** at; **3.** about; **4.** X; **5.** by; **6.** for; **7.** X; **8.** to; **9.** for; **10.** to

1. Part 2 may also be used as an in-class test to assess student performance, in addition to the Assessment CD-ROM with Exam*View*®. Have students read the direction line. Ask: *What are you going to write on the blanks?* (a preposition or *X* if no preposition is needed) Collect for assessment.

2. If necessary, have students review Lesson 10.

Expansion

These expansion activities provide opportunities for students to interact with one another and further develop their speaking and writing skills. Encourage students to use grammar from this lesson whenever possible.

CLASSROOM ACTIVITIES

10-15 mins per activity

1. Have students brainstorm ideas first and then discuss their likes and dislike in small groups.

2. Have students complete the chart individually. Then have students discuss their answers in groups or with the whole class.

3. Quickly brainstorm with students the types of questions that they may be asked during an interview. Ask volunteers to share experiences from interviews they may have had.

TALK ABOUT IT

15-20
mins

Have students discuss each topic in pairs, in groups, or as a class.

1. Ask students to talk about where they looked (ads in newspapers, on the Internet, window signs, etc.), how long they looked before they got an interview, and if they had to fill out an application.

2. Ask students to discuss the physical facility (the plant, the building, the store, etc.) and the social environment.

3. Have students talk about the advantages and disadvantages of the professions they're interested in.

4. Ask students to talk about the professions they are least interested in and to be specific about the reasons. Do they have experience in this profession, or do they know anyone who is in the profession?

WRITE ABOUT IT

20-30
mins

1. Ask students to bring in a résumé and cover letter(s) that they might already have. Provide samples of good résumés and cover letters. Have students bring in advertisements for jobs they are interested in applying for. Have them write their résumés and cover letters individually. Have students exchange résumés and cover letters with a partner. Collect for assessment.

2. Elicit from students jobs that they wouldn't like to have. Choose one of them and have students say why it wouldn't be a good job to have. Write their ideas on the board. Then have students choose another item from the list and write their paragraphs individually. Collect for assessment and/or have students share their paragraphs with the group.

3. Elicit from students jobs that they would like to have. Choose one of them and have students say why it would be a good job to have. Write their ideas on the board. Then have students choose another item from the list and write their paragraphs individually. Collect for assessment and/or have students share their paragraphs with the group.

Practice Idea: Speaking

Have students create a presentation on the profession they're most interested in. Ask them to include as many facts about the profession as possible (e.g., current needs for those professionals, salary ranges, the level and kind of education needed, etc.).

4. Have students read the direction line and the sample paragraph. Then have them write a list of ideas about the job they're going to write about. Have them talk about the job with a partner. Then have them write their compositions. Tell students to talk about at least three things they liked and three things they didn't like about the job. Collect for assessment and/or have students share their compositions with the group.

Practice Idea: Writing

Have students exchange first drafts with a partner. Ask students to help their partners edit their drafts. Refer students to the Editing Advice on pages 351–352.

INTERNET ACTIVITIES

1. Tell students to type career in a search engine and see how many results (or "hits") come up. Have them report back to the class.

2. Have students find some career counseling Web sites. Tell them to find a sample résumé in their field or close to their field. Have them print it out and bring it to class. Have them compare the résumés they found in groups.

3. Tell students to get information on one or more of the following topics from one of the career counseling Web sites they found:

- How to write a cover letter
- How to find a career counselor

- How to plan for your interview
- How to network
- What questions to ask an interviewer

Have them bring the information to class and discuss it in groups.

4. Have students find out if the local newspaper has a Web site. If it does, tell them to find the Help Wanted section of this newspaper and bring job listings that interest them into class. Have them discuss what they found in groups.

Lesson 11

Lesson Overview

GRAMMAR

1. Briefly review what students learned in the previous lesson. Ask: *What did we study in Lesson 10?* (gerunds and infinitives)

2. Ask: *What are we going to study in this lesson?* (adjective clauses) *Can anyone give me an example of an adjective clause?* (e.g., *This is the book <u>that I bought yesterday</u>.*) Have students give examples. Write the examples on the board.

CONTEXT

1. Ask: *What will we learn about in this lesson?* (finding old friends and making new friends) Activate students' prior knowledge. Ask: *Have you ever gotten in contact with an old friend you haven't seen in a long time? How do you make new friends? Have you ever used an online dating agency?*

2. Have students share their knowledge and personal experiences.

Presentation Ideas

The topic for this lesson can be enhanced with the following items:

1. A high school yearbook
2. Pages printed from social networking Web sites and online people-finding services

11.1 Adjective Clauses—An Overview ≡★

1. Have students cover up grammar chart **11.1** on page 358. Write the following on the board:

   Do you know your new neighbors?

   Do you know the people who live next door to you?

5–10 mins

Ask: *Which sentence has the adjective clause?* (the second sentence) *What is* new? (It's an adjective.) *Does the adjective come before or after the noun?* (before) *Where does the adjective clause come?* (after the noun)

2. Then have students look at grammar chart **11.1**. Review the example sentences in the chart. Say: *Relative pronouns introduce an adjective clause. What are the relative pronouns that introduce these adjective clauses?* (who and that)

Finding Old Friends READING

1. Have students look at the photo. Ask: *What is a high school yearbook?* (a book for high school students that records important events) *Do you have one?*

2. Have students look at the title of the reading. Ask: *What is the reading about?* Have students use the title and photo to make predictions about the reading.

3. Preteach any vocabulary words your students may not know, such as *lose touch, emerge,* and *reunion.*

Reading Glossary

emerge: to appear
lose touch: no longer have communication with
reunion: a time when people who have something in common (college, family) get together again

BEFORE YOU READ

1. Have students discuss the questions in pairs.

5–10 mins 2. Ask for a few volunteers to share their answers with the class.

Reading ≡★

CD 4 TR 01

1. Have students first read the text silently. Tell them to pay special attention to adjective clauses. Then play the audio and have students read along silently.

10–15 mins

2. Check students' comprehension. Ask questions such as: *Why do Americans often lose touch with old friends?* (Americans move a lot during their lives.) *When do Americans typically get interested in their old friends?* (when they're older, after building families and careers) *How did people find old friends before the Internet?* (They went to libraries and looked in phonebooks from other towns, and they hired detectives.) *Do Americans still have class reunions?* (yes)

Practice Idea: Listening

To practice listening skills, have students first listen to the audio alone. Ask a few comprehension questions. Repeat the audio if necessary. Then have them open their books and read along as they listen to the audio.

Context Note

Americans are a mobile group of people. The 2000 census found that almost half of all Americans had moved since 1995. Although many Americans move a number of times in their lifetimes, some people are more mobile than others. Hispanics tend to move more than whites. Mobility varies from state to state. Nevada has a very transient population. More than 60 percent of its population resided in a different place in 2000 than in 1995. In 2000, 60 percent of the population was living in their hometowns. The states with the most homebodies are Louisiana, Pennsylvania, and Michigan.

EXERCISE 1

ANSWERS: 1. F; **2.** T; **3.** T; **4.** T; **5.** F; **6.** T

 1. Say: *This exercise is based on the reading on pages 358–359.* Have students read the direction line. Go over the example.

2. Have students complete Exercise 1 individually. Remind them to review grammar chart **11.1** on page 358 if necessary. Go over the answers as a class.

EXERCISE 2

ANSWERS: 1. that has the diplomas of the graduates; **2.** that has lists of students from various high schools in the U.S.; **3.** that they had in high school; **4.** who get married; **5.** who graduate from high school; **6.** that help people make connections with old friends

 1. Say: *In this exercise, you're going to go back to Exercise 1.* Have students read the direction line. Go over the example. Have a volunteer model the example.

2. Have students complete Exercise 2 individually. Remind them to review grammar chart **11.1** on page 358 if necessary. Then have students compare answers in pairs. Go over the answers as a class.

11.2 Relative Pronoun as Subject ≡★

 1. Have students look at grammar chart **11.2** on page 360. Say: *Who, that, and* which *can be the subject of the adjective clause.* Who *and* that *are used for people.* That *and* which *are used for things.* Go over the examples and explanations. Ask: *How do you know if the relative pronoun is the subject?* Point out the first example sentence and say: *If the relative pronoun can be replaced by a subject and made into a complete sentence, then the relative pronoun is acting as the subject of the clause.* Point out the second example sentence. Show students how to replace the relative pronoun with the subject to make a sentence.

2. Direct students to the Language Notes. Point out that *which* is not used as often as *that*. Explain that the verb in the adjective clause has to agree with the subject. Say: *If the subject is plural, the verb is plural. If the subject is singular, the verb is singular.*

EXERCISE 3 ≡★

ANSWERS: 1. that has; **2.** who (OR that) go; **3.** that helps; **4.** that specialize; **5.** that (OR who) plan

 1. Have students read the direction line. Go over the example. Ask: *Can we use* that *for people?* (yes)

2. Have students complete Exercise 3 individually. Remind them to review grammar chart **11.2** on page 360 if necessary. Go over the answers as a class.

EXERCISE 4

ANSWERS: Answers will vary. Answers may begin with: 1. who exercise; **2.** who uses; **3.** who are; **4.** that don't have; **5.** that is; **6.** who have; **7.** that have; **8.** that has; **9.** who have

 10-15 mins

1. Have students read the direction line. Go over the example. Model the exercise for the class (e.g., *People who work hard are often too tired to have fun.*).

2. Have students complete Exercise 4 individually. Remind them to review grammar chart **11.2** on page 360 if necessary. Have students compare answers in pairs. Monitor pair work. Give help as needed. Have volunteers share some of their sentences.

EXERCISE 5

Answers will vary.

 10-15 mins

1. Have students read the direction line. Go over the example. Model the example for the class.

2. Have students complete Exercise 5 individually. Remind them to review grammar chart **11.2** on page 360 if necessary. Then have students compare answers in pairs. Monitor pair work. Give help as needed.

11.3 Relative Pronoun as Object

 5-10 mins

1. Have students look at grammar chart **11.3** on page 362. Say: *Who, whom, that, and which can be the object of the adjective clause.* Go over the examples and explanations.

2. Direct students to the Language Notes. Point out that the relative pronoun is often not said when it is the object of the adjective clause. Explain that *whom* is considered more formal than *who. Who* is more common than *whom*.

EXERCISE 6

ANSWERS: 1. The high school I attended is in another city. **2.** The teachers I had in high school are all old now. **3.** We didn't have to buy the textbooks we used in high school. **4.** She married a man she met in college. **5.** The friends I've made in this country don't know much about my country.

1. Have students read the direction line. Go over the example. Say: *Remember, in these sentences the relative pronoun has been left out.*

2. Have students complete Exercise 6 individually. Remind them to review grammar chart **11.3** on page 362 if necessary. Go over the answers as a class.

EXERCISE 7

CD 4 TR 02

ANSWERS: Answers may vary. Possible answers: 1. we had; **2.** wrote (to you); **3.** wrote OR put;

4. they had OR I called; **5.** has; **6.** graduated from OR attended; **7.** went OR were; **8.** who; **9.** she OR who(m) she OR that she; **10.** she OR that she OR who(m) she; **11.** I've OR that I've OR who(m) I've; **12.** choose

10-15 mins

1. Say: *In this conversation, a mother and daughter are talking about how to contact old friends.* Have students read the direction line. Go over the example. Remind students that answers may vary.

2. Have students complete Exercise 7 individually. Remind them to review grammar chart **11.3** on page 362 if necessary. Then have students compare answers in pairs. Play the audio and go over possible answers as a class.

Practice Idea: Listening

To provide practice with listening skills, have students close their books and listen to the audio. Repeat the audio as needed. Say: *In this conversation, a mother and daughter are talking about how to contact old friends.* Ask comprehension questions, such as: *Who wants to contact an old friend?* (the mother) *Why didn't they keep in touch by e-mail?* (E-mail didn't exist when they were younger.) *Are everyone's names on the* Classmates.com *Web site?* (No. Only the people who add their names.) Then have students open their books and complete Exercise 7.

Practice Idea: Speaking

Have students practice the conversation in pairs. Ask volunteers to role-play all or part of the conversation in front of the class.

EXERCISE 8

CD 4
TR 03

ANSWERS: Answers may vary. Possible answers:
1. who(m) I've met OR that I've met; **2.** (that) you have; **3.** that include; **4.** you describe(d) OR you mention(ed); **5.** that have; **6.** that has; **7.** that are free; **8.** that you've given (to me) OR (that) you gave (to me); **9.** (that) you like OR you enjoy

10-15 mins

1. Say: *In this conversation, two people are talking about making new friends.* Have students read the direction line. Go over the example. Remind students that answers may vary.

2. Have students complete Exercise 8 individually. Remind them to review grammar chart **11.3** on page 362 if necessary. Then have students compare answers in pairs. Play the audio and go over possible answers as a class.

Practice Idea: Listening

To provide practice with listening skills, have students close their books and listen to the audio. Repeat the audio as needed. Say: *In this conversation, two people are talking about making new friends.* Ask comprehension questions, such as: *Why is person A lonely?* (Person A doesn't have enough friends in the United States.) *What are person A's interests?* (reading, meditating, going for quiet walks) *What are Americans interested in?* (parties, TV, sports, movies, going to restaurants) Then have students open their books and complete Exercise 8.

Practice Idea: Speaking

Have students practice the conversation in pairs. Ask volunteers to role-play all or part of the conversation in front of the class.

Practice Idea: Speaking

Have students work in pairs to create a similar conversation, making it true for them. Ask volunteers to perform their conversations in front of the class.

EXERCISE 9
Answers will vary.

10-15 mins

1. Have students read the direction line. Go over the examples. Have a volunteer complete #1.

2. Have students complete Exercise 9 in pairs. Remind them to review grammar chart **11.3** on page 362 if necessary. Go over the answers as a class.

Practice Idea: Speaking

On a small piece of paper, have students write down one word they'd like to have a classmate define. Put the words in a hat, and ask each student to draw a paper and try to define the word on the spot.

11.4 *Where* and *When*

5-10 mins

1. Have students cover up grammar chart **11.4** on page 366. Have students go back to the reading on pages 358–359. Say: *Look for the sentences in bold that have* where *and* when. *What do you think* where *and* when *mean in these sentences?* (*in that place* and *at that time*) Write students' answers on the board.

2. Then have students look at grammar chart **11.4**. Say: Where *means* in that place. Go over the example sentences. Explain that *where* can't be omitted.

3. Say: When *means* at that time. Point out that *when* can often be omitted. Go over the example sentences.

4. Direct students to the Punctuation Notes. Go over the examples and explanations.

🔊 EXERCISE 🔟

CD 4
TR 04

ANSWERS: 1. when; **2.** when; **3.** when; **4.** where; **5.** where; **6.** when

10-15 mins

1. Say: *In this conversation, a father is talking to his son about how he met his wife.* Have students read the direction line. Go over the example. Point out the picture of the man and the woman at the soda shop.

2. Have students complete Exercise 10 individually. Remind them to review grammar chart **11.4** on page 366 if necessary. Then have students compare answers in pairs. Play the audio and go over the answers as a class.

Practice Idea: Listening

To provide practice with listening skills, have students close their books and listen to the audio. Repeat the audio as needed. Say: *In this conversation, a father is talking to his son about how he met his wife.* Ask comprehension questions, such as: *Where did he meet his wife?* (in typing class) *Why doesn't his son know what a typewriter is?* (They're not used anymore.) *Where did they use to meet?* (in a soda shop) Then have students open their books and complete Exercise 10.

Practice Idea: Speaking

Have students practice the conversation in pairs. Then ask volunteers to role-play the conversation in front of the class.

Practice Idea: Speaking

Have students work in pairs to write a similar conversation about meeting a boyfriend, girlfriend, husband, or wife. Ask volunteers to role-play the conversation in front of the class.

11.5 Formal vs. Informal

5-10 mins

Have students look at grammar chart **11.5** on page 367. Say: *Most native speakers put a preposition at the end of an adjective clause. In very formal speech, the preposition comes before the relative pronoun. If you use this formal style, only* whom *and* which *are used.* Go over the example sentences.

EXERCISE 🔢

ANSWERS: 1. He found his friend with whom he served in the military. **2.** I can't find the friend for whom I was looking. **3.** The high school from which she graduated was torn down. **4.** Do you remember the teacher about whom I was talking? **5.** In high school, the activities in which I was interested were baseball and band.

1. Say: *You're going to make these sentences formal by using prepositions before* whom *and* which. Have students read the direction line. Go over the example.

2. Have students complete the exercise individually. Remind them to review grammar chart **11.5** on page 367 if necessary. Go over the answers as a class.

Social Networking in the Twenty-First Century READING

1. Have students look at the photo. Ask: *What's the woman doing?* (She's doing something on her computer. She's thinking about something.)

2. Have students look at the title of the reading. Ask: *What is the reading about?* Have students use the title and photo to make predictions about the reading.

3. Preteach any vocabulary words your students may not know, such as *member* and *hooked on*.

Reading Glossary

hooked on: very interested in something, addicted to something

member: someone who is part of a group or club

BEFORE YOU READ

1. Have students discuss the questions in pairs.
2. Ask for a few volunteers to share their answers with the class.

Reading ≡★

CD 4
TR 05

1. Have students first read the text silently. Tell them to pay special attention to adjective clauses beginning with *whose*. Then play the audio and have students read along silently.

2. Check students' comprehension. Ask questions such as: *Why did Mark Zuckerman start Facebook?* (so busy students could find out what their friends were doing and thinking) *What are some of the reasons people join social networking sites?* (to meet people with the same interests, share photos, hear about events from friends, share links) *How is Meetup different from Facebook?* (members actually get together in person, not just online)

DID YOU KNOW?

Have students read the information. Then ask them what they think the advantages and disadvantages might be having in having advertisers pay for the sites, not the members.

11.6 *Whose* + Noun ≡★

1. Have students look at grammar chart **11.6** on page 369. Say: Whose *is the possessive form of* who. *It substitutes for possessive pronouns or the possessive form of the noun.* Review the example sentences.

2. Direct students to the Language Note. Say: Who *is used for a person.* Whose *is used for possession or relationship.* Go over the example sentences. Review the Punctuation Note.

EXERCISE 12

ANSWERS: 1. schoolwork; **2.** members; **3.** kids; **4.** photos; **5.** friends

1. Have students read the direction line. Go over the example in the book.

2. Have students complete Exercise 12 individually. Remind them to review grammar chart **11.6** on page 369 if necessary. Go over answers as a class.

EXERCISE 13
Answers will vary.

1. Say: *Complete these statements so that they are true for you.* Have students read the direction line. Go over the example. Model the example for the students.

2. Have students complete the exercise individually. Remind them to review grammar chart **11.6** on page 369 if necessary. Then have students compare answers in pairs. Monitor pair work. Give help as needed.

EXERCISE 14

ANSWERS: **1.** who(m) OR that I can trust. **2.** who(m) OR that don't take school seriously. **3.** who OR that like to play soccer. **4.** whose members speak French very well. **5.** that (OR which) isn't crowded in the morning. **6.** that (OR which) meets near my house. **7.** that (OR which) I found on Meetup.com.

10-15 mins

1. Say: *These are people's responses to the question: What kind of friends would you like to meet?* Have students read the direction line. Go over the example.

2. Have students complete the exercise individually. Remind them to review grammar chart **11.6** on page 369 if necessary. Then have students compare answers in pairs. Go over the answers as a class.

EXERCISE 15

CD 4
TR 06

ANSWERS: Answers may vary. Possible answers:
1. who(m) OR that I met; **2.** name; **3.** where; **4.** who(m) OR that I'm marrying OR I marry; **5.** where; **6.** we spend OR (that) we('ll) have

10-15 mins

1. Say: *In this conversation, a man is talking to his friend about his upcoming wedding.* Have students read the direction line. Go over the example.

2. Have students complete Exercise 15 individually. Remind them to review grammar chart **11.6** on page 369 if necessary. Then have students compare their answers in pairs. Play the audio and go over the answers as a class.

Practice Idea: Speaking

Have students practice the conversation in pairs. Ask volunteers to role-play the conversation in front of the class.

Practice Idea: Listening

To provide practice with listening skills, have students close their books and listen to the audio. Repeat the audio as needed. Say: *In this conversation, a man is talking to his friend about his upcoming wedding.* Ask comprehension questions, such as: *Does person B know the woman person A is going to marry?* (no) *Where did person A meet his fiancée?* (online) *Why are they going to live in the U.S.?* (He's got a good job here.) Then have students open their books and complete Exercise 15.

EXERCISE 16

ANSWERS: **1.** (who[m]) I see; **2.** who would lend me money; **3.** who knows everything about me; **4.** who has different political opinions; **5.** who doesn't speak my native language; **6.** whose religious beliefs are different from mine; **7.** who lives far away; **8.** whose interests are the same as mine; **9.** where I can make many new friends easily; **10.** when it is easy to make friends

10-15 mins

1. Have students read the direction line. Go over the example in the book. Say: *After you finish completing the statements, say if you agree or disagree with them.*

2. Have students complete Exercise 16 individually. Remind them to review grammar chart **11.6** on page 369 if necessary. Then have students compare answers in pairs. Monitor pair work. Give help as needed.

Practice Idea: Speaking

Have students discuss the statements in groups. Then take a class vote on each statement: who agrees and who disagrees?

Summary of Lesson 11

15-20 mins

Adjective Clauses Have students cover up the summary on page 373. Create a fill-in exercise on the board:

who, whom, that, which, whose, where, when

1. *I have a friend _____ brother lives in Japan.*
2. *She came to the U.S. at a time _____ she was young enough to learn English easily.*
3. *The book _____ I'm reading is very exciting.*
4. *The person about _____ I'm talking is my cousin.*
5. *The club _____ I am a member of meets at the community center.*
6. *The man _____ arrived late took a seat in the back.*

Say: *Fill in the blanks with the appropriate word. Answers may vary.* Then have students name the sentences where the relative pronoun is a subject, an object, or an object of a preposition. Finally, have students point out the one formal sentence. Have students look at page 373 to check their answers.

If necessary, have students review:

11.1 Adjective Clauses—An Overview (p. 358)
11.2 Relative Pronoun as Subject (p. 360)
11.3 Relative Pronoun as Object (p. 362)
11.4 *Where* and *When* (p. 366)
11.5 Formal vs. Informal (p. 367)
11.6 *Whose* + Noun (p. 369)

Editing Advice

15-20 mins

Have students close their books. Write the first few sentences without editing marks or corrections on the board. For example:

1. *I know a woman what has ten cats.*
2. *I know a man has visited every state in the U.S.*

Ask students to correct each sentence and provide a rule or an explanation for each correction. This activity can be done individually, in pairs, or as a class. After students have corrected each sentence, tell them to turn to pages 373–374. Say: *Now compare your work with the Editing Advice in the book.* Have students read through all the advice.

Editing Quiz

ANSWERS: 1. C; **2.** who(m) OR that OR ø; **3.** with whom; **4.** C; **5.** her roommate gave me; **6.** that OR who; **7.** C; **8.** ø; **9.** people who OR that; **10.** whose; **11.** where; **12.** C; **13.** C; **14.** has; **15.** who's; **16.** a hard search (*a search that is hard* is also correct but would be better changed); **17.** Whoever OR A person who (OR that)

10-15 mins

1. Tell students they are going to put the editing advice into practice. Have students read the direction line. Ask: *Do all the shaded words and phrases have mistakes?* (no) Go over the examples with the class. Then do #1 together.

2. Have students complete the quiz individually. Then have them compare answers with a partner before checking answers as a class.

3. For the items students had difficulties with, have them go back and find the relevant grammar chart and review it. Monitor and give help as necessary.

Lesson 11 Test/Review

20-30 mins

Use the Assessment CD-ROM with Exam*View*®, Online Workbook, and Web site for additional practice, review, and assessment materials.

PART 1

ANSWERS: 1. who(m) OR that; **2.** when; **3.** that OR ø; **4.** who(m) OR that; **5.** whose; **6.** where; **7.** that OR which; **8.** that OR who(m)

1. Part 1 may be used as an in-class test to assess student performance, in addition to the Assessment CD-ROM with Exam*View*®. Have students read the direction line. Collect for assessment.

2. If necessary, have students review Lesson 11.

PART 2

ANSWERS: Answers may vary. Possible answers:
1. whose children make a lot of noise OR whose children are noisy; **2.** (that) you had; **3.** who OR that speaks French; **4.** (who[m] OR that) I met; **5.** whose last names begin with A; **6.** (when) the reunion was held OR (when) they had the reunion

OR of the reunion, (who) I went to high school with OR with whom I went to high school;
7. whose mother

1. Part 2 may also be used as an in-class test to assess student performance, in addition to the Assessment CD-ROM with Exam*View*®. Have students read the direction line. Point out that they are going to read mini-conversations. Collect for assessment.

2. If necessary, have students review Lesson 11.

Expansion

These expansion activities provide opportunities for students to interact with one another and further develop their speaking and writing skills. Encourage students to use grammar from this lesson whenever possible.

CLASSROOM ACTIVITIES

⏱ **10-15 mins per activity**

1. To help students, write the names of objects and people on small cards and have students pick a card from a hat.

2. If possible, have students from different countries and cultures work together in groups.

3. If possible, bring in objects from other countries or cultures in case students forget theirs.

Practice Idea: Speaking

Put strange objects that students might not recognize on the table. Have students take guesses at what they are and demonstrate their use.

TALK ABOUT IT

Elicit a few ideas about friendship and making new friends. Ask questions such as: *What is important to you in a friendship? Do you find it easy or hard to make new friends? How do you make new friends?* Write students' ideas on the board. Then briefly ask what they think about making friends via the Internet. Have students discuss each topic in pairs or groups. Then have pairs or groups get together to compare their answers to the questions.

WRITE ABOUT IT

1. Have students read the direction line. Before they begin their compositions, have students make a list of all the qualities that describe the friend they're going to write about. Then have them talk about the friend with a partner. Have students write their paragraphs individually. Collect for assessment and/or have students share their paragraphs with the group.

2. Have students read the direction line. Brainstorm the different ways to make new friends. Write students' ideas on the board. Then have students write their compositions individually. Collect for assessment and/or have students share their paragraphs with the group.

3. Have students read the direction line and the sample paragraph. Then have students share their experiences with online social networking. Ask questions such as: *How much time do you spend a day on the social network site you use? Do you upload photos? Have you made new friends or are you just in touch with your existing friends? Have you met up with any old friends that you had lost touch with?* Write their ideas on the board. Then have them write their compositions. Collect for assessment and/or have students share their compositions with the group.

Practice Idea: Writing

Have students exchange first drafts with a partner. Ask students to help their partners edit their drafts. Refer students to the Editing Advice on pages 373–374.

INTERNET ACTIVITIES

1. Tell students to visit a social networking Web site and find out what they need to do to join. Have them report back to the class.

2. Have students visit Meetup.com. Tell them to find out what kind of meetup groups there are in their city. Have them report back on which ones interest them.

3. Tell students to visit a Web site that lists classmates. If they graduated from a high school in the U.S., have them see if their high school is listed.

4. Tell students to visit a Web site that plans reunions. Have them find out some of the steps that are necessary in planning a reunion. Have students compare the steps in pairs or small groups.

Lesson 12

Lesson Overview

GRAMMAR

1. Briefly review what students learned in the previous lesson. Ask: *What did we study in Lesson 11?* (adjective clauses)

2. Ask: *What are we going to study in this lesson?* (superlatives and comparatives) *Can anyone give me an example of a superlative?* (e.g., *the best book, the tallest mountain*) Have students give examples. Write the examples on the board. Then have students give examples of comparatives (e.g., *This winter was colder than winter last year.*).

CONTEXT

1. Ask: *What are we going to learn about in this lesson?* (sports and athletes) Activate students' prior knowledge. Ask: *Do you play any sports? What are your favorite sports? Who are your favorite athletes?*

2. Have students share their knowledge and personal experiences.

Presentation Ideas

The topic for this lesson can be enhanced with the following items:

1. Books and pictures of sports and famous athletes

2. Video clips of famous sports moments

12.1 Superlatives and Comparatives—An Overview ═★

1. Have students cover up grammar chart **12.1** on page 380. Write the following on the board:

   1. *Baseball is more popular than soccer in the U.S.*

5-10 mins

2. *He is as tall as a basketball player.*
3. *Jack is the tallest player on the basketball team.*

   Ask: *Which sentence shows equality?* (2) *Which sentence is comparing two things?* (1) *Which sentence points out the number one item out of a group of three or more?* (3)

2. Then have students look at grammar chart **12.1**. Review the example sentences and explanations in the chart.

Golf and Tiger Woods — READING

1. Have students look at the photos on page 380. Ask: *Who is this?* (Tiger Woods, a very successful golfer) *Have you ever seen him play?*

2. Have students look at the title of the reading. Ask: *What is the reading about?* Have students use the title and photos to make predictions about the reading.

3. Preteach any vocabulary words your students may not know, such as *remarkable* and *amateur*.

Reading Glossary

amateur: not professional
remarkable: amazing, incredible

BEFORE YOU READ

5-10 mins

1. Have students discuss the questions in pairs.

2. Ask for a few volunteers to share their answers with the class.

Reading

CD 4 TR 07

10-15 mins

1. Have students first read the text silently. Tell them to pay special attention to superlative forms. Then play the audio and have students read along silently.

2. Check students' comprehension. Ask questions such as: *Where did they first play golf?* (in Scotland) *Is golf the most popular sport in the U.S.?* (no) *Who did Woods first play golf*

with? (his father) *When did Woods become a professional golfer?* (in 1996 at age 21) *What happened in 2007?* (He was the highest-paid professional athlete.)

To practice listening skills, have students first listen to the audio alone. Ask a few comprehension questions. Repeat the audio if necessary. Then have them open their books and read along as they listen to the audio.

12.2 The Superlative Form

 1. Have students cover up grammar chart **12.2** on page 381. Write the following on the board:

Woods was the youngest winner.

Golf is not the most popular sport in the U.S.

Woods is one of the most successful golfers.

Woods is one of the best golfers who has ever lived.

Woods said, "My dad was my best friend."

Woods is one of the best golfers of all time.

Have students identify the adjective in each sentence. Have them identify any changes that have been made to the adjective. Briefly explain each sentence. Say:

For short adjectives, we add -est.

For longer adjectives, we add most *to the adjective.*

We often use the expression one of the *with superlatives.*

Some adjectives are irregular—and so their superlative forms will be irregular.

We often put a prepositional phrase after a superlative.

We often use an adjective clause with ever *with the superlative.*

2. Then have students look at grammar chart **12.2**. Review the example sentences and explanations in the chart.

3. Direct students to the Language Note. Point out the use of *the* before superlatives.

Explain that *the* is not used if there is a possessive form. Go over the examples.

Have students write three sentences about a famous athlete from their native countries. Say: *Use the sentences in the reading and grammar chart* **12.2** *as a model.*

EXERCISE 1

ANSWERS: 1. T, <u>lowest</u>; **2.** F, <u>the most popular</u>; **3.** F, <u>one of the best</u>; **4.** T, <u>best</u>; **5.** F, <u>one of the best</u>; **6.** T, <u>one of the richest</u>

1. Say: *This exercise is based on the reading on pages 380–381.* Have students read the direction line. Go over the example.

2. Have students complete Exercise 1 individually. Remind them to review grammar chart **12.2** on page 381 if necessary. Go over the answers as a class.

12.3 Comparative and Superlative Forms of Adjectives and Adverbs

1. Have students cover up grammar chart **12.3** on pages 382–383. Write the following adjectives on the board:

tall, fast
easy, happy
frequent, active
important, difficult

Ask: *What do you notice about each pair of adjectives?* If students have difficulty, give them a hint. Say: *Look at the syllables.*

2. Then have students look at grammar chart **12.3**. Say: *Let's look at how we form the comparative and superlative forms. For short adjectives, we usually add* -er *for the comparative form. For the superlative, we add* -est. *For longer adjectives, we add* more *before the adjective to form the comparative and* most *before the adjective to form the superlative.*

Go over the examples and explanations for each kind of adjective. Explain that some two-syllable adjectives have two forms. Direct students to the Language Notes and explain that there are exceptions to the rules. Say: Tired *and* bored, *which are one-syllable adjectives, use* more *and* most *for the comparative and superlative forms.* Point out the other two-syllable adjectives which have two forms.

3. Point out that -*ly* adverbs use *more* and *most.* The last category of adjectives and adverbs are irregular; their forms have to be memorized. Explain that except for *good/well* and *bad/badly,* the adjective and adverb are the same.

4. Direct students to the chart on page 383 to review the rules for spelling short adjectives and adverbs. Have students cover up the *rule* column of the chart. Say: *Study these adjectives and adverbs with their superlative and comparative forms. Can you guess the rules?*

5. Have volunteers write the rules on the board. Then have students look at the complete grammar chart. Say: *Now compare your work with the chart.* Go over the examples and rules. Point out that you don't double a final *w*.

EXERCISE 2

ANSWERS: 1. more interesting, the most interesting; **2.** younger, the youngest; **3.** more beautiful, the most beautiful; **4.** better, the best; **5.** more responsible, the most responsible; **6.** thinner, the thinnest; **7.** more carefully, the most carefully; **8.** prettier, the prettiest; **9.** worse, the worst; **10.** more famous, the most famous; **11.** luckier, the luckiest; **12.** simpler OR more simple, the simplest OR the most simple; **13.** higher, the highest; **14.** more delicious, the most delicious; **15.** farther, the farthest; **16.** more foolishly, the most foolishly

5-10 mins

1. Have students read the direction line. Go over the examples.

2. Have students complete Exercise 2 individually. Remind them to review grammar chart **12.3** on pages 382–383 if necessary. Then have students compare answers in pairs. Monitor pair work. Give help as needed.

Practice Idea: Writing

Put together a list of 40 or so adjectives. Divide the class into two teams. Give each team a word to change into the comparative and superlative. One member from each team writes the comparative and superlative on the board. The members of the team have to take turns going up to the board. The team that gets the most comparative and superlative forms correct wins.

EXERCISE 3

ANSWERS: 1. the fastest; **2.** the most difficult; **3.** the most popular; **4.** the fattest; **5.** the best; **6.** the most watched; **7.** the tallest; **8.** The most common OR The commonest; **9.** the hardest; **10.** the most interesting

5-10 mins

1. Have students read the direction line. Ask: *What form of the adjective are we going to use?* (superlative) Point out the photos of the sumo wrestler and of Yao Ming on page 384. Go over the example.

2. Have students complete Exercise 3 individually. Remind them to review grammar chart **12.3** on pages 382–383 if necessary. Then have students compare answers in pairs. Go over the answers as a class.

Practice Idea: Writing

Have students write similar sentences about other sports and athletes they know (e.g., *Pelé was the greatest soccer player in the history of the sport.*).

EXERCISE 4
Answers will vary.

1. Say: *In this exercise, you're going to use the present perfect with* ever. Have students read the direction line. Go over the example. Model the example for the class.

2. Have students complete Exercise 5 individually. Remind them to review grammar chart **12.3** on pages 382–383 if necessary.

Practice Idea: Speaking

Have volunteers share some of their statements with the class. How many students agree?

Practice Idea: Speaking

Have students write their answers on a small piece of paper without signing their names. Fold up the papers and put them all in a box. Read the papers randomly and have students guess who the answers refer to.

EXERCISE 5

ANSWERS: **Answers will vary but will include these phrases: 1.** the tallest building; **2.** the most beautiful actress; **3.** the most difficult subject; **4.** the farthest distance; **5.** the worst food; **6.** the best vacation; **7.** the best athlete; **8.** the hardest job; **9.** the most interesting sporting event

10-15 mins

1. Have students read the direction line. Tell the students they are going to give their own opinions on these topics. Go over the examples. Have a volunteer do #1.

2. Have students complete Exercise 4 individually. Remind them to review grammar chart **12.3** on pages 382–383 if necessary. Have students compare answers in pairs. Monitor pair work. Give help as needed.

Practice Idea: Speaking

Take a class survey for selected items in Exercise 5. Write the responses on the board.

EXERCISE 6

Answers will vary.

10-15 mins

1. Ask: *What kind of difficult situations have you been in?* Have students read the direction line. Go over the example. Model the example for the class.

2. Have students complete Exercise 6 individually. Remind them to review grammar chart **12.3** on pages 382–383 if necessary. Have students compare answers in pairs. Monitor pair work. Give help as needed.

12.4 Superlatives and Word Order

5-10 mins

1. Have students cover up grammar chart **12.4** on page 386. Write the following on the board:

   Who is the best American golfer?

   Interest in soccer is growing the most quickly in the U.S.

   Ask: *Where's the superlative adjective in the first sentence—before or after the noun?* (before) *Where's the superlative adverb in the second sentence?* (after the verb)

2. Then have students look at grammar chart **12.4**. Go over the examples and explanations. Explain that if an adjective and noun are connected to another noun by the verb *be*, there are two possible ways to write the sentence. Go over the examples. Remind students that *the best, the worst, the most,* and *the least* can be either adjectives or adverbs. Say: *If they're adjectives, they go before the noun. If they're adverbs, they go after the verb.*

EXERCISE 7 ≡★

ANSWERS: **Answers will vary, but may contain: 1.** drives the best; **2.** lives the farthest from me; **3.** speaks English the most confidently; **4.** spends the most money; **5.** is the best dressed; **6.** watches the most TV OR watches TV the most; **7.** worries the most; **8.** lives the best; **9.** works the hardest; **10.** is the most athletic; **11.** is the biggest sports fan; **12.** is learning English the most quickly

5-10 mins

1. Say: *You're going to talk about your family members: Who drives the best? Who's the best athlete?* Have students read the direction line. Go over the example. Say: *Remember to check*

if the phrase has an adjective and noun, or a verb and an adverb. Then you have to turn it into a superlative. Have a volunteer model the example.

2. Have students complete Exercise 7 in pairs. Remind them to review grammar chart **12.4** on page 386 if necessary. Go over the answers as a class. Ask for volunteers to share their answers.

Practice Idea: Speaking

Have students practice asking and answering questions about family members with a different partner (e.g., *Who drives the best in your family? My brother does.*).

Americans' Attitude Toward Soccer READING

1. Have students look at the photo. Ask: *Is this a familiar scene in your native country?*

2. Have students look at the title of the reading. Ask: *What is the reading about?* Have students use the title and photo to make predictions about the reading.

3. Preteach any vocabulary words your students may not know, such as *league* and *injury*.

Reading Glossary

injury: a wound; damage
league: a group of sports teams that compete against each other

BEFORE YOU READ

🕐
5-10 mins

1. Have students discuss the questions in pairs.

2. Ask for a few volunteers to share their answers with the class.

🔊
CD 4
TR 08

🕐
10-15 mins

Reading

1. Have students first read the text silently. Tell them to pay special attention to comparisons. Then play the audio and have students read along silently.

2. Check students' comprehension. Ask questions such as: *What did Americans use to say about soccer?* (It was boring.) *What big game was played in the U.S. in 1999?* (the Women's World Cup) *In elementary school, soccer is second to which sport?* (basketball) *Do more kids play baseball than soccer?* (no)

Practice Idea: Listening

To practice listening skills, have students first listen to the audio alone. Ask a few comprehension questions. Repeat the audio if necessary. Then have them open their books and read along as they listen to the audio.

Context Note

Two major American sports started out as imports, cricket and rugby, and then morphed into the very American sports we see today—baseball and American football. Soccer, in many an American's mind, never took on an American personality, and was forever doomed as an immigrant's game. These feelings were cemented during World War I and World War II when Americans sought refuge in isolationism. Attitudes are changing, especially as the world becomes smaller thanks to innovations in communication technology. As American teams get better and more competitive, the public's interest in the sport heightens.

12.5 Comparatives

🕐
10-15 mins

1. Have students look at grammar chart **12.5** on page 388. Say: *For short adjectives and adverbs, the comparative form ends in -er. Use more before longer adjectives and before adverbs that end in -ly.* Go over the examples. Refer students to chart **12.3** on pages 382–383 for irregular comparative forms.

2. Explain that the comparative is used to compare two items. Point out that *than* is used before the second item of comparison.

3. Say: *If there is no comparison with a second item, omit* than. Write the example from the chart on the board.

4. Say: Much *and* little *can be used in front of a comparative.* Go over the examples in the chart.

5. Explain that there are two ways to make comparisons when pronouns are used after *than*: a formal way and an informal way. Say: *In the formal way, you use an auxiliary verb after the pronoun. In the informal way, you use an object pronoun and no verb.* Go over the examples.

6. Explain that comparatives can be used to show cause and result. Go over the examples.

EXERCISE 8

ANSWERS: **1.** more; **2.** faster; **3.** more; **4.** less; **5.** less

5-10 mins

1. Have students read the direction line. Go over the example.

2. Have students complete Exercise 8 individually. Remind them to review grammar chart **12.5** on page 388 if necessary. Go over the answers as a class.

EXERCISE 9

ANSWERS: **1.** better, than; **2.** slower; **3.** more difficult; **4.** larger than; **5.** more easily than; **6.** better, than; **7.** more interesting than; **8.** more exciting than

10-15 mins

1. Have students read the direction line. Ask: *What form of the adjective are we going to use?* (comparative) Go over the example.

2. Have students complete the exercise individually. Remind them to review grammar chart **12.5** on page 388 if necessary. Go over the answers as a class.

EXERCISE 10

ANSWERS: **Answers will vary but will contain:**
1. more polite than; **2.** friendlier OR more friendly than; **3.** more formal than; **4.** more playful than; **5.** more responsible than; **6.** more serious than; **7.** more curious than; **8.** happier than

10-15 mins

1. Say: *Now you're going to make comparisons between adults and children.* Have students read the direction line. Go over the example. Have a volunteer model the example.

2. Have students complete the exercise in pairs. Remind them to review grammar chart **12.5** on page 388 if necessary. Monitor pair work. Give help as needed.

Practice Idea: Speaking

Have students get into groups to discuss their comparisons. If possible, have students from different cultures and nationalities work together.

EXERCISE 11

Answers will vary.

10-15 mins

1. Say: *Now compare the U.S. and your native country.* Have students read the direction line. Go over the examples. Remind students to explain their responses.

2. Have students complete the exercise in pairs. Remind them to review grammar chart **12.5** on page 388 if necessary. Monitor pair work. Give help as needed.

Practice Idea: Speaking

Have students get into groups to discuss their responses to Exercise 11. If possible, have students from different cultures and nationalities work together.

12.6 Comparatives and Word Order

5-10 mins

1. Have students cover up grammar chart **12.6** on page 390. Make a matching exercise on the board. Write the following sentences:

1. *Football is more popular than soccer in the U.S.*
2. *Woods played golf more successfully than his father.*
3. *There is less interest in hockey than there is in golf.*
4. *My sister likes soccer more than I do.*

a. *Put* more, less, better, *and* worse *after a verb.*

b. *Put comparative adverbs after the verb.*

c. *Put the comparative adjective after the verb* be *or other linking verbs:* seem, feel, look, sound, *etc.*

d. *Put* more, less, fewer, better, *and* worse *before a noun.*

Say: *Now match the examples with the explanations.* Have volunteers do the matching on the board. (**Matching Answers: 1.** c; **2.** b; **3.** d; **4.** a)

2. Have students look at grammar chart **12.6**. Say: *Now compare your work with the grammar chart.* Go over the examples and explanations.

EXERCISE **12**

ANSWERS: 1. C; **2.** A baseball game has less action than a soccer game. **3.** C; **4.** Tiger Woods plays golf more remarkably than most other players. **5.** I like baseball more than basketball. **6.** C; **7.** Team A played better than Team B.

1. Have students read the direction line. Go over the examples.

2. Have students complete Exercise 12 individually. Remind them to review grammar chart **12.6** on page 390 if necessary. Go over the answers as a class.

5–10 mins

EXERCISE **13**

ANSWERS: Answers will vary but will contain: 1. dress more stylishly than; **2.** work harder than; **3.** spend more than; **4.** speak English better than; **5.** worry less than; **6.** live more comfortably than; **7.** have more freedom than; **8.** have an easier life than; **9.** exercise more than

1. Say: *Now you're going to make comparisons between yourself and another person or between two people you know. You're going to use adverbs.* Have students read the direction line. Go over the example. Have a volunteer model the example.

2. Have students complete the exercise in pairs. Remind them to review grammar chart **12.6** on page 390 if necessary. Monitor pair work. Give help as needed.

10–15 mins

EXERCISE **14**

Answers will vary.

1. Say: *Now you're going to make comparisons between different schools.* Have students read the direction line. Go over the example. Have a volunteer model the example.

2. Have students complete the exercise in pairs. Remind them to review grammar chart **12.6** on page 390 if necessary. Monitor pair work. Give help as needed.

10–15 mins

EXERCISE **15**

ANSWERS: 1. softer than; **2.** the best; **3.** the tallest; **4.** more interested, than (I am interested); **5.** the most exciting; **6.** more muscular; **7.** slower, than; **8.** fewer, than; **9.** the coldest; **10.** farther; **11.** better

1. Have students read the direction line. Tell them that this time they have to decide if they need the superlative or comparative form. Go over the examples.

2. Have students complete the exercise individually. Remind them to review grammar chart **12.6** on page 390 if necessary. Go over the answers as a class.

10–15 mins

An Amazing Athlete READING

1. Have students look at the photo. Ask: *What's going on in this photo?* (A man is climbing a mountain.)

2. Have students look at the title of the reading. Ask: *What is the reading about?* Have students use the title and photo to make predictions about the reading.

3. Preteach any vocabulary words your students may not know, such as *tough* and *tolerate*.

Reading Glossary

tolerate: to endure; to suffer
tough: strong

BEFORE YOU READ

5-10 mins

1. Have students discuss the questions in pairs.
2. Ask for a few volunteers to share their answers with the class.

Reading

CD 4
TR 09

10-15 mins

1. Have students first read the text silently. Tell them to pay special attention to comparisons. Then play the audio and have students read along silently.
2. Check students' comprehension. Ask questions such as: *Was Erik always blind?* (No. He lost his sight in his early teens.) *What sports did he discover didn't require the athlete to see?* (first wrestling, then rock climbing) *Is he very different from sighted mountain climbers?* (No. He is skilled and strong.) *During the climb up Mount Everest, when did he have an advantage over his teammates?* (when visibility was zero because of the weather)

Practice Idea: Listening

To practice listening skills, have students first listen to the audio alone. Ask a few comprehension questions. Repeat the audio if necessary. Then have them open their books and read along as they listen to the audio.

DID YOU KNOW?

Have students read the information. Then ask them questions such as: *How old do you think the oldest person to climb Everest was? The youngest?*

Interesting Everest Facts:

Oldest person to climb Mount Everest—Yuchuiro Miura (age 70) Japan (2003)

Youngest person to climb Mount Everest—Temba Tseri (age 15) Nepal (2001)

Fastest ascent—Pemba Dorje Sherpa (8 hours, 10 minutes) Nepal (2004)

Fittest climber—Goran Kropp (Rode a bicycle from his home in Sweden to Everest, climbed the mountain without oxygen, and then rode his bike all the way home to Sweden.) Sweden (1996)

The worst year for deaths occurred in 1996, when 15 people lost their lives. The worst day was May 10, 1996, when eight died near the summit. That climb was detailed in the book *Into Thin Air* written by journalist and climber Jon Krakauer.

12.7 *As ... As*

5-10 mins

1. Have students look at grammar chart **12.7** on pages 393–394. Say: *We can show two things are equal or unequal by using: (not) as + adjective or adverb + as.* Go over the example sentences.
2. Say: *The lesser item goes first.* Go over the example sentences.
3. Explain that you can omit the second *as* if the second item is omitted. Go over the example.
4. Direct students to the Usage Notes. Go over the explanations and examples. Point out that *A.S.A.P.* is either pronounced as initials (*A-S-A-P*) or one word (*asap*).

EXERCISE 16

ANSWERS: 1. T; **2.** T; **3.** F; **4.** T; **5.** F; **6.** T

5-10 mins

1. Have students read the direction line. Go over the example.
2. Have students complete the exercise individually. Remind them to review grammar chart **12.7** on pages 393–394 if necessary. Go over the answers as a class.

EXERCISE 17

Answers will vary.

10-15 mins

1. Say: *In this exercise, you can compare yourself to other people or you can compare two other people.* Have students read the direction line. Go over the examples. Have volunteers model the examples.
2. Have students complete the exercise in pairs. Remind them to review grammar chart **12.7** on pages 393–394 if necessary. Monitor pair work. Give help as needed.

Practice Idea: Speaking

Have students compare themselves to each other. Have students take turns with their partners asking and answering questions (e.g., *Are you as old as I am? No, I'm not. I'm only 17.*).

EXERCISE 18
Answers will vary.

10-15 mins

1. Say: *Now compare yourself to me.* Have students read the direction line. Go over the example. Have a volunteer model the example.

2. Have students complete the exercise individually. Remind them to review grammar chart **12.7** on pages 393–394 if necessary. Then have students compare answers in pairs. Monitor pair work. Give help as needed.

Practice Idea: Speaking

Have volunteers share their answers with the class.

12.8 As Many/Much . . . As

5-10 mins

1. Have students look at grammar chart **12.8** on page 395. Say: *We can show two things are equal or not equal in quantity by using:* as many + *count noun* + as *or* as much + *noncount noun* + as. Go over the example sentences.

2. Say: *We can use* as much as *after a verb phrase.* Go over the examples.

EXERCISE 19
Answers will vary.

10-15 mins

1. Say: *First complete the statements to make them true for you. Then compare your information with a partner and make new statements.* Have students read the direction line. Go over the examples in Parts A and B. Have two volunteers model the exercise.

2. Have students complete the statements individually. Remind them to review grammar chart **12.8** on page 395 if necessary. Then have students compare answers in pairs. Monitor pair work. Give help as needed.

Practice Idea: Speaking

Have volunteers share some of their answers with the class.

EXERCISE 20

ANSWERS: Answers will vary but contain:
1. earn as much as; **2.** spend as much money as; **3.** talk as much as; **4.** gossip as much as; **5.** like to go shopping as much as; **6.** have as many responsibilities as; **7.** have as much freedom as; **8.** have as much free time as

10-15 mins

1. Have students read the direction line. Say: *You're going to compare yourself with another person, or compare two other people.* Go over the example in the book.

2. Have students complete Exercise 20 in pairs. Remind them to review grammar chart **12.8** on page 395 if necessary. Monitor pair work. Give help as needed.

EXERCISE 21
Answers will vary.

10-15 mins

1. Say: *Now compare schools.* Have students read the direction line. Go over the example in the book.

2. Have students complete Exercise 21 in pairs. Remind them to review grammar chart **12.8** on page 395 if necessary. Monitor pair work. Give help as needed.

EXERCISE 22
Answers will vary.

10-15 mins

1. Have students read the direction line. Explain that students will be comparing their city with another city they know. Go over the example in the book.

2. Have students complete Exercise 22 individually. Remind them to review grammar chart **12.8** on page 395 if necessary. Then have students compare answers in pairs. Monitor pair work. Give help as needed.

Practice Idea: Speaking

Have a class discussion about cities. Find out which cities students wrote about. Write them on the board. Ask students to share their opinions.

12.9 *The Same ... As*

5–10 mins

1. Have students look at grammar chart **12.9** on page 397. Say: *We can show two things are equal or not equal by using:* the same + *noun* + as. Go over the example sentences.

2. Say: *There are two ways to write the comparison with* same as. Point out Pattern A and Pattern B. Go over the examples.

3. Direct students to the Language Note. Say: *You can use many nouns with* the same ... as: the same size as, the same color as, the same religion as, *etc.*

EXERCISE 23

ANSWERS: 1. A soccer ball is the same shape as a volleyball. **2.** A soccer player isn't the same height as a basketball player. **3.** An amateur athlete doesn't have the same ability as a professional athlete. **4.** A soccer player isn't the same weight as a football player. **5.** Team A's uniforms aren't the same color as team B's uniforms.

5–10 mins

1. Have students read the direction line. Go over the examples.

2. Have students complete the statements individually. Remind them to review grammar chart **12.9** on page 397 if necessary. Go over the answers as a class.

EXERCISE 24
Answers will vary.

10–15 mins

1. Say: *Now compare two relatives or two friends of yours.* Have students read the direction line. Go over the example. Have two volunteers model the example.

2. Have students complete the statements individually. Remind them to review grammar chart **12.9** on page 397 if necessary. Then have students compare answers in pairs. Monitor pair work. Give help as needed.

EXERCISE 25
Answers will vary.

10–15 mins

1. Have students read the direction line. Go over the examples. Have two volunteers model the examples.

2. Have students complete the exercise in pairs. Remind them to review grammar chart **12.9** on page 397 if necessary. Monitor pair work. Give help as needed.

12.10 Equality with Nouns or Adjectives

5–10 mins

1. Have students cover up grammar chart **12.10** on pages 398–399. Say: *To show equality with nouns, use* the same ... as. *To show equality with adjectives or adverbs, use* as ... as. (*For example: A soccer player is not the same height as a basketball player. A soccer player is shorter. A soccer player is not as tall as a basketball player.*) Write the examples on the board.

2. Go through the list of nouns and adjectives and the example sentences.

EXERCISE 26
Answers will vary.

5–10 mins

1. Have students read the direction line. Go over the example.

2. Have students complete the statements individually. Remind them to review grammar chart **12.10** on page 399 if necessary. Go over the answers as a class.

Football and Soccer READING

1. Have students look at the photos. Say: *Describe what's going on in these photos.*

2. Have students look at the title of the reading. Ask: *What is the reading about?* Have students use the title and photos to make predictions about the reading.

3. Preteach any vocabulary words your students may not know, such as *tackle* and *block.* For *tackle,* point out the photo on page 400.

Reading Glossary

block: to stand in the way
tackle: the act of knocking a player carrying the ball to the ground

BEFORE YOU READ

5-10 mins

1. Have students discuss the questions in pairs.

2. Ask for a few volunteers to share their answers with the class.

 Reading
CD 4
TR 10

10-15 mins

1. Have students first read the text silently. Tell them to pay special attention to similarities and differences. Then play the audio and have students read along silently.

2. Check students' comprehension. Ask questions such as: *Do American football and soccer have anything in common?* (Yes. For example, many of the rules are the same. Both have 11 players. You score by getting the ball past the goal. And the playing fields are similar.) *Can all American football players kick the ball?* (no, only the kickers) *Do soccer players tackle?* (no) *Do football players wear shorts?* (no)

Practice Idea: Listening

To practice listening skills, have students first listen to the audio alone. Ask a few comprehension questions. Repeat the audio if necessary. Then have them open their books and read along as they listen to the audio.

12.11 Similarity with *Like* and *Alike*

5-10 mins

1. Have students cover up grammar chart **12.11** on page 401. Write the four sentences from the grammar chart on the board. Label them *Pattern A* and *Pattern B.* Say: *Find the patterns in the two groups of sentences.* Elicit the two patterns from students, and write them on the board.

2. Have students look at grammar chart **12.11**. Say: *Now check your work.* Point out the illustrations of a football player, a soccer player, and a rugby player.

3. Review the patterns. Then direct students to the Language Note. Point out that sense perception verbs are often used with *like* and *alike.* Review the list of verbs.

EXERCISE 27 =★
Answers will vary.

10-15 mins

1. Have students read the direction line. Go over the example. Say: *You can use Pattern A or Pattern B.*

2. Have students complete the exercise in pairs. Remind them to review grammar chart **12.11** on page 401 if necessary. Go over the answers as a class.

Practice Idea: Writing

Ask students to rewrite each sentence from Exercise 27 using the pattern they didn't use the first time they completed the exercise.

EXERCISE 28

ANSWERS: 1. look; **2.** alike; **3.** acts like; **4.** looks like; **5.** dress alike; **6.** like; **7.** sound like; **8.** dress; **9.** like; **10.** act like

---

10-15 mins

1. Have students read the direction line. Go over the example. Say: *Sometimes you may need to provide the verb, sometimes just* like *or* alike, *and sometimes you'll need to provide both.*

2. Have students complete the exercise individually. Remind them to review grammar

chart **12.11** on page 401 if necessary. Go over the answers as a class.

12.12 *Be Like*

 5-10 mins

1. Have students look at grammar chart **12.12** on page 403. Say: *We can show that two things are similar or not similar in internal characteristics with* be like *and* be alike. Tell students to look down at the bottom of the chart. Say: *Compare these two sentences. One describes physical characteristics, and the other describes internal characteristics.* Go over the examples.

2. Have students look at the top of the grammar chart. Say: *There are two patterns for* be like *and* be alike: *Pattern A and Pattern B.* Write the patterns on the board. Say: *Use* be like *when the two nouns being compared are separated, and use* be alike *when the two nouns being compared are together.*

EXERCISE 29 ≡★

ANSWERS: Student responses will vary. Correct questions: 1. Is an English class in the U.S. like an English class in your native country? **2.** Is your house (or apartment) in the U.S. like your house (or apartment) in your native country? **3.** Is the weather in this city like the weather in your hometown? **4.** Is food in your county like American food? **5.** Are women's clothes in your native country like women's clothing in the U.S.? **6.** Is a college in your native country like a college in the U.S.? **7.** Are American teachers like teachers in your native country? **8.** Are American athletes like athletes in your native country?

10-15 mins

1. Have students read the direction line. Go over the example. Say: *Remember, only use* be like.

2. Have students complete the exercise in pairs. Remind them to review grammar chart **12.12** on page 403 if necessary. Monitor pair work. Give help as needed.

Practice Idea: Writing

Now have students rewrite the questions from Exercise 29 using *be alike*.

12.13 Same or Different ≡★

5-10 mins

1. Have students look at grammar chart **12.13** on page 404. Say: *We can show that two things are the same or are not the same by using* the same as. *We can show that things are different by using* different from.

2. Say: *There are two patterns for* the same as *and* different from: *Pattern A and Pattern B.* Write the patterns on the board. Say: *Use* the same as *and* different from *when the two nouns being compared are separated, and use* the same *and* different *when the two nouns being compared are together.* Go over the example sentences.

3. Direct students to the Language Note. Say: *Some Americans say* different than *and not* different from.

EXERCISE 30 ≡★

ANSWERS: 1. Michael Jordan and Michael Phelps are different. **2.** A century is the same as one hundred years. **3.** Rock climbing and mountain climbing are different. **4.** A kilometer is the same as 1,000 meters. **5.** L.A. is the same as Los Angeles. **6.** A mile and a kilometer are different. **7.** Football and rugby are different. **8.** Football rules and soccer rules are different.

10-15 mins

1. Have students read the direction line. Go over the examples. Say: *You can use Pattern A or Pattern B.*

2. Have students complete the exercise in pairs. Remind them to review grammar chart **12.13** on page 404 if necessary. Go over the answers as a class.

Practice Idea: Writing

Ask students to rewrite each sentence using a different pattern than the one they used the first time they completed the exercise.

 EXERCISE 31
CD 4
TR 11 **ANSWERS: 1.** doesn't; **2.** like; **3.** from; **4.** same; **5.** the same; **6.** height; **7.** alike; **8.** different;

9. better; **10.** like; **11.** am OR 'm like; **12.** alike; **13.** seems OR sounds; **14.** the same

1. Say: *In this conversation, one friend talks about his twin brother with another friend.* Have students read the direction line. Go over the example. Say: *You may need to use* like/alike; be like/be alike; the same . . . as; *or the same as/ different from.*

2. Have students complete the exercise individually. Remind them to review grammar charts **12.9** on page 397, **12.10** on pages 398–399, **12.11** on page 401, **12.12** on page 403, and **12.13** on page 404. Then have them compare answers in pairs. Play the audio and go over the answers as a class.

  EXERCISE 32

CD 4
TR 12
ANSWERS: **1.** as; **2.** as; **3.** like; **4.** as; **5.** from; **6.** more; **7.** than; **8.** like; **9.** like; **10.** alike OR the same; **11.** more; **12.** from; **13.** more; **14.** like; **15.** as; **16.** as; **17.** as; **18.** as much; **19.** alike

1. Say: *In this conversation, two women are talking about their husbands' interest in football.* Have students read the direction line. Go over the example.

2. Have students complete the exercise individually. Remind them to review Lesson 12 if necessary. Have students compare answers in pairs. Play the audio and go over the answers as a class.

Practice Idea: Listening

To provide practice with listening skills, have students close their books and listen to the audio. Repeat the audio as needed. Say: *In this conversation, one friend talks about his twin brother with another friend.* Ask comprehension questions, such as: *Do the twin brothers look alike?* (No. They're fraternal twins.) *Is person B shorter or taller than his brother?* (taller) *Does person B's brother like sports?* (no) *Do they dress alike?* (no) Then have students open their books and complete Exercise 31.

Practice Idea: Speaking

Have students practice the conversation in pairs. Then ask volunteers to role-play all or part of the conversation in front of the class.

Practice Idea: Speaking

Have students write a similar conversation about one of the students and a brother or sister. Then ask volunteers to role-play all or part of the conversation in front of the class.

Practice Idea: Listening

To provide practice with listening skills, have students close their books and listen to the audio. Repeat the audio as needed. Say: *In this conversation, two women are talking about their husbands' interest in football.* Ask comprehension questions, such as: *What is the name given to women whose husbands watch too much football?* (football widows) *When person B complains, what does her husband say?* (to come sit down and join him) *Do the two women like football?* (No. They like soccer better.) *What is their favorite sport?* (shopping) Then have students open their books and complete Exercise 32.

Practice Idea: Speaking

Have students practice the conversation in pairs. Ask volunteers to role-play all or part of the conversation in front of the class.

Summary of Lesson 12

20-30 mins

1. **Simple, Comparative, and Superlative Forms** Have students cover up the summary of Lesson 12 on page 407. Create a fill-in exercise on the board:

   (tall)

   1. *Jacob is _____ .*
   2. *Mark is _____ Jacob.*
   3. *Bart is _____ member of the basketball team.*

   (popular)

   4. *Golf is _____ in the U.S.*
   5. *Baseball is _____ golf.*
   6. *Soccer is _____ game in the world.*

   Say: *Fill in the blanks with the appropriate form of the adjective.*

   If necessary, have students review:

   > **12.2** The Superlative Form (p. 381)
   > **12.3** Comparative and Superlative Forms of Adjectives and Adverbs (pp. 382–383)
   > **12.5** Comparatives (p. 388)

2. **Other Kinds of Comparisons** Create an exercise on the board:

   1. *She looks (as young/as young as) her daughter.*
   2. *She speaks English (as fluently/as fluently as) her husband.*
   3. *She is (the same age/the same age as) her husband.*
   4. *She and her husband are (the same age/the same age as).*
   5. *She works (as many hours/as many hours as) her husband.*
   6. *She doesn't have (as much time/as much time as) her husband.*
   7. *She works (as much/as much as) her husband.*

   Say: *Circle the correct answer.*

   If necessary, have students review:

   > **12.7** As … As (pp. 393–394)
   > **12.8** As Many/Much … As (p. 395)

3. **Comparisons with *Like*** Create an exercise on the board. Say: *Rewrite the sentence with* like *or* alike.

   1. *She's like her mother. _____ .*
   2. *She and her sister look alike. _____ .*
   3. *Lemons don't taste like limes. _____ .*
   4. *Western music and Asian music don't sound alike. _____ .*

   If necessary, have students review:

   > **12.11** Similarity with *Like* and *Alike* (p. 401)
   > **12.12** *Be Like* (p. 403)

4. **Comparisons with *Same* and *Different*** Create an exercise on the board. Say: *Complete the sentences with the appropriate forms of* same *and* different.

   1. *Football is _____ soccer.*
   2. *My uniform is _____ my teammates' uniforms.*

   If necessary, have students review:

   > **12.13** Same or Different (p. 404)

Editing Advice

10-15 mins

Have students close their books. Write the first few sentences without editing marks or corrections on the board. For example:

1. *He is more older than his teacher.*
2. *He is younger that his wife.*

Ask students to correct each sentence and provide a rule or an explanation for each correction. This activity can be done individually, in pairs, or as a class. After students have corrected each sentence, tell them to turn to pages 407–408. Say: *Now compare your work with the Editing Advice in the book.* Have students read through all the advice.

Editing Quiz

ANSWERS: 1. C; **2.** than; **3.** the most exciting sport; **4.** C; **5.** C; **6.** teams; **7.** C; **8.** sounds like; **9.** C; **10.** like; **11.** as; **12.** C; **13.** as; **14.** better; **15.** practiced more; **16.** C; **17.** as; **18.** C

10-15 mins

1. Tell students they are going to put the editing advice into practice. Have students read the direction line. Ask: *Do all the shaded words and phrases have mistakes?* (no) Go over the examples with the class. Then do #1 together.

2. Have students complete the quiz individually. Then have them compare answers with a partner before checking answers as a class.

3. For the items students had difficulties with, have them go back and find the relevant grammar chart and review it. Monitor and give help as necessary.

Lesson 12 Test/Review

 Use the Assessment CD-ROM with Exam*View*®, Online Workbook, and Web site for additional practice, review, and assessment materials.

30-40 mins

PART 1

ANSWERS: 1. the most popular; **2.** more popular than; **3.** the most interesting; **4.** heavier than; **5.** more exciting than; **6.** more difficult than; **7.** the tallest; **8.** better than; **9.** the lowest; **10.** the fastest

1. Part 1 may be used as an in-class test to assess student performance, in addition to the Assessment CD-ROM with Exam*View*®. Have students read the direction line. Collect for assessment.

2. If necessary, have students review:
   12.2 The Superlative Form (p. 381)
   12.3 Comparative and Superlative Forms of Adjectives and Adverbs (pp. 382–383)
   12.5 Comparatives (p. 388)

PART 2

ANSWERS: 1. the same; **2.** much as; **3.** looks; **4.** the same; **5.** from; **6.** size as; **7.** height; **8.** taste; **9.** is; **10.** alike; **11.** as soon as; **12.** the same; **13.** alike

1. Part 2 may also be used as an in-class test to assess student performance, in addition to the Assessment CD-ROM with Exam*View*®. Have students read the direction line. Collect for assessment.

2. If necessary, have students review:
   12.7 *As…As* (pp. 393–394)
   12.11 Similarity with *Like* and *Alike* (p. 401)
   12.12 *Be Like* (p. 403)
   12.13 Same or Different (p. 404)

Expansion

These expansion activities provide opportunities for students to interact with one another and further develop their speaking and writing skills. Encourage students to use grammar from this lesson whenever possible.

CLASSROOM ACTIVITIES

 1. Try to have students work with a partner they don't know very well. To encourage students to use all of the grammar learned in this lesson, direct students to the summary on page 407.

10-15 mins per activity

2. Have groups report the results of their discussions to the class.

3. Have each pair report to the class. Compile students' comparisons on the board.

4. Have students complete the chart individually. Then have students get into groups to discuss their answers.

5. Have students complete the statements individually. Then have students get into groups to discuss their answers.

TALK ABOUT IT

Briefly discuss sports in the students' different countries. Ask: *What sports are the most popular? Are sports part of schools' curricula? Do sports players have an important status?* Then have students discuss each topic in pairs or groups.

WRITE ABOUT IT

Have students read the direction line and the sample paragraph. Choose one of the sets of items and have students brainstorm qualities that are the same or different for those items. Write their ideas on the board. Have students help you begin writing a paragraph comparing the items on the board. Next have students make a list of all the qualities that are the same or different for the set of items they've decided to write about. Then have them write their compositions. Collect for assessment and/or have students share their compositions with the group.

Practice Idea: Writing

Have students exchange first drafts with a partner. Ask students to help their partners edit their drafts. Refer students to the Editing Advice on pages 407–408.

OUTSIDE ACTIVITY

Ask students to interview someone who was born in the U.S. Tell them to find out his or her opinion about the superlative of each of the following items:

- prestigious job in the U.S.
- beautiful city in the U.S.
- popular TV program
- terrible tragedy in American history
- big problem in the U.S.
- handsome or beautiful actor
- good athlete
- good sports team

Have students share their findings with the class. Have students prepare the questions in class before carrying out the interview (e.g., *What is the most prestigious job in the U.S.?*).

Practice Idea: Speaking

Have students practice the interview in class with another student before doing the interview with someone who was born in the U.S. Later students can compare answers. How many of them were the same? Different?

INTERNET ACTIVITIES

1. Have students find an article about Mount Everest on the Internet. Tell then to print the article and circle some interesting facts. Have students share their articles in groups and discuss what they found out.

2. Have students find an article about an athlete that they admire. Tell them to print the article and circle some interesting facts. Have students report orally on the athlete they chose and what they found out about him or her.

3. Have students visit the Olympics Web site or a Web site with sports statistics and information. Tell them to find out which country has won the most medals in a particular sport, which sport is the newest to be an Olympic event, and which athlete has the most Olympic medals. Have them report back to the class either orally or in writing.

4. Have students find an article about Enrique Oliu. Tell them to summarize the article and report back to the class on Oliu and what makes him so special.

Context Note

Enrique Oliu is a sportscaster who has been blind since birth. For a number of years, he has been providing color commentary for Spanish-speaking radio for the Tampa Bay Devil Rays—a minor league baseball team. How does he do it? He has an amazing memory. His wife, Debbie Oliu, reads him articles about the games and the players, and he also memorizes information about the players, including their game statistics. During the game, his wife sits behind him and describes what's going on.

Lesson 13

Lesson Overview

GRAMMAR

1. Briefly review what students learned in the previous lesson. Ask: *What did we study in Lesson 12?* (superlatives and comparatives)

2. Ask: *What are we going to study in this lesson?* (passive voice and active voice) *Can you give an example of the passive voice and the active voice?* (e.g., *Someone stole the bicycle; the bicycle was stolen.*) Have students give examples. Write the examples on the board.

CONTEXT

1. Ask: *What are we going to learn about in this lesson?* (the law) Activate students' prior knowledge. Ask: *Does the system of law in your native country include a jury of peers?*

2. Have students share their knowledge and personal experiences.

Presentation Ideas

The topic for this lesson can be enhanced with the following items:

1. A juror's notice and a pamphlet for prospective jurors
2. A video of *The People's Court* or *Judge Hatchett*

13.1 The Passive Voice and the Active Voice—An Overview ≡★

5-10 mins

1. Have students cover up grammar chart **13.1** on page 416. Create a matching exercise. Write the following on the board:
   1. *The thief was arrested by the police.*
   2. *The bicycle will be returned tomorrow.*
   3. *The police arrested the thief.*

a. *The active voice focuses on the person who performs the action.*
   b. *The passive voice focuses on the receiver of the action.*
   c. *Many passive sentences do not contain a* by *phrase.*

Say: *Match the sentences with the explanations.* (**Matching Answers: 1.** b; **2.** c; **3.** a)

2. Then have students look at grammar chart **13.1**. Say: *Compare your work with the chart.* Review the example sentences and explanations in the chart.

Jury Duty READING

1. Have students look at the photo. Ask: *What is going on in this photo?* (a lawyer is talking to a jury) *Do you know anyone who has served on a jury?*

2. Have students look at the title of the reading. Ask: *What is the reading about?* Have students use the title and photo to make predictions about the reading.

3. Preteach any vocabulary words your students may not know, such as *protect, charge, consider,* and *open-minded*.

Reading Glossary

charge: a statement of blame against
consider: to regard, think, believe
open-minded: willing to listen to or consider the opinions and ideas of others
protect: to defend against harm or loss

BEFORE YOU READ

5-10 mins

1. Have students discuss the questions in pairs.
2. Ask for a few volunteers to share their answers with the class.

Reading ≡★

CD 4 TR 13

10-15 mins

1. Have students first read the text silently. Tell them to pay special attention to the passive voice. Then play the audio and have students read along silently.

2. Check students' comprehension. Ask questions such as: *Who decides if a person is innocent or guilty?* (a jury) *Where does the court get names of prospective jury members?* (from lists of taxpayers, licensed drivers, and voters) *How many people are chosen to be on a jury?* (12) *Can the jurors talk with friends and family about the case?* (no) *Are jurors paid for their work?* (Yes. They are paid a small amount.)

Practice Idea: Listening

To practice listening skills, have students first listen to the audio alone. Ask a few comprehension questions. Repeat the audio if necessary. Then have them open their books and read along as they listen to the audio.

13.2 The Passive Voice

5-10
mins

1. Have students look at grammar chart **13.2** on page 417. Go over the examples and explanations. Explain how to form the passive (a form of *be* + the past participle). Ask: *How do you form the past participle for regular verbs?* (It's the same as the past form: *talk/talked; walk/walked.*)

2. Explain that in the active voice, the performer is the subject. The verb is the action that the subject performs. Go over the example. Say: *In the passive, the action is performed on the subject. When a performer is included, use by + noun or object pronoun.* Go over examples.

EXERCISE 1

ANSWERS: 1. A; **2.** A; **3.** P; **4.** P; **5.** P; **6.** A; **7.** P; **8.** P; **9.** A; **10.** A

5-10
mins

1. Have students read the direction line. Go over the examples.

2. Have students complete Exercise 1 individually. Remind them to review grammar chart **13.2** on page 417 if necessary. Go over the answers as a class.

13.3 Passive Voice—Form and Uses

10-15
mins

1. Have students cover up grammar chart **13.3** on pages 418-419. Create a matching exercise. Write the following on the board:

   1. *They have taken a vote.*
   2. *They took a vote.*
   3. *They will take a vote.*
   4. *They must take a vote.*
   5. *They take a vote.*
   a. *Simple Present*
   b. *Simple Past*
   c. *Future*
   d. *Present Perfect*
   e. *Modal*

   Say: *Match the verb tense with the example sentence. Then write a passive sentence from the active sentence.* (**Matching Answers: 1.** d; **2.** b; **3.** c; **4.** e; **5.** a)

2. Then have students look at grammar chart **13.3**. Say: *Compare your work with the chart.* Review the example sentences and explanations in the chart. Go over any trouble spots with the class.

3. Direct students to the Language Notes. Point out that an adverb can be placed between the auxiliary verb (*be, have, will,* or a modal) and the past participle. Tell students that there is no need to repeat the verb *be* when two verbs are connected by *and*. Go over the example.

4. Have students look at the section of the grammar chart on page 419. Say: *The passive voice is used more frequently without a performer than with a performer.* Go over each example and explanation.

5. Direct students to the first example. Ask: *How would these sentences be written if there were performers?* (e.g., *People speak English in the U.S.; People celebrate Independence Day in July.*) Ask: *Is* people *important? What is important in these sentences?* (The language that is spoken in the U.S., and not that people speak the language, is important. When Independence Day is celebrated, not who celebrates it, is important.) Review the remaining examples in this way.

EXERCISE 2

ANSWERS: 1. He will be chosen. **2.** You are always chosen. **3.** They can't be chosen. **4.** We have never been chosen. **5.** I wasn't chosen. **6.** She shouldn't be chosen.

 5-10 mins

1. Have students read the direction line. Go over the example.

2. Have students complete Exercise 2 individually. Remind them to review grammar chart **13.3** on pages 418–419 if necessary. Go over the answers with the class.

EXERCISE 3

ANSWERS: 1. are selected; **2.** are sent; **3.** is filled, returned; **4.** are called; **5.** is chosen; **6.** are asked; **7.** are not permitted; **8.** are given

5-10 mins

1. Have students read the direction line. Go over the example. Remind students that the verbs in this exercise should be in the present tense.

2. Have students complete Exercise 3 individually. Remind them to review grammar chart **13.3** on pages 418–419 if necessary. Then have students compare answers in pairs. Go over the answers as a class.

EXERCISE 4

ANSWERS: 1. was told; **2.** was called; **3.** was given; **4.** was shown; **5.** were taken; **6.** was asked; **7.** wasn't chosen; **8.** was sent

5-10 mins

1. Have students read the direction line. Go over the example. Remind students that the verbs in this exercise should be in the past tense.

2. Have students complete Exercise 4 individually. Remind them to review grammar chart **13.3** on pages 418–419 if necessary. Have students compare answers in pairs. Go over the answers as a class.

EXERCISE 5

ANSWERS: 1. have been written; **2.** have been made; **3.** have been chosen; **4.** has been selected; **5.** have been paid; **6.** has been left; **7.** has been put

5-10 mins

1. Have students read the direction line. Go over the example. Remind students that the verbs in this exercise should be in the present perfect tense.

2. Have students complete Exercise 5 individually. Remind them to review grammar chart **13.3** on pages 418–419 if necessary. Then have students compare answers in pairs. Go over the answers as a class.

EXERCISE 6

ANSWERS: 1. will be told; **2.** will be asked; **3.** will be introduced; **4.** will be given; **5.** will not be allowed; **6.** will be selected; **7.** will not be picked; **8.** will be chosen; **9.** will be sent; **10.** will be paid

10-15 mins

1. Have students read the direction line. Explain that this exercise is about instructions for jury duty. Go over the example. Remind students that the verbs in this exercise should be in the future tense.

2. Have students complete Exercise 6 individually. Remind them to review grammar chart **13.3** on pages 418–419 if necessary. Have students compare answers in pairs. Go over the answers as a class.

EXERCISE 7

ANSWERS: 1. were asked; **2.** will be paid; **3.** were told; **4.** were given; **5.** are paid; **6.** should be used; **7.** were shown

🕐 **10-15 mins**

1. Have students read the direction line. Go over the example. Remind students to use the same tense as the underlined verb.

2. Have students complete Exercise 7 individually. Remind them to review grammar chart **13.3** on pages 418–419 if necessary. Then have students compare answers in pairs. Go over the answers as a class.

13.4 Negatives and Questions with the Passive Voice

🕐 **5-10 mins**

1. Have students look at grammar chart **13.4** on page 422. Go over each sentence in the simple past and the present perfect.

2. Direct students to the Language Note. Remind students that the verb *be* is used in the passive—so you can't use *do, does,* or *did* with the passive.

EXERCISE 8

ANSWERS: 1. aren't paid; **2.** weren't chosen; **3.** aren't allowed; **4.** weren't told; **5.** haven't been given

🕐 **5-10 mins**

1. Have students read the direction line. Go over the example.

2. Have students complete Exercise 8 individually. Remind them to review grammar chart **13.4** on page 422 if necessary. Go over the answers as a class.

EXERCISE 9

ANSWERS: 1. Why aren't some people selected?
2. When are the jurors given a lunch break?
3. Why weren't you chosen for the jury? **4.** What kind of information were you given about the case? **5.** When will the film be shown? **6.** Which jurors have been sent home? **7.** Why should the jurors be paid more money? **8.** When were we (OR you) told to go to the courtroom? **9.** Why has the jury been instructed by the judge?

🕐 **10-15 mins**

1. Have students read the direction line. Go over the example.

2. Have students complete Exercise 9 individually. Remind them to review grammar chart **13.4** on page 422 if necessary. Have students compare answers in pairs. Go over the answers as a class.

> **Practice Idea: Writing**
>
> In pairs, ask students to write answers for the questions in Exercise 9. Some of the answers can be found in the reading; others can be made up.

Unusual Lawsuits   READING

1. Have students look at the photo. Ask: *What's happening in this picture?* (A woman is eating a bagel, holding a cup of coffee, and talking on her cell phone while driving.)

2. Have students look at the title of the reading. Ask: *What is the reading about?* Have students use the title and photo to make predictions about the reading.

3. Preteach any vocabulary words your students may not know, such as *lawsuit.*

Reading Glossary

lawsuit: a legal action bringing a problem or claim to a court of law

BEFORE YOU READ

🕐 **5-10 mins**

1. Have students discuss the questions in pairs.

2. Ask for a few volunteers to share their answers with the class.

🔊 Reading

**CD 4
TR 14**

🕐 **10-15 mins**

1. Have students first read the text silently. Tell them to pay special attention to the active and the passive voice. Then play the audio and have students read along silently.

2. Check students' comprehension. Ask questions such as: *What happened to the 79-year-old woman in New Mexico?* (She spilled hot coffee

on herself while she was driving. She suffered serious burns.) *How much did she win in the lawsuit?* (Eventually, she won $3 million.) *Did the teenagers win their lawsuit against a fast-food chain?* (No. The lawsuit was thrown out of court.) *Who was killed by a driver talking on a cell phone?* (a teenage girl)

Practice Idea: Listening

To practice listening skills, have students first listen to the audio alone. Ask a few comprehension questions. Repeat the audio if necessary. Then have them open their books and read along as they listen to the audio.

DID YOU KNOW?

Have students read the information. Briefly discuss with students why it might be dangerous to text or talk on the cell phone while driving. Ask them if they think it is safer if you have a hands-free phone. Then share the following information with them.

Many states are now creating laws regulating the use of cell phones while driving. Many states are now mandating the use of hands-free devices based on studies that indicate that the driver is most distracted while dialing or locating the phone. However, the National Safety Council has new evidence that suggests it is the phone conversation that distracts the driver the most.

13.5 Choosing Active Voice or Passive Voice =★

10-15 mins

1. Have students look at grammar chart **13.5** on page 425. Say: *When the sentence has a specific performer, we can use an active or a passive construction. In English, we usually use active constructions when there is a choice. When we do use a passive construction, the performer is mentioned in a* by *phrase.* Go over the examples.

2. Say: *When there is no specific performer, we use a passive construction.* Go over the examples.

3. Say: *The passive voice is often used after* it *when talking about findings, discoveries, or general beliefs.* Go over the examples.

4. Say: *With some verbs, you can't use the passive. These verbs do not take an object.* Go over the examples.

5. Demonstrate the difference in pronouns in active and passive constructions. Go over the examples.

6. Direct students to the Language Note. Say: Have *and* want *are generally not used in passive constructions.* Go over the examples.

EXERCISE 10 =★

ANSWERS: 1. Cell phones are used by employees. **2.** A pedestrian was hit by a driver. **3.** The case was thrown out by the court. **4.** Accidents are caused by distracted drivers. **5.** The laws are made by Congress. **6.** Should cell phone use be controlled by the government? **7.** New laws are signed by the president. **8.** The case has been decided by the court. **9.** A decision will be made by the judge. **10.** Hamburgers and fries are sold by (OR at) fast-food restaurants.

 10-15 mins

1. Have students read the direction line. Go over the example.

2. Have students complete the exercise individually. Remind them to review grammar chart **13.5** on page 425 if necessary. Go over the answers as a class.

Practice Idea: Writing

Have students write five sentences in the active voice. Ask students to use all the tenses, including modals. Then have students exchange sentences with a partner. Have the partner change the active sentence into a passive sentence.

EXERCISE 11 =★

ANSWERS: 1. A questionnaire was sent to me. OR I was sent a questionnaire. **2.** We have been taken to a separate room. **3.** We were told not to discuss the case. **4.** Twelve people will be chosen. **5.** Has your name been selected? **6.** We weren't permitted to read any newspapers.

7. He will not (OR won't) be selected again for jury duty. **8.** Will you be paid? **9.** We aren't allowed to eat in the courtroom. **10.** My name has been called.

10-15 mins

1. Have students read the direction line. Go over the example.

2. Have students complete the exercise individually. Remind them to review grammar chart **13.5** on page 425 if necessary. Then have students compare answers in pairs. Go over the answers as a class.

EXERCISE 12 =★

ANSWERS: **1.** The driver had a cell phone. **2.** The driver spilled hot coffee. **3.** Do you use a cell phone? **4.** I have driven the car. **5.** Lawyers make a lot of money. **6.** Drivers with cell phones should use an earpiece. **7.** I conduct business from my car. **8.** We watch the news every night. **9.** Teenagers eat a lot of fast food. **10.** They'll report the accident.

10-15 mins

1. Have students read the direction line. Go over the example. Remind students to use the same tense as the underlined verb.

2. Have students complete the exercise individually. Remind them to review grammar chart **13.5** on page 425 if necessary. Then have students compare answers in pairs. Go over the answers as a class.

EXERCISE 13

CD 4 TR 15

ANSWERS: **1.** is banned; **2.** depends; **3.** live; **4.** is prohibited; **5.** is permitted; **6.** doesn't obey; **7.** have started; **8.** has become; **9.** need; **10.** will be punished; **11.** can be sent; **12.** are caused; **13.** determined; **14.** are distracted; **15.** need

10-15 mins

1. Say: *This exercise is about the use of cell phones while driving.* Have students read the direction line. Go over the example.

2. Have students complete the exercise individually. Remind them to review grammar chart **13.5** on page 425 if necessary. Then have students compare answers in pairs. Play the audio and go over the answers as a class.

Practice Idea: Listening

To provide practice with listening skills, have students close their books and listen to the audio. Repeat the audio as needed. Say: *This listening selection is about the use of cell phones while driving.* Ask comprehension questions, such as: *Are the laws about cell phone use while driving the same in every state in the U.S.?* (No. The laws vary from state to state.) *Is the cell phone the only distraction in the car?* (No. Eating, putting on makeup, reading, reaching for things, and changing stations on the radio are all distractions that have caused accidents.) Then have students open their books and complete Exercise 13.

EXERCISE 14

CD 4 TR 16

ANSWERS: **1.** was arrested; **2.** interviewed; **3.** didn't understand; **4.** didn't speak; **5.** told; **6.** gave; **7.** weren't chosen; **8.** were you asked; **9.** wanted; **10.** said; **11.** weren't selected; **12.** Did you talk; **13.** went; **14.** were told; **15.** told; **16.** didn't agree; **17.** talked; **18.** Did your boss pay; **19.** was chosen

10-15 mins

1. Say: *In this conversation, two friends are talking about jury duty.* Have students read the direction line. Go over the example.

2. Have students complete the exercise individually. Remind them to review grammar chart **13.5** on page 425 if necessary. Then have students compare answers in pairs. Play the audio and go over the answers as a class.

Practice Idea: Listening

To provide practice with listening skills, have students close their books and listen to the audio. Repeat the audio as needed. Say: *In this conversation, two friends are talking about jury duty.* Ask comprehension questions, such as: *How long did it take to choose the jury?* (half a day) *How many people were interviewed?* (more than 50) *Why were some people rejected?* (They couldn't speak English very well. Others had bad experiences with police officers.) Then have students open their books and complete Exercise 14.

Practice Idea: Speaking

Have students practice the conversation in pairs. Ask volunteers to role-play all or part of the conversation in front of the class.

Summary of Lesson 13

20-30 mins

1. **Active and Passive Voice: Forms** Have students cover up the summary of Lesson 13 on page 430. Create an exercise on the board:

   1. *He drove the car.*
   2. *The car wasn't driven by him.*
   3. *The car will be driven by him.*
   4. *He has driven the car.*
   5. *The car is often driven by him.*
   6. *He should drive the car.*
   7. *Did he drive the car?*
   8. *When was the car driven by him?*

   Say: *If the sentence is active, make it passive. If it's passive, make it active.* If necessary, have students review:

   13.3 The Passive Voice—Form and Uses (pp. 418–419)

2. **The Active Voice: Use** Say: *The active voice is preferred in English. With verbs that don't take an object, only the active voice can be used.* Go over the examples. If necessary, have students review:

   13.5 Choosing Active Voice or Passive Voice (p. 425)

3. **The Passive Voice: Use** Create a matching exercise on the board:

   1. *My cell phone was made in Japan.*
   2. *The criminal was taken to jail.*
   3. *Cell phones are used all over the world.*
   4. *The court paid me. I was paid at the end of the day.*
   5. *It was discovered that many accidents are the result of driver distraction.*
   6. *A fast-food company was sued by a woman in New Mexico.*

   a. *Use the passive when the emphasis shifts from the performer to the receiver.*
   b. *Use the passive voice when the performer is not known or is not important.*
   c. *Use the passive when the performer is obvious.*
   d. *Use the passive with* it *when talking about findings, discoveries, and beliefs.*
   e. *Use the passive when the performer is everybody or people in general.*
   f. *Use the passive when we want to emphasize the receiver more than the performer.*

   Say: *Match the example with the explanation. Read through all of the choices before making a decision.* (**Matching Answers: 1.** b; **2.** c; **3.** e; **4.** a; **5.** d; **6.** f) If necessary, have students review:

   13.5 Choosing Active Voice or Passive Voice (p. 425)

Editing Advice

10-15 mins

Have students close their books. Write the first few sentences without editing marks or corrections on the board. For example:

1. *The money didn't find.*
2. *Where did the jurors taken?*

Ask students to correct each sentence and provide a rule or an explanation for each correction. This activity can be done individually, in pairs, or as a class. After students have corrected each sentence, tell them to turn to page 431. Say: *Now compare your work with the Editing Advice in the book.* Have students read through all the advice.

Editing Quiz

ANSWERS: 1. C; **2.** became; **3.** C; **4.** Were; **5.** C; **6.** C; **7.** was asked; **8.** C; **9.** was chosen; **10.** C; **11.** C; **12.** was badly damaged; **13.** Was the woman injured? **14.** was; **15.** C; **16.** C; **17.** C; **18.** happened; **19.** C; **20.** was taken; **21.** was driving; **22.** C; **23.** C; **24.** was never told

10-15 mins

1. Tell students they are going to put the Editing Advice into practice. Have students read the direction line. Ask: *Do all the shaded words and phrases have mistakes?* (no) Go over the examples with the class. Then do #1 together.

2. Have students complete the quiz individually. Then have them compare answers with a partner before checking answers as a class.

3. For the items students had difficulties with, have them go back and find the relevant grammar chart and review it. Monitor and give help as necessary.

Lesson 13 Test/Review

 30-40 mins Use the Assessment CD-ROM with Exam*View*®, Online Workbook, and the Web site for additional practice, review, and assessment materials.

PART 1

Answers: 1. English is spoken in the U.S. **2.** A dictionary can be used during the test. **3.** The criminal was taken to jail. **4.** The president has been seen on TV many times. **5.** You will be taken to the courtroom. **6.** The mirror has broken into small pieces. **7.** You are expected to learn English in the U.S. **8.** Cameras aren't allowed in the courtroom.

1. Part 1 may be used as an in-class test to assess student performance, in addition to the Assessment CD-ROM with Exam*View*®. Have students read the direction line. Collect for assessment.

2. If necessary, have students review:
   13.3 The Passive Voice—Form and Uses (pp. 418–419)

PART 2

Answers: 1. The teacher has told you to write a composition. **2.** You must pay your phone bill. **3.** The teacher does not allow you to use your books during a test. **4.** The teacher will return the tests. **5.** When do the bride and groom open wedding gifts? **6.** The police did not find your missing car.

1. Part 2 may also be used as an in-class test to assess student performance, in addition to the Assessment CD-ROM with Exam*View*®. Have students read the direction line. Collect for assessment.

2. If necessary, have students review:
   13.3 The Passive Voice—Form and Uses (pp. 418–419)
   13.4 Negatives and Questions with Passive Voice (p. 422)

PART 3

Answers: 1. was taken; **2.** will visit; **3.** saw OR have seen; **4.** was seen OR has been seen; **5.** have; **6.** have been helped; **7.** died; **8.** were rescued; **9.** comes; **10.** was driven; **11.** isn't known OR wasn't known; **12.** doesn't know OR didn't know

1. Part 3 may also be used as an in-class test to assess student performance, in addition to the Assessment CD-ROM with Exam*View*®. Have students read the direction line. Collect for assessment.

2. If necessary, have students review:
   13.5 Choosing Active Voice or Passive Voice (p. 425)

Expansion

These expansion activities provide opportunities for students to interact with one another and further develop their speaking and writing skills. Encourage students to use grammar from this lesson whenever possible.

CLASSROOM ACTIVITIES

 10-15 mins per activity
1. Have students fill out the chart on the judicial system in their native countries. Then have students get together in groups to talk about one or more countries.

2. Divide the class into two groups to make presentations on cell phone use in cars. Ask students to display their main points on the board, on posters, on a handout, or in some other form of presentation.

TALK ABOUT IT

 15-20 mins Elicit a few ideas from students about reasons why they would or wouldn't like to be on a jury. Write their ideas on the board. Briefly ask them what they think about the legal system in the U.S. Write their ideas on the board. Then have students discuss each topic in pairs or in groups.

WRITE ABOUT IT

20-30 mins

1. Have students read the direction line. Have them think about an experience they've had and then talk about what happened with a partner. Before they begin writing, have students make an outline of the events that happened, if relevant. Then have them write their compositions individually. Collect for assessment and/or have students share their compositions with the group.

2. Have students read the direction line and the sample paragraph. With the class, think of a famous court case that most students know about. Have students brainstorm ideas related to that case. Write their ideas on the board. Have students help you begin a paragraph on the board about the case. Then have them write their compositions individually. Encourage them to give their opinions as well as the details about the case. Collect for assessment and/or have students share their compositions with the group.

Practice Idea: Writing

Have students exchange first drafts with a partner. Ask students to help their partners edit their drafts. Refer students to the Editing Advice on pages 431–432.

OUTSIDE ACTIVITIES

1. Tell students to watch a court movie, such as *The Firm, Witness to the Prosecution, Inherit the Wind, A Time to Kill, To Kill a Mockingbird, Presumed Innocent, Twelve Angry Men, A Civil Action,* or *The Client.* Have them write about their impressions of the American court system after watching one of these movies. Have them share these impressions with the class or in groups. Try to make sure not all students watch the same movie.

2. Tell students to watch a court TV show. Have them report back to the class on one of the cases they saw and what they thought of the judge's decision. Have them discuss their impression of these shows.

3. Have students ask an American if he or she has ever been selected for a jury. Tell them to ask him or her about this experience. Have students report back to the class orally or in writing on what they found out. Have students prepare questions for the interview beforehand in class.

INTERNET ACTIVITIES

1. Tell students to type *Insurance Information Institute* and *cell phones* into a search engine and find some statistics about drivers who use cell phones. Have them bring the information to class and discuss in groups if there is anything that surprises them in the statistics. Before students search the Internet, have them brainstorm the types of statistics they might find, as well as additional key words they may use to help narrow their searches, such as *statistics* or *deaths.*

2. Tell students to look for information about one of these famous American trials:

   a. the O.J. Simpson trial
   b. the Leopold and Loeb trial
   c. the Sacco and Vanzetti trial
   d. the Amistad trials
   e. the Scopes trial
   f. the Rosenberg trial
   g. the Bruno Hauptmann trial

   Have students answer these questions about the trial they choose:

   • What was the defendant accused of?
   • When did the trial take place?
   • How long did the trial last?
   • Was the defendant found guilty?

   Have them report on their findings either orally or in writing. For example:

   a. The O.J. Simpson trial—O.J. Simpson, a famous American and former football player, was accused of killing his wife, Nicole Brown, and her friend, Ron Goldman. After a controversial nine-month trial, Simpson was found not guilty in 1995. Many feel that regardless of the outcome of the trial, he was guilty. He was found responsible for her death in the civil trial.

b. The Leopold and Loeb trial—Two intelligent and educated sons of wealthy families, in an attempt to commit the perfect crime, kidnapped and murdered a young boy in 1924. They pleaded guilty and were sentenced to life in prison. Loeb died in prison, and Leopold was released after 34 years.

c. The Sacco and Vanzetti trial—Sacco and Vanzetti were aliens, atheists, anarchists, and conscientious objectors of the war (WWI). They were accused of the murder of a guard at a shoe company in Massachusetts. They both had guns and lied about their activities. Supporters felt they were victims of communist hysteria. They were convicted in 1921 and later executed. The trial lasted two months. Their appeals were denied.

d. The Amistad trials—In 1839, a slave ship sailing from Cuba was taken over in a mutiny led by African slave, Cinque. The slaves were eventually captured by the American Navy and put on trial in Connecticut. The case was eventually taken to the Supreme Court, where the Court ordered the slaves to be freed immediately. The trials lasted for approximately one year.

e. The Scopes trial—John Scopes was a biology teacher who taught evolution in his Tennessee classroom, even though it had just been made illegal in Tennessee and in other states. Townspeople who wanted to generate some publicity for their depopulated town decided to test the law in court. At the end of the long two-month trial in 1925, Scopes was found guilty and was fined. It was the hope of the defense to take the trial to the Supreme Court. It was thrown out of the appeals court.

f. The Rosenberg trial—Husband and wife Julius and Ethel Rosenberg were tried and executed for selling secrets about U.S. efforts to build atomic weapons to the Soviets. The prosecution was built on very poor evidence. People all around the world, including the Pope, begged for leniency. They were executed in 1953.

g. The Bruno Hauptmann trial—Bruno Hauptmann was convicted and executed in 1936 for the kidnapping and murder of famous aviator Charles Lindbergh's baby. The trial took place in 1935 and lasted one month.

Lesson 14

Lesson Overview

GRAMMAR

1. Briefly review what students learned in the previous lesson. Ask: *What did we study in Lesson 13?* (passive voice and active voice)

2. Ask: *What are we going to study in Lesson 14?* (articles; *other/another*; indefinite pronouns) *What are some articles?* (a, the) Have students give examples. Write the examples on the board. Then ask for examples of sentences using indefinite pronouns (e.g., *I don't have a car. But I'm going to need one next year when I move to the suburbs.*).

CONTEXT

1. Ask: *What are we going to learn about in this lesson?* (money) Activate students' prior knowledge. Ask: *How old were you when you started earning money? Did you save it or did you spend it?*

2. Have students share their knowledge and personal experiences.

> ### Presentation Ideas
>
> The topic for this lesson can be enhanced with the following items:
>
> 1. Catalogs from state and private colleges and universities with tuition and housing costs
> 2. American money: new and old
> 3. Coins and bills from other countries

14.1 Articles— An Overview

5-10 mins

Have students look at grammar chart **14.1** on page 438. Say: *The indefinite articles are* a/an, *and the definite article is* the. Point out that nouns are sometimes used without an article. Go over the examples.

Kids and Money READING

1. Have students look at the photo. Ask: *What is going on in this photo?* (two kids/girls are shopping)

2. Have students look at the title of the reading. Ask: *What is the reading about?* Have students use the title and photo to make predictions about the reading.

3. Preteach any vocabulary words your students may not know, such as *gratitude, generosity, guilt, allowance,* and *chores.*

Reading Glossary

allowance: money for everyday expenses
chores: routine tasks or jobs
generosity: readiness to give; giving
gratitude: thankfulness
guilt: feeling of having done something wrong or shameful; remorse

BEFORE YOU READ

5-10 mins

1. Have students discuss the questions in pairs.
2. Ask for a few volunteers to share their answers with the class.

Reading

CD 4
TR 17

10-15 mins

1. Have students first read the text silently. Tell them to pay special attention to nouns and the articles that precede them. Then play the audio and have students read along silently.

2. Check students' comprehension. Ask questions such as: *In 2009, how much did kids on average spend a week?* ($100) *Why are some parents buying their children things?* (because they feel guilty for not spending a lot of time with them) *What do some children receive an allowance for?* (Some children have regular chores they do in exchange for an allowance.) *When should parents start talking to their children about money?* (when they start saying *I want…*)

To practice listening skills, have students first listen to the audio alone. Ask a few comprehension questions. Repeat the audio if necessary. Then have them open their books and read along as they listen to the audio.

DID YOU KNOW?

Have students read the information. Then share the following with them and ask them if they have any similar traditions in their countries: When young children (6–8 years of age) in the U.S. lose a tooth, they put it under their pillow at night. The next day, money "magically" appears in its place, compliments of the Tooth Fairy. Parents are now complaining that children expect more than the traditional quarter these days because of what they hear friends at school are getting. Tooth Fairy inflation has caused parents to fork over more money or to be creative. Many parents now give their children special gold dollar coins available at the post office or online at the U.S. mint.

14.2 The Indefinite Article— Classifying or Identifying the Subject

⏱ **5-10 mins**

1. Have students look at grammar chart **14.2** on page 439. Say: *To tell who or what the subject is, we use* a *or* an *with a singular count noun after* be. Go over the examples.

2. Explain that when we classify a plural subject, we don't use an article. Go over examples.

3. Direct students to the Language Note. Say: *We can also classify things in the past.* Go over the examples.

EXERCISE 1

ANSWERS: **Answers may vary. Possible answers:**
1. A teenager is a person between 13 and 19 years old. **2.** A quarter is a coin. Four of them make a dollar. **3.** A dime is also a coin. It is smaller than a quarter and is worth less. Ten dimes make a dollar. **4.** A credit card is a plastic card that lets you buy things and pay for them later. **5.** A wallet is something that holds your money and credit cards. **6.** Gold is a valuable metal that is used for jewelry and coins. **7.** Silver and gold are metals that are worth a lot of money.

⏱ **5-10 mins**

1. Have students read the direction line. Go over the example.

2. Have students complete Exercise 1 individually. Remind them to review grammar chart **14.2** on page 439 if necessary. Go over the answers as a class.

EXERCISE 2

ANSWERS: **Answers will vary. Possible answers:**
1. Albert Einstein was a scientist. **2.** Tiger Woods is a golfer OR is a professional athlete. **3.** Erik Weihenmayer is a blind mountain climber. **4.** Barack Obama is the president of the United States. **5.** George Dawson was an African-American author. **6.** Navajos are American Indians.

⏱ **5-10 mins**

1. Have students read the direction line. Go over the example.

2. Have students complete Exercise 2 individually. Remind them to review grammar chart **14.2** on page 439 if necessary. Go over the answers as a class.

Have students write five sentences telling who some important or famous people from their native countries or cultures are. Then have students exchange papers with a partner from a different country.

14.3 The Indefinite Article— Introducing a Noun

⏱ **5-10 mins**

1. Have students look at grammar chart **14.3** on page 440. Say: A *and* an *introduce a singular noun.* Go over the examples.

2. Say: Some *or* any *introduce a plural noun or a noncount noun.*

3. Direct students to the Language Notes. Say: Some *is used in affirmatives,* any *is used in negatives, and* some *or* any *are used in questions.* Some *and* any *do not have to be used.* Go over the examples.

EXERCISE 3

ANSWERS: 1. an; **2.** any OR some; **3.** a; **4.** some; **5.** some; **6.** any OR some; **7.** any; **8.** a; **9.** some; **10.** a; **11.** a; **12.** an

 5-10 mins

1. Have students read the direction line. Go over the example.

2. Have students complete Exercise 3 individually. Remind them to review grammar chart **14.3** on page 440 if necessary. Go over the answers with the class.

EXERCISE 4

CD 4 TR 18

ANSWERS: 1. some; **2.** an; **3.** a; **4.** a; **5.** a; **6.** any; **7.** a; **8.** any; **9.** some; **10.** a; **11.** a; **12.** a; **13.** a; **14.** a; **15.** a; **16.** a

 10-15 mins

1. Say: *In this conversation, a mother and her son are talking about getting a job.* Have students read the direction line. Go over the example.

2. Have students complete the exercise individually. Remind them to review grammar chart **14.3** on page 440 if necessary. Then have students compare answers in pairs. Play the audio and check answers as a class.

Practice Idea: Listening

To provide practice with listening skills, have students close their books and listen to the audio. Repeat the audio as needed. Say: *In this conversation, a mother and her son are talking about getting a job.* Ask comprehension questions, such as: *Why does he want to get a job?* (to make money) *What is his mother worried about?* (that he won't have enough time for school work) *What does he want to buy with his money?* (clothes, a car) Then have students open their books and complete Exercise 4.

Practice Idea: Speaking

Have students practice the conversation in pairs. Ask volunteers to role-play all or part of the conversation in front of the class.

14.4 The Definite Article

 10-15 mins

1. Have students cover up grammar chart **14.4** on pages 442–443. Create a matching exercise on the board:

   1. *Did you read the article about money?*
   2. *Many kids in the world are poor.*
   3. *I'm going to the store after work. Do you want anything?*
   4. *The author wants to teach kids to be responsible with money.*
   5. *Where's the teacher? I have a question about the homework.*
   a. *Refers to a specific object or person present*
   b. *When there is only one of something*
   c. *When we refer to something (such as a classroom text) that we share with others*
   d. *When we refer to a specific noun that is defined in the phrase after the noun*
   e. *When we refer to the thing or the one that we usually use*

   Say: *Match the example with the explanation.* (**Matching Answers: 1.** d; **2.** b; **3.** e; **4.** a; **5.** c)

2. Then have students look at grammar chart **14.4** on pages 442–443. Say: *Compare your work with the chart.* Go over the examples and the explanations.

3. Explain that when a noun is first introduced, it has an indefinite article. When you refer to it again, you use the definite article *the.* Go over the examples.

4. Explain that you don't use the definite article with possessive forms. Go over the examples.

EXERCISE 5

CD 4 TR 19

ANSWERS: Conversation 1: 1. a; **2.** The; **3.** an; **4.** an; **5.** the; **6.** some; **7.** The; **8.** an; **9.** the.

Conversation 2: 1. a; **2.** the; **3.** a; **4.** the; **5.** a; **6.** any; **7.** a; **8.** the. **Conversation 3: 1.** the; **2.** the; **3.** a; **4.** the; **5.** the; **6.** the; **7.** a.

10-15 mins

1. Say: *There are three short conversations in this exercise.* Have students read the direction line. Go over the example. Point out the photo of the ATM and the illustration of the dollar-bill changer.

2. Have students complete the exercise individually. Remind them to review grammar chart **14.4** on pages 442–443 if necessary. Then have students compare answers in pairs. Play the audio and check the answers as a class.

Practice Idea: Listening

To provide practice with listening skills, have students close their books and listen to the audio. Repeat the audio as needed. Say: *You'll hear three short conversations.* Ask comprehension questions, such as: *What do they want to do in conversation 1?* (get cash from a bank or an ATM) *What does the student want to do in conversation 2?* (get coffee) *What's happening in conversation 3?* (The teacher is late.) Then have students open their books and complete Exercise 5.

Practice Idea: Speaking

Have students practice the conversations in pairs. Ask volunteers to perform all or part of the conversations in front of the class.

14.5 Making Generalizations

5-10 mins

1. Have students look at grammar chart **14.5** on page 445. Say: *When we make a generalization, we say that something is true of all members of a group.* Explain that to make a generalization with a singular count noun, we use *a* or *an*. To make a generalization about a plural noun, we don't use an article. Go over the examples.

2. Say: *For noncount nouns, don't use an article.* Go over the examples.

3. Explain that when you're making a generalization about the object of a sentence, you use a plural noun and no article with count nouns. With objects that are noncount nouns, don't use an article. Go over the examples.

4. Direct students to the Language Note. Point out that you don't use *some* or *any* with generalizations.

EXERCISE 6 =★

ANSWERS: 1. An; **2.** The; **3.** ø, ø; **4.** ø; **5.** The; **6.** ø; **7.** The; **8.** ø; **9.** ø; **10.** The; **11.** ø; **12.** The; **13.** ø; **14.** The; **15.** The

10-15 mins

1. Say: *In this exercise, you're going to talk about the specific things on this page, or you're going to make generalizations with singular, plural, and noncount nouns.* Have students read the direction line. Go over the examples. Remind students that to make generalizations with singular nouns, we use *a* or *an*.

2. Have students complete Exercise 6 individually. Remind them to review grammar chart **14.5** on page 445 if necessary. Have students compare answers in pairs. Go over the answers with the class.

Practice Idea: Writing

Have students work in pairs to write four sentences about specific things in the room and four sentences with generalizations.

EXERCISE 7 =★
Answers will vary.

1. Say: *You're going to talk about what you like and what you don't like.* Have students read the direction line. Go over the examples.

2. Have students complete Exercise 7 in pairs. Remind them to review grammar chart **14.5** on page 445 if necessary. Monitor pair work. Give help as needed.

EXERCISE 8

 CD 4
TR 20

ANSWERS: 1. some OR ø; **2.** a; **3.** the; **4.** Some OR ø; **5.** a; **6.** some OR ø; **7.** ø; **8.** the; **9.** a; **10.** a; **11.** the; **12.** an; **13.** the; **14.** the; **15.** ø; **16.** some OR ø; **17.** the; **18.** the

10-15 mins

1. Say: *In this conversation, you'll hear two friends talk about sending money through the mail.* Have students read the direction line. Go over the example. Remind students that some nouns won't need an article.

2. Have students complete the exercise individually. Remind them to review grammar chart **14.5** on page 445 if necessary. Then have students compare answers in pairs. Play the audio and check the possible answers as a class.

Practice Idea: Listening

To provide practice with listening skills, have students close their books and listen to the audio. Repeat the audio as needed. Say: *In this conversation, you'll hear two friends talk about sending money through the mail.* Ask comprehension questions, such as: *What is person A going to send at the post office?* (a package to her family) *What's in the package?* (shirts, a coat, and money) *Why does she need to get a money order?* (It's not safe to send cash in the mail.) Then have students open their books and complete Exercise 8.

Practice Idea: Speaking

Have students practice the conversation in pairs. Ask volunteers to role-play all or part of the conversation in front of the class.

 EXERCISE 9

CD 4
TR 21

ANSWERS: 1. the; **2.** ø OR some; **3.** the; **4.** ø; **5.** ø; **6.** a; **7.** ø; **8.** ø; **9.** a; **10.** ø; **11.** the; **12.** a; **13.** some OR ø; **14.** The; **15.** some OR ø; **16.** a; **17.** some OR ø

10-15 mins

1. Say: *In this conversation, you'll hear two friends talk about money.* Have students read the

direction line. Go over the example. Remind students that some nouns won't need an article.

2. Have students complete the exercise individually. Remind them to review grammar chart **14.5** on page 445 if necessary. Then have students compare answers in pairs. Play the audio and check the possible answers as a class.

Practice Idea: Listening

To provide practice with listening skills, have students close their books and listen to the audio. Repeat the audio as needed. Say: *In this conversation, you'll hear two friends talk about money.* Ask comprehension questions, such as: *Who has to set a good example for kids?* (the parents) *What do they use instead of cash?* (credit cards) *What did person A put in the basement?* (their old TV) Then have students open their books and complete Exercise 9.

Practice Idea: Speaking

Have students practice the conversation in pairs. Ask volunteers to role-play all or part of the conversation in front of the class.

Practice Idea: Speaking

Have students work in pairs to create a similar conversation with their own information. Ask volunteers to perform all or part of the conversation in front of the class.

14.6 General or Specific with Quantity Words

5-10 mins

1. Have students look at grammar chart **14.6** on page 448. Say: *When we put* of the *after a quantity word, we are making something specific.* Go over the examples. Explain that without *of the* we're making generalizations.

2. Then have students read the sentences with *of the*. Explain that after *all*, the word *of* can be omitted. *None* is singular and should be followed by a singular verb. But point out that many native speakers use a plural verb after *none*. Go over the example.

3. Direct students to the Language Note. Point out that by omitting *a* before *few* and *little*, you make the emphasis negative. Go over the examples.

Presentation Idea

Have students change the general sentences in the grammar chart to specific sentences by adding *of the* and some additional information (e.g., *All of the children at the party liked the toys.*).

EXERCISE 10
Answers will vary.

🕐 10–15 mins

1. Say: *In this exercise, you're going to make general statements about Americans.* Have students read the direction line. Go over the example.

2. Have students complete the exercise individually. Remind them to review grammar chart **14.6** on page 448 if necessary. Then have students compare answers in pairs. Monitor pair work. Give help as needed.

Practice Idea: Speaking

Have students discuss their answers in groups. Who agrees? Who disagrees? Have groups report to the class.

EXERCISE 11
Answers will vary.

🕐 10–15 mins

1. Have students read the direction line. Say: *Now you're going to be completing specific statements.* Go over the examples. Say: *Remember that* none *is singular and so the verb has to be singular.*

---

2. Have students complete the exercise individually. Remind them to review grammar chart **14.6** on page 448 if necessary. Then have students compare answers in pairs. Monitor pair work. Give help as needed.

Practice Idea: Speaking

Do a class survey. Did most of the class have the same answers? Write the results on the board.

Bills, Bills, Bills 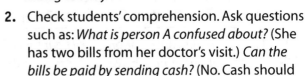 READING

1. Have students look at the picture. Say: *What do you think the woman is doing?*

2. Have students look at the title of the reading. Ask: *What is the reading about?* Have students use the title and picture to make predictions about the reading.

3. Preteach any vocabulary words your students may not know such as *figure something out*, *insurance*, and *direct debit*. For *direct debit*, direct students to the footnote at the bottom of page 450.

Reading Glossary

figure something out: work something out, understand something, solve something

insurance: a policy you pay on a regular basis to cover unexpected costs. For example: health insurance, car insurance, home insurance

BEFORE YOU READ

🕐 5–10 mins

1. Have students discuss the questions in pairs.

2. Ask for a few volunteers to share their answers with the class.

🔊 Reading

CD 4 TR 22

🕐 10–15 mins

1. Have students first read the text silently. Tell them to pay attention to *other* and *another*. Then play the audio and have students read along silently.

2. Check students' comprehension. Ask questions such as: *What is person A confused about?* (She has two bills from her doctor's visit.) *Can the bills be paid by sending cash?* (No. Cash should

---

never be sent by mail.) *What does person B suggest to avoid worrying about bills every month?* (setting up a direct debit for each bill)

14.7 *Another* and *Other*

 5-10 mins

1. Have students look at grammar chart **14.7** on page 451. Say: The other *with a singular and plural noun is definite.* Other *with a plural noun and* another *with a singular noun are indefinite.* The other + *singular noun indicates that there is only one remaining.* The other + *plural noun indicates all the remaining ones.* Go over the examples.

2. Say: Another *is indefinite.* Another + *singular noun indicates that it is one of several.* Other + *plural noun indicates that they are some of several.* Go over the examples.

14.8 More About *Another* and *Other*

5-10 mins

1. Have students cover up grammar chart **14.8** on page 452. Create a matching exercise:
   1. *I received one doctor's bill. Then I received another one.*
   2. *I have two bank accounts. One is for savings. My other account is for checking.*
   3. *Can we talk any other time?*

4. *One number is the phone number. The other one is the fax number.*
5. *Some people pay by check. Others pay by credit card.*

a. *We can use* one *or* ones *in place of the noun.*
b. *When the plural noun or pronoun (*ones*) is omitted, change* other *to* others.
c. *The* is omitted when we use a possessive form.
d. *After* some *or* any, another *is changed to* other.
e. *Another* is sometimes used to mean a different one.

Say: *Match the example to the explanation.* (**Matching Answers: 1.** e; **2.** c; **3.** d; **4.** a; **5.** b)

2. Then have students look at grammar chart **14.8** on page 452. Say: *Check your work with the chart.* Review all the examples and explanations.

EXERCISE 12

ANSWERS: 1. the other; **2.** another; **3.** The other; **4.** The other; **5.** other; **6.** other; **7.** Other; **8.** Others; **9.** the other; **10.** another

5-10 mins

1. Have students read the direction line. Go over the example.

2. Have students complete the exercise individually. Remind them to review grammar charts **14.7** on page 451 and **14.8** on page 452 if necessary. Then go over the answers as a class.

EXERCISE 13

CD 4 TR 23

ANSWERS: 1. the other; **2.** Other; **3.** another; **4.** the other; **5.** other; **6.** The other; **7.** other; **8.** the other; **9.** another

10-15 mins

1. Say: *In this conversation, a grandfather and his grandson are talking about buying sneakers.* Have students read the direction line. Go over the example.

2. Have students complete the exercise individually. Remind them to review grammar charts **14.7** on page 451 and **14.8** on page 452 if necessary. Then have students compare answers in pairs. Play the audio and check the answers as a class.

Practice Idea: Listening

To provide practice with listening skills, have students close their books and listen to the audio. Repeat the audio as needed. Say: *In this conversation, a grandfather and his grandson are talking about buying sneakers.* Ask comprehension questions, such as: *How many pairs of sneakers does the boy have?* (six) *How many pairs of sneakers don't fit him anymore?* (five) *What's wrong with the other pair?* (They're not in style anymore.) *What does the grandfather think he should do with the shoes that don't fit?* (He thinks the boy should give them to other boys in the neighborhood.) Then have students open their books and complete Exercise 13.

Practice Idea: Speaking

Have students practice the conversation in pairs. Then ask volunteers to role-play all or part of the conversation in front of the class.

The High Cost of a College Education READING

1. Have students look at the photo. Ask: *What's going on in this photo?* (A father and son are having a serious conversation about something.)

2. Have students look at the title of the reading. Ask: *What is the reading about?* Have students use the title and photo to make predictions about the reading.

3. Preteach any vocabulary words your students may not know such as *potential* and *diploma*.

Reading Glossary

diploma: an academic certificate; an official paper stating that someone has passed a course of study

potential: capacity to be or do something

BEFORE YOU READ

⏱ 5-10 mins

1. Have students discuss the questions in pairs.

2. Ask for a few volunteers to share their answers with the class.

Reading

CD 4
TR 24

⏱ 10-15 mins

1. Have students first read the text silently. Tell them to pay attention to *one, some, any, it,* and *them.* Then play the audio and have students read along silently.

2. Check students' comprehension. Ask questions such as: *Why is the father concerned?* (His son is telling him that he doesn't want to go to college.) *Why does the father want his son to go to college?* (He'll earn a better living with a college degree. He'll earn more money in his lifetime.) *How will he pay for college?* (The father has been saving money since his son was born.) *What else will the son need to do in order to pay for college?* (He'll need to get a scholarship and apply for grants and loans.)

Practice Idea: Listening

To practice listening skills, have students first listen to the audio alone. Ask a few comprehension questions. Repeat the audio if necessary. Then have them open their books and read along as they listen to the audio.

DID YOU KNOW?

Have students read the information. Ask them who they think pays for scholarships and grants. Then share the following information with them: The federal government provides about 70 percent of all financial aid for postsecondary education. In 2005, federal aid was more than 60 billion dollars.

14.9 Definite and Indefinite Pronouns ▭★

⏱ 5-10 mins

1. Have students cover up grammar chart **14.9** on page 457. Create an exercise on the board:

   1. *I've always thought about your education. I started to think about _____ when you were born.*

   2. *I received two college applications. I have to fill _____ out.*

3. *A college degree is important. It's hard to make a lot of money without _____ .*

4. *The father knew it was important to save money. He saved _____ every month.*

5. *You received five brochures for colleges. Did you read _____?*

Say: *Complete the sentences with* some, any, one, it, *or* them.

2. Then have students look at grammar chart **14.9** on page 457. Say: *Check your work with the chart.* Review all the examples and explanations.

3. Direct students to the Language Note. Say: *We often use* any *and* some *before* more. Go over the examples.

 EXERCISE 14

CD 4
TR 25   **ANSWERS: 1.** it; **2.** it; **3.** one; **4.** it; **5.** it; **6.** it; **7.** one; **8.** it; **9.** it; **10.** it

 1. Tell students this is a conversation between a mother and daughter. Have students read the direction line. Go over the example.

10-15 mins

2. Have students complete the exercise individually. Remind them to review grammar chart **14.9** on page 457 if necessary. Then have students compare answers in pairs. Play the audio and check the answers as a class.

Practice Idea: Listening

To provide practice with listening skills, have students close their books and listen to the audio. Repeat the audio as needed. Say: *In this conversation, a mother and her teenage daughter are talking about art school.* Ask comprehension questions, such as: *What does the mother want her daughter to do?* (look at information about the state university) *Why doesn't the daughter want to do it?* (She doesn't want to go to college. She wants to go to art school.) *What does the mother suggest she do?* (look at art schools) Then have students open their books and complete Exercise 14.

Practice Idea: Speaking

Have students practice the conversation in pairs. Ask volunteers to perform all or part of the conversation in front of the class.

EXERCISE 15
Answers will vary.

1. Have students read the direction line. Go over the examples.

10-15 mins

2. Have students complete the exercise in pairs. Remind them to review grammar chart **14.9** on page 457 if necessary. Monitor pair work. Give help as needed.

Practice Idea: Speaking

Take turns asking and answering the questions with a partner.

 EXERCISE 16

CD 4
TR 26   **ANSWERS: 1.** some OR ø; **2.** it; **3.** it; **4.** any; **5.** one; **6.** it; **7.** the; **8.** any; **9.** it; **10.** ø; **11.** some; **12.** it; **13.** any OR ø; **14.** any; **15.** a; **16.** one; **17.** the; **18.** an; **19.** ø; **20.** ø; **21.** ø; **22.** a; **23.** an

1. Say: *In this conversation, a mother and her daughter talk about the value of money.* Have students read the direction line. Go over the example.

10-15 mins

2. Have students complete the exercise individually. Remind them to review the grammar charts in Lesson 14 if necessary. Go over the answers as a class.

Practice Idea: Listening

To provide practice with listening skills, have students close their books and listen to the audio. Repeat the audio as needed. Say: *In this conversation, a mother and her daughter talk about the value of money.* Ask comprehension questions, such as: *Why does the daughter want money?* (She wants to buy a poster.) *What happened to all the money she received from her grandfather?* (She spent all of it.) *What does the mother suggest she do?* (She wants her daughter to work for the money.) Then have students open their books and complete Exercise 16.

Practice Idea: Speaking

Have students practice the conversation in pairs. Ask volunteers to perform all or part of the conversation in front of the class.

Practice Idea: Speaking

Have students work in pairs to write similar conversations using their own information. Ask volunteers to perform all or part of the conversation in front of the class.

Summary of Lesson 14

20-30 mins

1. **Articles** Have students cover up the summary of Lesson 14. Create a fill-in exercise on the board:

   1. _____ child likes toys.
   2. I love _____ children.
   3. Everyone needs _____ money.
   4. I bought _____ toy.
   5. I bought _____ toys.
   6. I didn't buy _____ games.

   Say: *Fill in the blanks with a/an, some, any, the, or ø if no article is needed.* If necessary, have students review:

2. ***Other/Another*** Have students cover up the summary on page 461. On one side of the board, reproduce the chart without the phrases. On the other side of the board, list the phrases in random order. For example:

   > *the other book*
   > *other books*
   > *my other books*
   > *the other*

   Ask: *Where does each phrase belong? Put the phrases in the correct box: singular/definite; plural/definite; singular/indefinite; plural/indefinite.* If necessary, have students review:

3. **Indefinite Pronouns** Have students cover up the summary on page 461. Write the following on the board:

   > *I need a quarter. Do you have* _____*?*
   > *I need some pennies. You have* _____*.*
   > *I don't have any change. Do you have* _____*?*

   Say: *Fill in the blanks with the correct indefinite pronouns.*

   If necessary, have students review:

Editing Advice

10-15 mins

Have students close their books. Write the first few sentences without editing marks or corrections on the board. For example:

1. *Most of students in my class are from Romania.*
2. *Almost my teachers are very patient.*

Ask students to correct each sentence and provide a rule or an explanation for each correction. This activity can be done individually, in pairs, or as a class.

After students have corrected each sentence, tell them to turn to pages 461–462. Say: *Now compare your work with the Editing Advice in the book.* Have students read through all the advice.

Editing Quiz

ANSWERS: 1. money; **2.** C; **3.** ø; **4.** a; **5.** C; **6.** Most of; **7.** C OR ø; **8.** C; **9.** one; **10.** friends; **11.** a big bookstore; **12.** C; **13.** another; **14.** Most people; **15.** some OR ø; **16.** C; **17.** Other; **18.** the sidewalks; **19.** ø; **20.** C; **21.** the Internet; **22.** Some songs OR Some of the songs; **23.** the others; **24.** C; **25.** C; **26.** another one; **27.** C; **28.** C

10-15 mins

1. Tell students they are going to put the Editing Advice into practice. Have students read the direction line. Ask: *Do all the shaded words and phrases have mistakes?* (no) Go over the examples with the class. Then do #1 together.

2. Have students complete the quiz individually. Then have them compare answers with a partner before checking answers as a class.

3. For the items students had difficulties with, have them go back and find the relevant grammar chart and review it. Monitor and give help as necessary.

Lesson 14 Test/Review

30-40 mins

Use the Assessment CD-ROM with Exam*View*®, Online Workbook, and the Web site for additional practice, review, and assessment materials.

PART 1

ANSWERS: 1. some OR ø; **2.** some OR ø; **3.** a; **4.** the; **5.** the; **6.** some OR ø; **7.** ø; **8.** ø; **9.** ø OR any; **10.** the; **11.** a; **12.** a; **13.** a; **14.** some OR ø; **15.** some OR ø; **16.** ø; **17.** a; **18.** a; **19.** a; **20.** the; **21.** the; **22.** the

1. Part 1 may be used as an in-class test to assess student performance, in addition to the Assessment CD-ROM with Exam*View*®. Have students read the direction line. Collect for assessment.

2. If necessary, have students review:
   14.3 The Indefinite Article—Introducing a Noun (p. 440)
   14.4 The Definite Article (pp. 442–443)
   14.5 Making Generalizations (p. 445)

PART 2

ANSWERS: 1. other; **2.** others; **3.** the other; **4.** another; **5.** the other; **6.** the other; **7.** another

1. Part 2 may also be used as an in-class test to assess student performance, in addition to the Assessment CD-ROM with Exam*View*®. Have students read the direction line. Collect for assessment.

2. If necessary, have students review:
   14.7 *Another* and *Other* (p. 451)
   14.8 More About *Another* and *Other* (p. 452)

PART 3

ANSWERS: 1. it; **2.** it; **3.** any; **4.** any; **5.** them; **6.** some; **7.** it; **8.** some; **9.** any

1. Part 3 may also be used as an in-class test to assess student performance, in addition to the Assessment CD-ROM with Exam*View*®. Have students read the direction line. Collect for assessment.

2. If necessary, have students review:
   14.9 Definite and Indefinite Pronouns (p. 457)

Expansion

These expansion activities provide opportunities for students to interact with one another and further develop their speaking and writing skills. Encourage students to use grammar from this lesson whenever possible.

CLASSROOM ACTIVITIES

10-15 mins

First have students fill out the chart individually. Then have students compare charts in pairs.

TALK ABOUT IT

1. Ask students if they have any sayings or proverbs in their language about money. Have them share them. Then have students discuss each saying in pairs, in groups, or as a class.

2. Have students discuss this topic in small groups. Then have groups report to the class with suggestions for saving money.

3. Have students discuss the meaning of this saying, as well as whether they agree or disagree with it.

WRITE ABOUT IT

1. Have students read the direction line. Before they begin writing, have a quick class discussion on the topic. Elicit students' answers to the questions and write their ideas on the board. Then have them write their paragraphs individually. Collect for assessment and/or have students share their compositions with the group.

2. Have students read the direction line and the sample paragraph. Have students brainstorm ideas for teenagers to make money. Write their ideas on the board. Then have them write their compositions individually. Encourage them to write as much as possible. Collect for assessment and/or have students share their compositions with the group.

Practice Idea: Writing

Have students exchange first drafts with a partner. Ask students to help their partners edit their drafts. Refer students to the Editing Advice on pages 461–462.

INTERNET ACTIVITIES

1. Tell students look for bank rates on the Internet and compare the interest on a one-year CD (certificate of deposit) at two banks. Have them report back to the class on what they found out.

2. Tell students to find a currency converter on the Web and convert the American dollar to the currency of another country. Have them report back to the class on the currency they chose.

3. Tell students to go online to find an application for financial aid. Have them print the application form and bring it to class. Have them compare the forms in pairs or small groups and discuss any questions they have on how to fill it out.

4. Tell students to find the Web site of a college or university they are interested in. Have them find out the cost of tuition. In small groups, have them compare tuition fees.